Devotions for a Healthy Faith

Devotions for a Healthy Faith

Get to Know God through His 66 Books

Bill Nichols, PhD

Devotions for a Healthy Faith:
Get to Know God through His 66 Books

Published by GWN Publishing

ISBN: 978-1-7344522-8-0 (paperback)
ISBN: 978-1-7344522-9-7 (ebook)

CONTENTS

NEW TESTAMENT

ACKNOWLEDGMENTS

MY INSIGHTS INTO THE HISTORICAL BACKGROUNDS of each of the sixty-six books of the Bible, the biblical truth I discovered, and the inspirational stories I shared in *Devotions for a Healthy Faith* were a result of years of diligent work and life-experiences of many of my fellow faith-writers, teachers, friends and family members. I am indebted and grateful to far more people than I can possibly acknowledge here. But I am especially appreciative for the following people.

First and above all, I thank my best friend and the love of my life, Phyllis Clark Nichols, who is a novelist, seminary graduate, musician, and my most patient writing mentor. Because of her tender tenacity, persistent encouragements, and our stimulating conversations, writing this book has been an enriching spiritual journey for me.

I am grateful to Leslie Peterson, my editor. I could not have worked with a more gentle and more thoughtful guide and yet highly professional expert.

I am thankful for Jordan Smith, my production and marketing manager who graciously and skillfully handled the many responsibilities that go on behind the scenes in the book-publishing world that most of never think about. Working with Jordan was my daughter, Christy Nichols Quinn of Q2 Promotions & Marketing, who produced the book cover using one of my original paintings as her inspiration.

I am beholden to those mentioned in the book, some whose names are not real and some who are family members and friends, but all whose lives and experiences are real and illustrate the reality of the truths of God's Word and a healthy faith.

And always, I bow my knee in humble gratitude to my Heavenly Father who has led me throughout this process. During the writing of this book, I have fought a difficult battle with advanced kidney cancer that required major abdominal surgery, the miseries of serious chemotherapy, and the possibility of my death. Through the entire experience, the Spirit of our Living Lord has always been near, always comforting, always assuring, and always all I needed. What better time to be writing a devotional book? This has been for me a personal spiritual journey through His 66 books and a testimony to His all-sufficiency. I hope, in reading these devotionals and spending time in God's Word, you too will have a deeply meaningful spiritual journey by getting to know God more fully and thereby growing a healthy faith.

INTRODUCTION

God's Greatest Desire for You

IF GOD HAD WRITTEN AN INTRODUCTION to the Bible, I imagine He would have said something like this: "I give you this Bible to help you get to know me."

Our heavenly Father's greatest desire for you is that you have a close relationship with Him. He knows you inside and out and wants you to know Him—not just information about Him, but to know Him in a personal, intimate, transforming, everything-you-are way.

If you look at some of the Bible heroes, you will see their greatest desire was to know God. The apostle Paul considered everything in life worthless compared to knowing God. It was his supreme longing (see Philippians 3:8). After Jesus returned to heaven, the apostle Peter told Jesus's followers that what they needed above anything in life was to get to know God. Peter said, "God has given us everything we need for living a godly life. We have received all of this by coming to know him" (2 Peter 1:3 NLT).

Why Did God Give Us the Bible?

Some think God gave us the Bible as an answer book to explain things. Others think the Bible is God's instruction manual designed to help us know what we should and should not do to have a successful life. But perhaps those were not His primary motives for giving us His Bible.

As valuable as the Bible is for explaining, instructing, inspiring, comforting, and challenging us, not one of those benefits encapsulates the main value of the Bible. God gave us His Holy Word because He loves us. He wants us to know the truth about Him from His own perspective and to help us get close to Him. Your best ideas, thoughts, and theories about God will always be far from an accurate knowledge of Him. Without His personal revelation of Himself, you would not be able to know Him on your own.

How Do You Get to Know Anyone?

If you want to get to know anyone in more than a superficial way, you need to spend time with that person and closely examine the person over time. A quick glance now and then will not work. You need to observe the way that person acts and reacts to adversities, evil, and suffering as well as fun, love, and pleasantries.

The same is true for getting to know your God. G. Ernest Wright's classic book *The God Who Act*s became internationally famous for clarifying an almost forgotten but important truth in his day. He explained that other religions say we can get to know God by studying, contemplating, thinking, and theorizing about Him. But Wright showed how the Bible teaches the opposite. Our heavenly Father gives us sixty-six storybooks and personal letters that are mainly historical records of His activities.

Don't ever forget: the Bible is much more than a collection of teachings to accept, laws to memorize, and truths to believe. The Bible is more about real-life stories of non-sugar-coated-situations where God openly discloses His character, His thoughts, His heart, His emotions, His values, and His behavior. God is the Author of His story and has always been active in human history. When He knew the time was just right, He stepped down out of heaven, took on flesh, and became a human. And as Jesus walked around the dusty villages and cities in and around Jerusalem, His disciples followed Him and observed His behavior in all kinds of circumstances. They examined His every move. From their observations they got to know Him. They began to feel close to Him, respected Him, loved Him, served Him, wanted to please Him, and eventually were willing to give their lives for Him. And some of them recorded the stories in the Bible.

Jesus told His followers, "If you had really known me, you would know who my Father is" (John 14:7 NLT). He told them they could get to know God: "No one has ever seen God, but the one and only Son, who is himself God and is in closest relationship with the Father, has made him known" (John 1:18 NIV).

The first book in my Healthy Faith series was entitled *Healthy Faith: A Strategic Lifestyle Plan to Transform Your Head, Heart and Hands*. It is a step-by-step action plan to create a faith that works, a faith that has intellectual, emotional, and biblical integrity. This book is the second in this series. I have entitled it *Devotions for a Healthy Faith: Get to Know God through His Sixty-Six Books* because that is what I hope you will experience. As you go through the entire Bible book by book, letter by letter, and story by story, I hope you will get closer to your God. Perhaps you will begin to see patterns of your God's loving, redemptive nature and the unique ways He relates to you and others. And my prayer is that as His Spirit speaks to you through His Word and my stories, you will get to know Him more intimately and recognize Him more often as He moves in your life.

Why This Kind of Devotional Book?

If you have used other devotional books, you will notice this one is different in its design and purpose. For every book in the Bible, you will find a devotion that contains four elements: (1) a brief overview of the Bible book, (2) a devotion on one of the book's themes, (3) a few favorite scriptures from the focus book and related books, and (4) a few questions to help you apply the devotion to your life. My hope is that through this format, as we explore God's people, stories, and words, you will come to a closer relationship with Him.

HOLY BEGINNINGS: THE PENTATEUCH

Five Books on Beginnings and God's Laws for Living God's Way

GOD LAUNCHES HIS SIXTY-SIX STORYBOOKS and letters with five story-packed books about beginnings. In these initial books God reveals a great deal about Himself through His activities in creation and in developing a relationship with individuals and families. These books especially show us the planning, caring, powerful, and purposeful side of our Father. If you look closely, you will recognize characteristics of God that you'll find throughout the rest of the Bible.

Genesis, which is the Hebrew word for "beginnings," is a storybook filled with—you guessed it—beginnings. In this real-life record, God shows you His work in Creation. You will learn much about the mind, the heart, and the way God relates to His children even when they become rebellious.

Exodus is a storybook that records true accounts of God's deliverance of His covenant people from slavery in Egypt. Through the miracles and sufferings in this beginning book, God gives you some clear pictures you will never forget.

Leviticus is an instructive book that will show you how much God loves order, details, and sincere gratitude through worship. You will get a glimpse of God's heart for helping His people when they don't respond to Him in faith and when they ignore the seriousness of sin.

Numbers is a helpful book filled with heartbreaking stories that assist you to know more about the responsible side of our God. God does not just record stories about His faithful children. He also reports the painful stories of those He loved and blessed and yet who turned on Him and were ungrateful.

Deuteronomy is the last of the five beginning books of the Bible. It records Moses's final sermons before the children of Israel cross over into the Promised Land. As God speaks through Moses, you will get to know more of His merciful and responsible love.

Get to Know God through Genesis

Brief Overview

THE HEBREW WORD FOR *genesis* means "beginnings." So it's no surprise that this first book of the Bible is a series of true stories about beginnings. The beginning of everything God created out of nothing. The beginning of family life. The beginning of good and evil. And the beginning of God's plan to bring His willful and wayward children back into a close relationship with Him.

Genesis introduces you to some of the most famous characters in the Bible: Adam and Eve, Cain and Abel, Noah, Abraham, Isaac, and the most famous of them all, Joseph. Woven like a golden thread through the fabric of each of these fascinating stories is God's introduction of Himself. It is a glimpse of His character, His values, His deepest desires, and His way of acting in everyday life.

By the time you finish Genesis, you recognize the four main characteristics of your Creator God.

- God is *all-powerful*. Nothing is impossible for Him.
- God is *all-knowing*. He knows everything and has a plan and purpose for each of us.
- God is *all-loving*. He is personal, caring, and gracious and wants an intimate relationship with us.
- God is *all-present*. He is always with us no matter what happens.

Genesis ends with the Joseph story. In a dream, God tells the child Joseph that one day he will be great. Joseph's boastings about this fact lead his brothers to sell him into slavery. He ends up in prison in Egypt, but he rises to be second only to Pharaoh and uses his power to save his distressed family in Israel. He forgives them for rejecting him and gives them a new beginning.

The Joseph story is a true account of Joseph, but it is also a preview of God's coming to earth through Jesus to forgive and save His disobedient children. Genesis is God's introduction of Himself and the great themes of the rest of the Bible.

An Inspirational Theme of Genesis

God's Plan or Your Plan?

Originally, the famous Loretto Chapel in Santa Fe, New Mexico, had no staircase to the second-floor choir loft. The architect had died before he finished the plans, and the contractor simply followed the incomplete drawings, which did not include stairs. Because there was no plan in place when it was needed, for many years the nuns had to climb a ladder to the loft in order to sing. Thankfully, they did finally get their staircase (and there's a wonderful story that goes with it, if you want to look it up).

Having a good plan makes a big difference in almost everything you do. As you make important life decisions each day, you will follow some plan or another—one others make for you, one you make for yourself, or the one your all-knowing God designed specifically for you. And that's the main message of the book of Genesis.

I know it's beyond anyone's imagination and understanding, but the Bible tells us that God created you and had a plan for your life before you were born. Sounds mind-blowing, doesn't it? Think about it. God knows all about you, will lead you to accomplish His plan, and will go with you every step of the way. That is the kind of God He is. He created everything, including you, with a purpose in mind.

The Joseph story is a good example of how the Spirit of God works behind the scene carrying out His plans. When Joseph was a boy, God told him in a dream He had a plan for Joseph's life to be a great leader for Him. After many obstacles, including being sold into slavery by his brothers, Joseph eventually became second-in-command of Egypt. Joseph used his God-given power to save his family from the distress of famine. He forgave his brothers and told them, "You intended to harm me, but God intended it all for good" (Genesis 50:20 NLT).

Put another way, "Even though on the outside it often looks like things are falling apart on us, on the inside, where God is making new life, not a day goes by without his unfolding grace" (2 Corinthians 4:16 MSG).

Begin this day and every day looking for and following God's Spirit as He moves in the circumstances of your life. As the Bible says, "So we fix our eyes not on what is seen, but on what is unseen, since what is seen is temporary, but what is unseen is eternal" (2 Corinthians 4:18 NIV).

Related Scriptures from Genesis

[God] settled on [Abraham] as the one to train his children and future family to observe God's way of life, live kindly and generously and fairly, so that God can complete in Abraham what he promised him.

(Genesis 18:19 MSG)

You intended to harm me, but God intended it all for good.

(Genesis 50:20 NLT)

Other Related Scriptures

And I am certain that God, who began the good work within you, will continue his work until it is finally finished on the day when Christ Jesus returns.

(Philippians 1:6 NLT)

I knew you before I formed you in your mother's womb. Before you were born, I set you apart and appointed you as my prophet to the nations.

(Jeremiah 1:5 NLT)

What Is God Saying to You?

When you think about the creation story, what are some of God's characteristics that come to your mind?

What are some advantages of discovering God's plan for you compared to coming up with your own plan?

Dear Father, the better I get to know You, the more I see that You have a plan for my life and are working Your plan. Thank You. Amen.

Get to Know God through Exodus

A Brief Overview

Exodus comes from a Hebrew word that means "a way out." In story after story in this fascinating account-based book, God tell us about the many ways He provides a way out of painful and sometimes seemingly impossible situations. The book's main message is simple: if you'll turn to Him, God wants to and is able to save you and make "a way out" from any problem, no matter how bad things look.

Exodus begins where Genesis ends. In Genesis God saved Joseph from prison, made him the leader of Egypt, saved his family from famine in Israel, and gave them a new start. When Exodus begins, Joseph has died. A new pharaoh, who fears the growing number of Hebrews, enslaves them and orders that all male Hebrew babies be cast into the Nile River.

God saves baby Moses when his mother places him in a basket in the Nile. A princess finds the baby, and young Moses grows up enjoying all the advantages as Pharaoh's son. Over time, he becomes second in power to Pharaoh. But one day, in a moment of anger, Moses kills an Egyptian officer for beating a Hebrew slave. Moses flees, and God again saves Moses by showing him a way out from a death sentence.

During his years in the desert, Moses starts a family. Then one day, God speaks to him from a burning bush, telling him to return to Egypt to save his people from slavery. Through Moses, God uses ten plagues to convince Pharaoh to let the

Hebrews go. While escaping, the Hebrews come to the Red Sea and face what seems to be certain death. The sea is stretched in front of them, and the Egyptian army is behind them. There is no way out in sight until Moses looks up to God. Again God rescues them, this time by miraculously parting the sea, and they cross over on dry ground.

During their journey through the desert to God's promised land, God gives the Hebrews the Ten Commandments and other instructions on how to build successful families and a godly nation. In spite of their continual rebellion against His ways, God saves them repeatedly from hunger, thirst, sickness, and other challenges. The book of Exodus ends with God's glory filling the tabernacle.

The main message of Exodus and its key stories are retold throughout the Bible, showing in all of history how God continues to provide salvation and "a way out" for all who turn to Him.

An Inspirational Theme of Exodus

When It Seems There's No Way Out

Have you ever been in a situation when you felt like there was no way out? I've been there, and it was a frightening and discouraging place. You may be in one of those places now—a relationship, a job, a health condition, a family matter, a spiritual or moral problem. When we end up in that kind of situation, what we want most is "a way out."

God's children were in that kind of situation when they stood with the Red Sea in front of them and the entire army of the most powerful nation on the earth at their backs. They were scared to death. They saw no way out and were about to give up. Then Moses looked up to his God, who alone does the seemingly impossible. Moses asked God for a miracle, and God told Moses to raise his hands toward the sea and tell his terrified followers, "Fear ye not, stand still, and see the salvation of the Lord" (Exodus 14:13 KJV).

The rest of this true story is so miraculous that people for over three thousand years and from all around the world have known what happened next. God sent a powerful and perfectly guided wind that parted the sea and left dry ground for His children to cross to the other side. They had all thought there was no way out. They forgot that their God always has a solution. He always wants to, always knows how, and is always able to deliver us from our situation.

When a crowd questioned Jesus about a seemingly impossible situation, the Bible says, "Jesus looked at them intently and said, 'Humanly speaking, it is impossible. But with God everything is possible'" (Matthew 19:26 NLT). And when Jeremiah faced insurmountable trials, he reminded his people of what happened to their fellow Israelites at the Red Sea. Then he turned to God and said, "O Sovereign Lord! You made the heavens and earth by your strong hand and powerful arm. Nothing is too hard for you!" (Jeremiah 32:17 NLT).

I don't know what you're facing today. And even if I did, more than likely I wouldn't know what to do or be able to offer you a solution. But this I do know, along with those who walked on that dry sea bottom: if you put your faith in the God of the Exodus, the God of a way out, the God who wants to and is able to set you free, He will be your rescuer by intervening in your situation or by working inside your mind and heart to bring you peace.

Related Scriptures from Exodus

I will claim you as my own people, and I will be your God. Then you will know that I am the LORD your God who has freed you.

(Exodus 6:7 NLT)

Fear ye not, stand still, and see the salvation of the LORD.

(Exodus 14:13 KJV)

With your unfailing love you lead/ the people you have redeemed. / In your might, you guide them/ to your sacred home.

(Exodus 15:13 NLT)

Other Related Scriptures

Jesus looked at them intently and said, “Humanly speaking, it is impossible. But with God everything is possible.”

(Matthew 19:26 NLT)

Now all glory to God, who is able, through his mighty power at work within us, to accomplish infinitely more than we might ask or think.

(Ephesians 3:20 NLT)

What Is God Saying to You?

Can you recall a time when you felt like you were on the shores of the Red Sea with "no way out"? What is it about your Lord that can help you in such times?

After God freed the Israelites from bondage, they repeatedly forgot what He did for them. Why does the Lord keep forgiving and rescuing us? What are some things you can do so that you never forget God's goodness to you?

Dear Father, the better I get to know You, the more I see how much You love me and that, in Your time and in Your way, You are able to provide a way out. Amen.

Get to Know God through Leviticus

A Brief Overview

LEVITICUS CONTINUES GOD'S REVELATION OF HIMSELF where Genesis and Exodus leave off. But prepare yourself. You will not find more intriguing, fascinating, and inspiring stories like in Moses's first two books.

In Leviticus, Moses gives His children a hardnosed how-to book. It is a practical instruction manual designed to guide God's newly liberated but still undisciplined and confused people who have no idea what to do with their newfound freedom. They are still learning, still repeatedly falling and having to get up and start all over again.

Exodus ended with God miraculously parting the Red Sea and leading His disorganized children to Mount Sinai. Here, God enrolls them in His Desert School of Hard Knocks. Here, the Hebrews' rescuer Father teaches them how to stay free as they face the unfamiliar paths and formidable enemies before them.

The detailed lessons in Leviticus are designed to prepare God's frail children for their future freedom-journey from Egyptian slavery to His promised land. From personal, moral, and spiritual slavery to full and lasting freedom. From being lured back into their godless, self-centered, unhealthy, primitive culture to being transformed into a holy people. The word *holy* means being special, set apart, different from those around them.

Although barely out of Egypt, the freed Israelites slip and return to their old faithless, complaining ways. When Moses realizes how difficult it is going to be to lead such an unstable crowd, he asks God for help: "Let me know your ways so I may understand you more fully and continue to enjoy your favor" (Exodus 33:13–14 NLT).

God answers Moses by providing him with the ways he requested. God says, "Live holy lives before me because I, GOD, am holy. I have distinguished you from the nations to be my very own" (Leviticus 20:26 MSG).

So Moses records God's guidelines—new ways, new routines, and new habits designed to equip His children at that time and in their unique circumstances. Times change and specifics change, but underneath those time-sensitive instructions are His timeless principles for all people, including us.

God is so good to provide us with His unchanging, holy habits that make holy living possible. Principles such as unselfish sacrifice, clean living, continual worship, responsible obedience, and unlimited gratitude.

An Inspirational Theme of Leviticus

Ever Heard of Holy Habits?

Did you know that 99.99 percent of what you do comes from your habits? That's what William James, the father of modern psychology, discovered. In his book *The Principles of Psychology* he wrote that most of what we do is "purely automatic and habitual."

If you drive your car down the same dirt road long enough, you'll eventually make such deep tracks your car will practically steer itself. The same is true of your mental, moral, and spiritual grooves. The longer you repeat a task, the deeper the impressions are cut into the tracks of your mind until they automatically steer the way you think, feel, make choices, and act.

Ever heard of Holy Habits? If you haven't, you'll be glad to know about them. They are powerful, positive grooves that will lead you to life's best. You will never be able to make permanent, worthwhile, spiritual changes in your life until you develop Holy Habits.

That's why God had Moses write Leviticus. God had just freed His children from Egyptian slavery. But they carried with them some old, deeply grooved, harmful habits learned from their conqueror's pagan practices. For them to have the new quality life the Lord wanted for them and their future families, God knew they would first have to become a holy people—a special kind of people set apart from those around them. So He gave them a manual on how to develop some Holy Habits. He told them, "Keep all my decrees by putting them into practice, for I am the Lord who makes you holy" (Leviticus 20:8 NLT).

Being holy is not being strange or weird. It's not about acting super religious or better-than. It's seeing yourself as someone who thinks differently, values differently, and acts differently—the way God designed you to be and do.

You don't have to guess as to what it means to be holy. Look at the life of Jesus. He is your model. Despite all the evil forces and people who attempted to get him to compromise, Jesus maintained His holy life by developing routines and customs. For example, Jesus made it His habit to regularly get together with God's people: "On the Sabbath day, [Jesus] went into the synagogue, as was his custom" (Luke 4:16 NIV).

Holiness in its simplest form is being like Jesus. It is loving people who don't love you. It's being unselfish when others are selfish, acting responsibly when it costs, forgiving others when they don't deserve it, telling the truth when lying is easier, and graciously taking less that others might have more.

If you want to be able to handle life's worst storms and temptations, it is never going to happen until you make Jesus's Holy Habits your habits. He spent time every morning alone with His Father, studied God's Word, socialized with His spiritual family, thanked His Father in all circumstances, lived each day as a servant of others, giving Himself as a living sacrifice, and gave his heavenly Father the credit and thanks in everything.

We are all traveling in some deep-cut tracks. What grooves or habits have you chosen to guide your daily life?

Related Scriptures from Leviticus

You must faithfully keep all my commands by putting them into practice, for I am the LORD. Do not bring shame on my holy name, for I will display my holiness among the people of Israel. I am the LORD who makes you holy. It was I who rescued you from the land of Egypt, that I might be your GOD. I am the LORD.

(Leviticus 22:31–33 NLT)

So, set yourselves apart to be holy, for I am the LORD your GOD. Keep all my decrees by putting them into practice, for I am the LORD who makes you holy.

(Leviticus 20:7–8 NLT)

Other Related Scriptures

Give your bodies to God because of all he has done for you. Let them be a living and holy sacrifice—the kind he will find acceptable. This is truly the way to worship him.

(Romans 12:1 NLT)

Previously, you let yourselves be slaves to impurity and lawlessness, which led ever deeper into sin. Now you must give yourselves to be slaves to righteous living that you will become holy.

(Romans 6:19 NLT)

What Is God Saying to You?

What does God's manual for Holy Habits in Leviticus say about His nature?

List some areas of your life that are more a reflection of your culture than of the life of your Lord Jesus.

Dear Father, the better I get to know You, the more I see how holy You are and how important Your holy habits are to me. Amen.

Get to Know God through Numbers

A Brief Overview

NUMBERS WAS ORIGINALLY NAMED *Bamidbar* ("in the desert") because the book's opening verse basically says, "And God spoke to Moses in the desert of Sinai." It was later named Numbers because it begins and ends with a detailed census of Israel.

This fourth book of Moses is a record of real people, real places, and real events as God prepares His newly freed children to enter His Promised Land. Its main message is that God wants his wayward children to get reacquainted with Him and His special, holy way of living. They had been away from Him so long and had taken on so many of the customs and views of the wicked cultures surrounding them that their knowledge of God was greatly distorted.

Throughout Numbers, God is pictured as an all-loving, all-powerful, all-knowing, and personally involved God who overcomes their every crisis, supplies their every need, guides them through their every wandering, forgives their sins, and continually opens new doors for them. Yet despite all of His efforts to help and guide His rebellious children, they use their God-given free will to act as stubborn, distrustful, selfish, and complaining people. Their self-destructive ways result in thirty-seven more years of wandering through the brutal wilderness.

The book ends with the Israelites again at Canaan's borders. God announces that some, because of their unfaithfulness, will not enter the Promised Land. But those like Caleb, who had a different spirit, will receive God's final instructions and be able to enter their reward—the Promised Land.

An Inspirational Theme of Numbers

Why Am I Doing What I Do?

In Numbers, Moses tells about sending men to scout out the Promised Land. They return with two reports. The first group says, "The land is wonderful, but we shouldn't go over there. Our enemies are like giants." Caleb's report was different: "The people are strong, but our God is stronger. God saved us from Egypt. He can do it again" (see Numbers 13).

Caleb dared to stand alone, not in his own strength, but in God's. While others wanted to quit, Caleb wanted to do more, to do good. What made him different? It wasn't his size, intelligence, strength, or armor. Caleb had a different attitude. He trusted God (see Numbers 14:23–24).

Like all on life's desert roads, even with his different attitude, Caleb still experienced years of hardships, complaining family members, loss, and brutal resistances. Jesus experienced those same harsh realities and tried to prepare his disciples for them. Before He sent His disciples out to do good, He warned them: Don't be surprised. When you give kindness, you'll be repaid with meanness. When you try to help, you'll be hurt, treated unfairly, made fun of, and even hated.

For some of Jesus's followers, the negative responses were just too much. They became disillusioned or angry and just gave up. For others, the adversities seemed to motivate them to do even more. What made the difference? It was their attitude, sometimes called their spirit or motivation.

Paul explained how he kept going despite his hardships: "You must have the same attitude that Christ Jesus had" (Philippians 2:5 NLT). Peter said it this way: "You must arm yourselves with the same attitude [Jesus] had" (1 Peter 4:1 NLT).

The Bible's explanation of the word *attitude* is not the popular view of putting on a smiley face and thinking positive thoughts or having an unrealistic, unfounded optimism. It means having a realistic, grateful confidence. That's what kept Caleb and Peter and Paul going. The reason they never stopped doing good was not to get something in return but to demonstrate their gratitude for all God had done for them.

As you face today's challenges, choose right now to do what Peter, Paul, and Caleb did. Have a grateful and confident attitude even when hard times come. And ask yourself this important question: "Why am I doing what I do?"

Related Scriptures from Numbers

But because my servant Caleb has a different spirit and follows me wholeheartedly, I will bring him into the land he went to, and his descendants will inherit it.

(Numbers 14:24 NIV)

The land we [Joshua and Caleb] traveled through and explored is a wonderful land! And if the Lord is pleased with us, he will bring us safely into that land and give it to us. It is a rich land flowing with milk and honey.

(Numbers 14:7–8 NLT)

Other Related Scriptures

May the God who gives endurance and encouragement give you the same attitude of mind toward each other that Christ Jesus had.

(Romans 15:5 NIV)

So then, since Christ suffered physical pain, you must arm yourselves with the same attitude he had, and be ready to suffer, too.

(1 Peter 4:1 NLT)

What Is God Saying to You?

God had some things to say about Caleb. What does the fact that He said those words about Caleb say about God Himself?

How do you think God would describe your attitude and your motivation for doing the things you do? What are some of your attitudes toward others that are not like Jesus's?

Dear Father, the better I get to know You, the more I see how I want to have an attitude like Jesus. Amen.

Get to Know God through Deuteronomy

A Brief Overview

DEUTERONOMY MEANS "THE LAW THE SECOND TIME." Moses wrote the book for God's children who were about to enter the Promised Land with Joshua and Caleb as their new leaders. Except for those two men, none of those going into their long-awaited homeland had ever seen God's supernatural acts around the Exodus.

This last of the five Books of Moses is one of the most loved books in the Bible. Jesus quoted it often. It is a summary of the other four books. Moses is now one hundred and twenty years old. He writes these three sermons and an appendix from Mount Nebo. He knows the Israelites will face challenging days in an unfamiliar land controlled by fierce, primitive tribes who practiced immoral and superstitious religions. Moses sought to prepare them through these messages.

Moses knew that their future attitude and actions must be based on their knowledge of what God had done in the past and how they must follow God's instructions for holy living. His main focus was calling them to remember they were a holy people, chosen by God. He reminded them that God had dealt with them graciously and that they should respond by giving Him their loyalty, loving God with all their hearts, souls, and minds.

In Moses's first sermon in chapters 1 through 4, he looks back and gives serious challenges to the new nation. He stresses the importance of teaching their children and future generations the key stories surrounding the Exodus.

In Moses's second sermon in chapters 5 through 28, Moses restates the Ten Commandments, explaining the principles, laws, and traditions they will need to maintain a godly life as individuals, families, and God's chosen nation.

Moses's third sermon in chapters 29 and 30 contains a call to commitment and a warning. He strongly cautions about losing their moral distinction by gradually taking on the immoral customs of their culture.

Finally, in chapters 31 through 34, you'll see Moses, the one who has led the people of God the entire time, hand over his authority to Joshua. Moses then commissions Joshua for the new work, asks God to bless the people, and gives God the glory. Before Moses dies on Mount Nebo, God allows him to look over the valley into the Promised Land, a land Moses is not allowed to enter. But in Moses's faithfulness, he knows he is going to an even better land.

An Inspirational Theme of Deuteronomy

He Goes Ahead of You

Fear is a powerful emotion. If you don't take control of your fears, they will definitely take control of every part of you. And they'll cause you to miss out on some wonderful things God has planned for you—a meaningful relationship with Him and others, a fulfilling purpose, a deep inner peace, and many enjoyable adventures and exciting opportunities.

When you face something that you think could be embarrassing or dangerous, your mind produces feelings we call fear, stress, anxiety, or worry. You don't have to allow those feeling to control you. God wants to help you and has the answer for how you can overcome any fear.

Before writing this, I thought it would be interesting to see what answers others give to one of the most often asked questions on the internet: "How can I overcome my fears?" Would you believe Google found 3,350,000 articles on the subject? Some answers were helpful, but honestly, far too many were just plain wacky. So I returned to the Bible and found the answer your heavenly Father has been giving people for centuries.

When God's chosen people gazed wishfully across the valley at the unfamiliar and dangerous Promised Land, they asked, "What should we do? We're afraid to go in."

Most of their leaders answered, "Don't do it. It's too risky. Your enemies are too strong." But God gave them and Joshua, their new leader, the same answer He has always given people paralyzed by their fears: "Do not be afraid or discouraged, for the LORD will personally go ahead of you. He will be with you; he will neither fail you nor abandon you" (Deuteronomy 31:8 NLT).

Sounds too simple, doesn't it? Well, it *is* simple. It's not easy. But it works. It has worked for people since Bible times. It has worked for me, and it will work for you.

I was eight the first time I visited my Granddaddy Nichols on his farm in Virginia. Growing up on Pompano Beach, Florida, I had never milked a cow. So naturally, that's the job granddaddy gave me. One morning before daybreak, he handed me the milk bucket and told me to go on out to the barn and milk the cows. I was scared to death and didn't think

I could do it. So I told him, "Granddad, it's dark out there. I don't know how to milk a cow. And besides, what if there are snakes in that barn?"

Granddaddy put his hand on my shoulder and said, "Wait here."

He went out to the barn and returned shortly. "Bill, you can relax. You don't need to be afraid anymore. I've checked everything out. There are no snakes out there, and I turned the light on. And I'm going to be right by your side all the time. How's that?"

You guessed it. I had a great time milking my first cow. And in addition to that, our whole family had fresh milk for breakfast because I trusted my granddad and did my job.

You need to do the same thing with your fears. First, remember your heavenly Father says He has already scouted things out and gotten everything ready. He's checking for snakes and turning on lights. And He's going to be with you all along the way. That's God's part. It's simple because nothing is impossible for Him, and He's been handling folks' fears from the beginning of time.

The second part is not so easy. It's your part. It's called faith—believing your Father tells the truth and depending on Him as you leave the safety of your home and head for the barn.

Related Scriptures from Deuteronomy

The LORD your GOD has blessed you in everything you have done. He has watched your every step through this great wilderness. During these forty years, the LORD your GOD has been with you, and you have lacked nothing.

(Deuteronomy 2:7 NLT)

So be strong and courageous! Do not be afraid and do not panic before them. For the LORD your GOD will personally go ahead of you. He will neither fail you nor abandon you.

(Deuteronomy 31:6 NLT)

Other Related Scriptures

Don't be afraid, [Jesus] said. Take courage. I am here!

(Matthew 14:27 NLT)

So do not fear, for I am with you; do not be dismayed, for I am your God. I will strengthen you and help you; I will uphold you with my righteous right hand.

(Isaiah 41:10 NIV)

What Is God Saying to you?

What do the sermons of Moses tell us about the nature of our God?

List some of the things you fear most. Next, describe each one to God. Then, ask God what He thinks about your fears. Now, listen to Him.

Dear Father, the better I get to know You, the more I see there's nothing for me to fear since You are going ahead of me and will be with me. Amen.

HOLY HISTORY

Twelve Books on the Activities of God in Building a Community of Believers

THESE TWELVE RECORDS OF HISTORY are not recordings of everything happening in history. They are a record of a special and holy part of history—the activities of God among His chosen people who were called to be a light to all others on earth.

This section of God's written revelation of Himself focuses on His activities among the Israelites after forty years of their wandering in the desert and the death of Moses. The twelve storybooks reveal God's patience, mercy, and purposeful choices in His process of building a special family and nation. That growth was difficult for a young nation facing surrounding hostile states with superstitious beliefs, profane practices, and harmful human customs.

God gave each of His children a free will to make their own choices. In these historical stories you will see the persistent love of our Father toward His rebellious children, many who used their God-given free wills to make some bad choices. You will see them abandon their covenant with God and take on the customs of their godless neighbors.

You will also get to know more about your God as you continually witness His faithfulness to His ultimate purposes for His children. God discloses His unwavering merciful and dependable character in and through the lives of real leaders who are both faithfully sacrificial and unfaithfully self-centered.

God led the Israelites across the Jordan River and into the Promised Land by using His godly leaders Joshua and Caleb. From Joshua's story all the way through to Esther's, you will follow God and His children as they occupy their new Promised Land, build a nation, become divided and immoral, and finally get taken into slavery. You will see God use the pagan Babylonian Empire to show His children the painful path back to Him. In all of this, God again demonstrates His sovereignty and faithfulness as He works through Esther to lead Cyrus, king of Persia, to come to know God and set God's people free to go home.

Throughout every story in these twelve special storybooks, you will observe God loving and teaching His people the consequences of sin and the way to a close and rewarding relationship with Him.

Before God gave us His greatest revelation of Himself in Jesus, He worked with and through His children individually and collectively to demonstrate the eternal and unchanging principles that Jesus would fulfill. The God we know in Jesus is the same God we see in Joshua, Samuel, David, Ruth, and Esther.

Get to Know God through Joshua

A Brief Overview

JOSHUA, LIKE *JESUS*, means "God saves" or "God sets free." As you read this instructive and inspiring book, you'll realize just how fitting this name is. As God's chosen leader to take over the work of Moses, Joshua led his people to freedom from years of wandering in ignorance and self-destruction. Under his guidance, the new nation of Israel possessed God's Promised Land and began to carry out God's eternal purposes for them.

The book begins after Moses's death around 1400 BC. The Israelites are camped on the banks of the Jordan River across from the walled city of Jericho. But it will take nearly seven years for Joshua and his people to conquer Canaan.

The main message of Joshua is clear: God keeps His promises. Sometimes because things are going in the wrong direction, it appears that God is doing nothing and that His plans will fail. But as you continue to read this fascinating, historical record, you begin to discover that you can always count on our great Creator-Sustainer God to come through, no matter how bad things feel or how impossible they look. Time and again the records reveal God carrying out His plans through people like Rahab the harlot (see 2:1–21), Joshua in the battle of Jericho (see 6:1–27), and Caleb the young soldier (see 14:6–14).

Although it is heartbreaking and confusing in many ways to see God's children suffer, God is seen as one who is always dependable even when the consequences are devastating. For example, Achan's sin results in serious losses at Ai (see 7:2–5). Israel's armies fail to carry out God's commands, and their enemies become an ongoing immoral disease to Israel's culture and faith.

The book closes by highlighting the burials of three of Israel's heroes: Joshua (see 24:29–30), Joseph's bones (see 24:32), and Eleazar the high priest (see 24:33). Each chose to follow God's challenge, the challenge He offers each of us: "Choose you this day whom you will serve" (see 24:15). They each chose to serve God by following His plan rather than their own.

The book of Joshua is a reminder for all of God's children for all ages that it always pays to keep following God's lead, no matter the confusion and challenges.

An Inspirational Theme of Joshua

Breaking Down Your Walls

Don't you wish you could live in a perfect place that God created just for you? Let's call it God's Promised Land. Most people spend all their lives looking for it but never find it—that peace-filled, joy-filled, love-filled, hope-filled, and purpose-filled place God says He has prepared for each of us. It's what God's Word calls the abundant life (see John 10:10).

You don't have to be a part of that seeker group traveling the wide road that never reaches God's Promised Land. You can get on what Jesus called the narrow road that leads to God's personal Promised Land for you. However, before you can get on that special, promising road, you might need to knock down some big, ugly, old walls standing in the way.

That's what happened to God's children when they crossed the Jordan River. They were ready to enter their long-awaited Promised Land and wanted so much to begin their new abundant life. But before they could go in, they faced a wall—a real wall. The Jericho wall, the oldest and biggest fortification in the world at that time, surrounded what was considered the most wicked city in the world. Modern excavations reveal that the wall's stone foundation was eleven feet high and fourteen feet wide, with a sloped wall on top of it that rose another thirty-five feet. This was the foundation for the final stone-wall lookout.

The people of Jericho were known throughout that part of the world for their impenetrable wall and for their greedy, brutal, and immoral practices. After years of mercy, God decided their time was up. He would use His small band of followers to demolish Jericho's presumed impermeable wall and rescue the region.

Before the massive wall would come tumbling down, God instructed Joshua to do something that seemed ridiculous. He told Joshua to march His unarmed leaders around the wall for six days and on the seventh day to blow their rams' horns and thank God for what He was about to do.

Joshua did exactly what God instructed. And when those horns began to blast, those so-called impenetrable walls began to crumble, bringing an end to a wicked people and their supposed indestructible wall. It was a timely lesson for the Israelites: they could now enter the Promised Land and face other ungodly and seemingly impossible walls of resistance.

And it's an important lesson for each of us as we attempt to enter the abundant life God has for each of us. The lesson is clear: if you want to reach your Promised Land, you cannot ignore the walls standing between you and God's future for you. The most difficult walls any of us face are not usually physical barriers but harmful internal walls of self-reliance, greed, hate, unforgiveness, pride, and immoral practices that over time have grown big and strong inside us. These barricades keep out God's love, peace, joy, and hope.

You'll need to recognize them, confront them, and admit that they are obstacles you can't possibly overcome alone. Like Joshua, you must acknowledge that you can't possibly overcome such impenetrable walls by your own strength. But you can bring them down the same way Joshua did.

Begin today by naming each wall that is separating you from God's awaiting abundant life. Admit your need for God's help. Turn daily to His Word for instructions. Join other abundant life-seekers on a regular basis for strength and encouragement. Listen and look for the leading of God's Spirit in your mind and heart. And you'll begin to see God breaking down those Jericho walls in you.

Related Scriptures from Joshua

Purify yourselves, for tomorrow the LORD will do great wonders among you.

(Joshua 3:5 NLT)

Not a single one of all the good promises the LORD had given to the family of Israel was left unfulfilled; everything he had spoken came true.

(Joshua 21:45 NLT)

Other Related Scriptures

It was by faith that the people of Israel marched around Jericho for seven days, and the walls came crashing down.

(Hebrews 11:30 NLT)

The night is almost gone; the day of salvation will soon be here. So, remove your dark deeds like dirty clothes, and put on the shining armor of right living.

(Romans 13:12 NLT)

What Is God Saying to You?

God gave Joshua specific instructions about marching around the Jericho wall for seven days before God made it fall. What do you think that says about God?

What are some things God wants you to do to get rid of the sinful walls in your inner life?

Dear Father, the better I get to know You, the more I see that You desire to give me an abundant life, and You have the ability to make it happen. Amen.

Get to Know God through Judges

A Brief Overview

JUDGES, IN THIS TIME IN BIBLE HISTORY, were more like political and military leaders than legal arbitrators. God appointed them to help His people carry out His purposes for them as families and a new nation.

Before Joshua's death, instead of having a king like the surrounding nations, God gave His young nation judges who were supposed to be representatives of the people. They were to lead Israel as God's Spirit directed them. But after Joshua, the people changed their minds and wanted a king. They demanded that Saul be crowned king by the prophet Samuel in 1051 BC (see 1 Samuel 10:24).

The events described in Judges were not written chronologically but were designed to give an overview of some of the struggles and victories God's children experienced in settling the Promised Land and developing a moral society in the middle of a longstanding immoral culture.

Throughout the Bible you find a realistic and honest record of the facts without an attempt to cover up the bad that God's people did or to overstate the good. The accounts in Judges are a mixture of great rebellion and great faithfulness under pressure. Time and again in this book you'll face the age-old problem of evil and suffering—how can a good and powerful God do or even allow such horrible things to happen to His own children? And you'll come to see the consequences of

God's giving us a free will so we can choose to love Him or not. You'll witness the devastating results of lives lived apart from God's moral laws and personal leadership.

The main message of Judges is simple. Our loving Creator God is a responsible parent. He is both merciful and honest, forgiving and just. Without overpowering our free wills, He does all He can to help His children choose what is best. But He will not ignore rejection or let those who turn their backs on Him go unpunished, hurting those touched by their evil or apathetic choices.

Many of the Israelites forgot the miraculous events that brought them to their Promised Land. Most of them were no longer a people living and serving out of gratitude. Judges is a good book for helping each of us ask ourselves some critical questions: Have I forgotten the great things God has done for me? Am I living in constant gratitude or oblivious to the reality and presence of God? Will God need to discipline me to get my attention?

An Inspirational Theme of Judges

Turn "Making No Sense" Into "Making Good Sense"

My friend Maggie was eighty when Neil Armstrong became the first man on the moon. Maggie was a smart, likable, commonsense person who loved farming but wouldn't use the remote control for her television and refused to get on a plane. Nor would she believe that Armstrong walked on the moon. She told me, "It just doesn't make sense that such a huge hunk of metal can get off the ground, much less fly to the moon."

It is hard to believe in something or commit to it if you cannot personally figure it out. But that's what faith is. It's doing what God says when you can't completely figure it out and moving forward when you cannot see the future. Faith is the way your heavenly Father helps you experience more than the physical world. It's how He introduced you to the eternal dimension of your life, His spiritual world.

God will never force you to enjoy His miraculous gifts and the amazing future He has planned for you, but He will open doors for you. He will invite you to trust Him, to follow Him, and to do what He says is best even when it seems impossible or when you can't begin to understand it. God's Word says, "Trust in the LORD with all your heart and lean not on your own understanding" (Proverbs 3:5 NIV).

Gideon's story in Judges 6 and 7 is a fascinating real-life example of God's way of transforming the life of a man who puts his faith in God. When God invited a humble, insecure, peace-loving farmer named Gideon to lead Israel's army against their worst enemy, Gideon was shocked. No doubt he thought, "Lord, you must have the wrong address. You've come to the wrong house. I am no warrior. I've always been just a simple farmer. I know nothing about fighting or leading armies. I can't possibly do that. It makes no sense."

After showering the Lord with reasons as to why God's invitation made no sense, Gideon finally accepted God's challenge. From that point on, Gideon saw God take care of him. God gave Gideon and his straggly little army of three hundred untrained soldiers the means to defeat the Midianite army of 135,000 well-trained soldiers. Even with 450-to-1 odds against him, Gideon saw God go to work and perform remarkable and mighty acts when Gideon stopped trying to figure out God's plans and simply started doing what God planned. Gideon saw a whole new dimension in life when he started depending on God's wisdom instead of his own understanding and abilities.

Remember my friend Maggie? Her beliefs did not alter the truth: remote controls work, planes fly, and Armstrong walked on the moon. She just missed out on knowing it.

Could it be that your all-loving, all-powerful, all-knowing, and all-present God is doing the same for you? Is He inviting you to experience His miraculous future? Is it possible that He is offering you a chance to do something you can't do by yourself—become His close, personal friend and get in on His plan for your life and eternity?

Are you willing to risk going beyond your own understanding and reach out to your Creator-Savior God who knows everything about you and loves you? The more you think about it, doesn't trusting Him turn your "This makes no sense" into "This make good sense"?

Related Scriptures from Judges

The LORD turned to [Gideon] and said, "Go in the strength you have and save Israel out of Midian's hand. Am I not sending you?"

(Judges 6:14 NIV)

The LORD said to [Gideon], "I will be with you. And you will destroy the Midianites as if you were fighting against one man.

(Judges 6:16 NLT)

Other Related Scriptures

Trust in the Lord with all your heart; do not depend on your own understanding.

(Proverbs 3:5 NLT)

That's why I take pleasure in my weaknesses, and in the insults, hardships, persecutions, and troubles that I suffer for Christ. For when I am weak, then I am strong.

(2 Corinthians 12:10 NLT)

What Is God Saying to You?

Gideon felt inadequate for the job God called him to do. Why might God call a farmer with no military experience to be the leader of Israel's army? What does that say about God?

Since God is all-powerful and nothing is impossible for Him, why do we sometimes still hesitate to do what He wants us to do?

Dear Father, the better I get to know You, the more I see that following You is my best choice and is much better than following my own understanding. Amen.

Get to Know God through Ruth

A Brief Overview

THE BOOK OF RUTH WAS WRITTEN by the prophet Samuel. It has been called the most beautiful and heartwarming short story ever written. Ruth's story took place between 1160 BC and 1100 BC, during the end to the period of the judges (see Ruth 1:1). Those were sad and destructive days filled with judgment and suffering resulting from the Israelites' rejection of their families' faith-based heritage and their own spiritual and social immoral practices.

In contrast to the overall darkness of the masses, you see in this little book a brief picture of one family in a small town seeking to put God first and to follow His way in their everyday activities. Written from the perspective of Naomi, Ruth's mother-in-law, Ruth is unique by being the first story that looks at God through the eyes of a woman. Naomi relates the stories of her husband's and sons' deaths, her daughters-in-law, her return to Bethlehem, her relative Boaz, her land to sell, and her view of God.

Naomi's story is much like Job's. Although a child of God, she lost everything: her home, husband, her sons, and her source of income. She was homeless and almost hopeless, but in faith she turned to her God. He gave her Ruth.

Ruth's emotional and loyal vow of love to Naomi has often been considered one of the most meaningful expressions of true love in the Bible. In modern days it is often included in wedding ceremonies to communicate the depth of love newlyweds should have one for the other: "Where you go, I will go, and where you stay, I will stay. Your people will be my people and your God my God. Where you die, I will die" (Ruth 1:16–17 NIV).

The book of Ruth demonstrates to us the blessings that God gives to those who have faithful love and reminds us that God always answers the prayers of people. He provided for people like Naomi and Ruth throughout history. He cared about the small, the lowly, and these two poor widows with seemingly no hope for a future.

Like Naomi, Ruth, Boaz, and our Lord Jesus, we are called to be faithful to each other, reaching out to help others with that same humble, divine grace in spite of our immoral and selfish culture.

An Inspirational Theme of Ruth

Above All Else

One freezing November night in Times Square, NYPD Officer Lawrence DePrimo was working a counterterrorism post when he noticed an elderly homeless man who sat barefooted. The officer's heart was moved. He slipped away, but in only a few minutes he returned with a new pair of boots.

If a tourist hadn't taken a cellphone photo of him kneeling to help the man put on the boots and lace them up, his selfless act of love would have gone unnoticed. The tourist was so touched by the scene she posted the photo and story on the NYPD Facebook page. No surprise, it went viral.

Why are we so stirred by such stories? It's simple. Selflessness is the pearl of great price. A glimpse of God's heart. The greatest gift you can ever get or give. It's thinking about, wanting to, and then actually putting another's needs before your needs or wants (see Philippians 2:4).

The Bible story of Ruth is one the most beautiful examples of selfless love in all of literature. Due to a devastating famine, a godly woman named Naomi left her hometown of Bethlehem and moved to the nearby nation of Moab. It was there her husband and two sons died, leaving her broken, penniless, homeless, and alone except for her two daughters-in-law.

When Naomi decided to return to Bethlehem, her widowed daughter-in-law Ruth decided to leave everything she had and the only home she had ever known to stay by Naomi's side. Naomi thanked Ruth for her generous offer but told her such a sacrifice was too much. But as noted above, Ruth's reply was one of absolute selflessness as she committed herself to remain with Naomi.

Selflessness is at the core of our Christian faith. It is the main message of the Bible, a snapshot of God's heart and character. Selflessness is the basic reason relationships succeed, and selfishness is the main reason relationships fail.

If you had to choose just one word to characterize the life and message of Jesus, what would it be? I would choose *selfless*. Above everything else, Jesus was selfless. He cared more for others than he did himself.

God created you and selflessly gave His Son to die on the cross for you. Now He is giving you a chance to have life at its best. This can only happen by living a selfless life like Jesus. Remember, everything you have is a gift from God. So decide now to go counter-culture. Choose to follow the example of your Lord, and throughout this day think and do all you can to give yourself away. As Jesus said, "Only those who throw away their lives for my sake and for the sake of the Good News will ever know what it means to really live" (Mark 8:35 TLB).

Related Scriptures from Ruth

Naomi said to her, "your sister-in-law has gone back to her people and to her gods. You should do the same." But Ruth replied, "Don't ask me to leave you and turn back. Wherever you go, I will go; wherever you live, I will live. Your people will be my people, and your God will be my God.

(Ruth 1:15–16 NLT)

May the Lord, the God of Israel, under whose wings you have come to take refuge, reward you fully for what you have done.

(Ruth 2:12 NLT)

Other Related Scriptures

Don't be selfish; don't try to impress others. Be humble, thinking of others as better than yourselves.

(Philippians 2:3 NLT)

The Son of Man came not to be served but to serve others and to give his life as a ransom for many.

(Matthew 20:28 NLT)

What Is God Saying to You?

What does it say about God that He would want Ruth and Naomi's story in His story?

What are some ways Jesus demonstrated selfless behavior? What are some simple, practical things you could do to be selfless?

Dear Father, the better I get to know You, the more I see how utterly selfless You are. Thank You, Lord. Amen.

Get to Know God through 1 Samuel

A Brief Overview

ORIGINALLY, 1 AND 2 SAMUEL were one book. The Greek translation of the Bible, the Septuagint, was the first version to divide them into two books. First Samuel covers some of the key activities of God in the lives of His people for a period of 110 years, from the closing days of the judges when Samuel was born (1120 BC) until Saul's death (1011 BC).

The book gives you a glimpse of a significant transitional time in the lives of God's people in Israel. They move from being a disorganized group of slaves freed from Egypt to being led by God-chosen judges to demanding that they have a king like the nations around them. In 1 Samuel, you will read about Samuel's birth, his calling, and ministry. You will follow the rise and fall of King Saul and God's preparing of young David for his historic role as king of Israel—the voice of God and the one called "a man after God's own heart" (see 1 Samuel 13:14).

Saul, the first king, was a big man—a tall, handsome warrior whom the people thought would be the perfect king. Their thinking was wrong. Saul was big—a big disappointment in every way that counted. He did not have a heart for God, and his life showed it. His reign was stormy, embarrassing, hurtful to his people, and short lived.

Soon God told the prophet Samuel that the people had made a mistake in choosing Saul. So this time God would make the choice of who would lead His people. God led Samuel to David, who was anointed king.

The remainder of 1 Samuel follows David's activities as a young shepherd and warrior. You will find fascinating reading in the accounts of David winning the battle over the giant Goliath (see 17:1–58), his close relationship with Jonathan (see 18:1–4), his many victories in battle (see 18:5–30), and his patience in waiting to become the next king following the death of Saul (see 31:1–13).

The main message of 1 Samuel is clear: God has a plan for your life, and the only way to find life at its best, the way God designed it, is to follow His Spirit and the guidelines He has given His children. You will see this great truth in the lives of Samuel, Saul, and David. This truth is summarized in Samuel's words from God: "To obey is better than sacrifice" (1 Samuel 15:22 KJV).

An Inspirational Theme of 1 Samuel

Giants Greater Than Goliath

Sooner or later you're going to have to take on a Goliath. Not one that looks like David's Goliath—a tall, muscular, sword-slinging, ugly warrior. More than likely, your giants will come at you in the form of an intimidating boss, a seemingly impossible task, a devastating illness, the death of a loved one, or some other challenge.

As difficult as those tangible Goliaths can be, there are other giants even greater. You'll need to face those first. They're not intruders from without but attitudes from within. Attitudes that hide in your mind and heart and keep you from being able to handle your physical giants.

The famous story of David and Goliath is about a young shepherd boy who, with a single rock from his trusty slingshot, miraculously killed the supposed unbeatable, God-mocking giant Goliath. No soldier or other adult would stand up to Goliath, but the boy David did. How did he do it? While faithfully protecting his sheep over the years from all sorts of dangerous wild animals and natural elements, David developed a habit of defeating his outer enemies by first defeating his own personal inner enemies of fear, distraction, and pride. For years as a shepherd, David grew up having to choose between favoring his fears or his flock. Would he put his sheep before himself? Or would he put his responsibilities before his own safety?

First, David chose faithfulness over his self-centeredness. So, when Goliath showed up, it was business as usual for David. You'll always struggle with handling your physical Goliaths until you start daily following David's example in handling your smallest, common everyday fears with God's help.

Second, David kept his focus. He didn't let discouraging and critical voices distract him. King Saul, an expert in war, tried to discourage him by saying, "You're too young and too inexperienced. You're not a soldier, and you have no chance against this giant warrior" (see 1 Samuel 17). David stayed focused on God's voice rather all the other negative voices from his past and present. You'll never be able handle your Goliaths until you daily practice listening to the encouraging word of

God and His Spirit instead of the negative naysayers around and inside you.

Finally, David considered himself a humble servant. He didn't see himself as a giant slayer. After all, he was the smallest, youngest, and least qualified male in his family. When everyone said he was not big enough, strong enough, or skilled enough, David already knew all that. He admitted it. But he told all of them that he didn't plan on defeating Goliath on his own abilities but by doing what he had always done. David put his faith in one who was bigger, stronger, and more skilled than any giant.

You'll be able to defeat your Goliaths when you start putting aside pride and saying in humility what David said: "You come against me with sword and spear and javelin, but I come against you in the name of the LORD Almighty" (1 Samuel 17:45 NIV). If you're not already daily practicing God's proven ways, start today by asking Jesus to help you defeat your secret, every-day, inner Goliaths. Then trust Him to provide what you need.

Related Scriptures from 1 Samuel

The LORD doesn't see things the way you see them. People judge by outward appearance, but the LORD looks at the heart.

(1 Samuel 16:7 NLT)

It has pleased the LORD to make you his very own people . . . But be sure to fear the LORD and faithfully serve him. Think of all the wonderful things he has done for you.

(1 Samuel 12:22–24 NLT)

Other Related Scriptures

For I can do everything through Christ, who gives me strength.

(Philippians 4:13 NLT)

Commit everything you do to the LORD. / Trust him, and he will help you.

(Psalm 37:5 NLT)

What Is God Saying to You?

What does the fact that God chose a shepherd boy to become king and lead His people say about Him?

What are some of the physical or social Goliaths in your life that you are dealing with now?

What are some of the inner giants you are dealing with these days?

Dear Father, the better I get to know You, the more I see that nothing is impossible for You. Help me overcome my inner giants. Amen.

Get to Know God through 2 Samuel

A Brief Overview

AS YOU READ 2 SAMUEL, you continue the story of King David's forty-year reign from about 1011 to 971 BC. The book begins with David's deep grief over the deaths of Saul, his predecessor, and Jonathan, his close friend (see 2 Samuel 1:19–27). Then, not long after David became king over the two tribes of the southern kingdom of Israel, he united all twelve tribes into one nation called Israel.

Chapters 1 through 10 tell exciting and memorable accounts of why David was so greatly revered and loved. By following God's leadership as a child and young man, David rose from a common shepherd boy to become the most honored and successful king in Israel's history. He was victorious in battle after battle. He was loved by the people for his tender care for the sick and poor. He brought back to Jerusalem the cherished Ark of the Covenant that had been captured and lost for years. He showed compassion for Mephibosheth, Jonathan's crippled son, by moving him into his home and treating him as his own son. Greatly admired by the nation's leaders and common people and feared by his enemies, David gave God the glory for all his accomplishments.

However, the Bible writers did not minimize or ignore David's weaknesses, misfortunes, and moral failures. Even with all David's wrongdoing, God showed him mercy. You get to know God in a new and different way by observing the way

He dealt with David. God said, "I have found David, son of Jesse, a man after my own heart" (Acts 13:22 NLT).

God and David had a close personal relationship, and God used David's commitment in many ways in spite of his troubles and bad choices. David disappointed God and wounded their relationship in his adultery with Bathsheba (see 2 Samuel 11:1–27), his part in the death of his own child (see 12:18), his daughter Tamar's rape by his son Amnon (see 13:1–39), Amnon's murder (see 13:28–30), David's political overthrow by his hate-filled son Absalom (see 15:1–37), and Absalom's heartbreaking death (see 18:1–33). Yet even with all of David's sins, he repented and asked the Lord for mercy. God willingly offered him forgiveness and a second chance to carry out His purposes. Because of David's relationship with his heavenly Father, he later received a special, divine promise called the Davidic Covenant: "Your house and your kingdom will endure forever before me; your throne will be established forever" (2 Samuel 7:16 NIV).

The fulfillment of this divine covenant was seen in Jesus, the Messiah, who was providentially in the lineage of David.

An Inspirational Theme of 2 Samuel

I've Sinned. What Will God Do?

Do you ever wonder if the bad things that happen to you are God's punishment for your sins? Is it true that God keeps a list of every sin, failure, mistake, or wrong you've ever done, and when you die and face His final judgment, you pay for all your sins before you can get into heaven?

As you would imagine, there are many misleading and hurtful beliefs about this subject. Often such beliefs look true because they are supported by Bible verses taken out of context. Holding on to such false beliefs can cause you a great deal of confusion, worry, and fear. So, how can you know the truth as to what God does about your sins? The best thing you can do is to turn to the source of all truth, God Himself.

When you look at what God has been saying and doing for centuries, you find a twofold message about this subject repeated throughout the Bible. First, the Bible gives numerous stories describing what happens to those who say, "I'll do it my way. I don't need God." Those lives are filled with needless suffering, pain, brokenness, anger, and hopelessness. That is not what God wants for you, but it is what many choose.

Second, the Bible gives other stories describing what happens to those who say, "I've sinned. I'm sorry for my sins. I can't handle my sins. I need God's forgiveness and inner strength." Those stories describe lives filled with gratitude, joy, peace, purpose, and eternal hope. That is what God wants for you, and it's what you can have.

The truth is God already dealt with your sins when His son, Jesus, died on the Cross. He took all of our sins on Himself. That means He, who had no sin, suffered and died in your place. You don't ever have to pay for your sins.

God has done His part. Now it's up to you. Will you accept or reject His amazing, supernatural gift?

Remember David? God loved him unreservedly. David was His child even with all his sins. God wanted to forgive him completely and held no grudges. He erased David's sins. And God will do no less for you. He understands you fully and is sympathetic about your failures and faults. God offers you hope and will use your past to make you a useful and grateful servant in the future.

You may think, "I've messed up too many times. God has given up on me." No. He hasn't. He still loves you and wants you to return to Him. His Spirit is tugging at your heart and mind. He is reaching out to you with open arms. In the Bible, He tells you of many repentant sinners who had serious moral failures. Yet they sought God's mercy and found forgiveness and an amazingly meaningful life. God made them outstanding servants in His eternal work.

So, what will God do about your sins? It all depends on what you choose to do with His invitation. He wants you to begin every day saying with David, "I confessed all my sins to you [God] and stopped trying to hide my guilt . . . And you forgave me! All my guilt is gone" (Psalm 32:5 NLT).

Now, go and show Him how grateful you are.

Related Scriptures from 2 Samuel

The Lord is my rock, my fortress, and my savior; my God is my rock, in whom I find protection. He is my shield, the power that saves me, and my place of safety.

(2 Samuel 22:2–3 NLT)

[God] reached down from heaven and rescued me; / he drew me out of deep waters. / He rescued me from my powerful enemies, / from those who hated me and were too strong for me . . . You rescue the humble, / but your eyes watch the proud and humiliate them. O LORD, you are my lamp. / The LORD lights up my darkness.

(2 Samuel 22:17–18, 28–29 NLT)

Other Related Scriptures

He has removed our sins as far from us as the east is from the west.

(Psalm 103:12 NLT)

But if we confess our sins to him, he is faithful and just to forgive us our sins and to cleanse us from all wickedness.

(1 John 1:9 NLT)

What Is God Saying to You?

Think about those sins you want to forget. Now think about Jesus dying on the cross for those sins. What is your conclusion about God's forgiveness?

What is most harmful about trying to do enough good to balance all you've done wrong? What's different about God's way of handling wrongdoing?

Dear Father, the better I get to know You, the more I see how gracious and forgiving You are. Accept my appreciation in how I serve You this day. Amen.

Get to Know God through 1 Kings

A Brief Overview

LIKE SAMUEL, 1 AND 2 KINGS originally were one book in the Hebrew Bible called the Book of Kings. The prophets Ezra, Ezekiel, and Jeremiah were contributing authors. However, since the book covers more than four hundred years of history and has a common literary style, it is believed that an editor compiled the authors' messages into the one book.

The Book of Kings gives you additional insights into God's character and presence among His exiled people in Babylon and how they responded to their circumstances. It begins by describing the final days of King David around 971 BC and the conspiracies surrounding his succession. It continues through David's death and Solomon's rise to the throne.

Although geographically small, Israel was powerful and influential in its economy and military strength under Solomon's reign. After Solomon's death in 931 BC (see 11:43), the twelve tribes of Israel divided into the northern (Israel) and southern (Judah) kingdoms.

Solomon is the prominent figure in 1 Kings. Because of his close relationship with God, especially in his early years, the Lord gave him unparalleled wisdom and wealth that have been admired throughout history and around the world. He used God's gifts to serve God and His people and to build Israel's first great temple.

Unfortunately, in his later years, Solomon damaged his reputation. God brought judgment on him because of his unfaithfulness to God's command to never have but one wife (see Deuteronomy 17:17). Solomon married many women, and the Bible tell us that in his old age, his wives turned his heart away to other gods. Fortunately, Solomon is best known for his writing of Proverbs, an often-quoted book of the Bible.

First Kings closes in chapters 19 through 22 with a focus on the prophet Elijah and his confrontations with King Ahab. Ahab "did more evil in the eyes of the LORD than any of those before him" (1 Kings 16:30 NIV). Part of his infamous life was his marriage to the evil Jezebel, who hated God's people (see 1 Kings 18:4).

You get to know God better through 1 Kings by observing the way He relates to His children and, in particular, His leaders. When the Lord gives people leadership responsibilities, He expects them to use their gifts to serve others for His glory. When they are faithful, He blesses them. But when they use God's gifts to serve themselves, they receive God's curses. God is always both gracious and responsible.

An Inspirational Theme of 1 Kings

Watch Out or You'll Miss the Train

My dad took me to New York City when I was ten. We visited popular sites like the Empire State Building, the Statue of Liberty, and Circle Line Tour. My most memorable experience was the subway—not because it was the most amazing, but because of what happened.

As we waited for the subway car, Daddy warned me, "Bill, stay close to me. The train stops for only a few seconds." You guessed it. I didn't stay close. I got distracted. The next thing I heard was Daddy calling from inside the train as the door was closing.

The same thing happens in your everyday life. It is easy to get distracted with all the sights, sounds, and people competing for your attention. Then, before you know it, you've lost that closeness you once had with your heavenly Father. And if you don't get back quickly, you'll drift farther and farther away until you feel like you lost Him forever. The Bible says Satan is the "great deceiver" (see Revelation 12:9). So he uses all kinds of deceptive distractions to keep you from being close to Jesus.

That's what happened to Solomon. He was known for his wisdom and for being a close friend of God. Then he got distracted by the beauty of a woman who did not care about God or His ways. Quickly Solomon lost his relationship with his heavenly Father and ended up breaking all of God's ten commandments, even taking hundreds of immoral women into his palace as wives. Eventually, Solomon lost everything that mattered to him.

Today, your most important task is to stay close to Jesus. The greatest desire of Jesus's heart was to stay close to His heavenly Father. He called it being one with His Father (see John 10:30). That's His greatest desire for you—being so close to Him that you feel like you are one with Him.

You're going to face all kinds of distractions in your life. And if you let them, they'll separate you from Jesus. Keep your eyes, ears, and mind close to Him. And any time you begin to notice you are drifting away from your daily reading of His

Word, from talking to Him and meeting regularly with some of His family of faith, stop what you're doing. Get back on board with Him before it's too late.

And, by the way, I did squeeze onto that subway car just before the door closed. Daddy held the door open for me just like your heavenly Father is holding the door open for you. You won't be surprised to know that I didn't leave my daddy's side for the rest of my New York trip.

Related Scriptures from 1 Kings

May the LORD our God be with us as he was with our ancestors; may he never leave us or abandon us. May he give us the desire to do his will in everything and to obey all the commands, decrees, and regulations that he gave our ancestors.

(1 Kings 8:57–58 NLT)

Praise the Lord who has given rest to his people Israel, just as he promised. Not one word has failed of all the wonderful promises he gave through his servant Moses.

(1 Kings 8:56 NLT)

Other Related Scriptures

Remain in me, and I will remain in you. For a branch cannot produce fruit if it is severed from the vine, and you cannot be fruitful unless you remain in me.

(John 15:4 NLT)

One day Jesus told his disciples a story to show that they should always pray and never give up.

(Luke 18:1 NLT)

What Is God Saying to You?

What does God's treatment of Solomon teach you about Him?

List some things that distract you and cause you to not be close to God. How does staying close to God by reading His Word daily and talking with Him throughout each day help you?

Dear Father, the better I get to know You, the more I see how important it is for me to stay close to You. Amen.

Get to Know God through 2 Kings

A Brief Overview

AS I MENTIONED PREVIOUSLY, the books of 1 and 2 Kings were originally one book in the Hebrew Bible. No doubt Ezra, Ezekiel, and Jeremiah contributed to the book, but Bible scholars are not sure which prophet God chose to compile the various messages into one document. What we do know is that 2 Kings gives helpful insights into how God feels, thinks, and acts. It does that in the context of an accurate history of Israel's divided kingdoms following the reign of Solomon.

In 722 BC, the world's most powerful empire, Assyria, invaded the northern kingdom. The results were devastating. The people and land were brutally torn apart. Most of the people were either murdered or taken captive. Only Judah remained. But it wasn't long before the prophets' warnings came true and Assyria fell to the mighty Babylonian armies, which destroyed the Assyrian capital of Nineveh in 612 BC and took over Judah.

Many Israelites, such as Daniel, became slaves and were carried to Babylon. In 586 BC, the Babylonians leveled Jerusalem and the temple. By the end of 2 Kings, the Israelites no longer lived in their once Promised Land.

Some of the most memorable events in Bible history are recorded in 2 Kings.

- God raising two people from the dead (see 4:32–37; 13:20–21)
- God taking Elijah to heaven without dying (see 2:1–18)
- God parting the Jordan River twice (see 2:8, 14)
- God using the prophet Elisha in powerful ways (see 4:1–7, 32–37; 5:8–16)
- God defeating the Assyrian army that threatened King Hezekiah (see 19:35–37)

Such miraculous events give us excellent knowledge of God's graciousness and responsibility to do what He says.

A few of the kings, such as Good King Hezekiah who reigned over the southern kingdom, followed the Lord's commands and Spirit. But all of the kings in the northern kingdom did evil in the sight of the Lord and led the people to follow the ways of their immoral, godless culture.

Even with the continued warnings from God's prophets, the Israelites turned their backs on God. So God kept His promises and brought judgment on His rebellious children. However, He did not forget His promise to David. He rescued and blessed a remnant and kept the royal linage of David so that one day His people could return to their land and Jesus would come as promised.

An Inspirational Theme of 2 Kings

It's Not My Fault

I wanted to impress my little brother Frank by cutting down a tree. So although Daddy had told me never to get into his toolbox without his permission, I took his hatchet. Frank was only five, so he quietly and obediently followed me, his big brother, into the woods across the street from our house.

Frank was standing right behind me when I raised the hatchet to whack that tree. And as you might guess, the backside of that hatchet struck him right on his forehead. Blood went everywhere. After a while, it stopped bleeding and a huge red knot came up. There was no way to hide that. So when Daddy came home that night, I tried to explain it was all Frank's fault for standing right behind me. Daddy did not fall for it.

We're all guilty of trying to hide our wrongdoing, of blaming others for our messes, of dodging consequences of bad choices, and of trying to escape anything that might cause us pain or embarrassment. I would have done well to have learned from the good King Hezekiah. He was facing Sennacherib, the king of Assyria. This savage king threatened the Israelites and mocked their God, saying He wouldn't help them. He then promised to destroy their sacred Jerusalem.

Now the people knew that the Assyrians had the largest army around, and so they told King Hezekiah just to do whatever Sennacherib wanted to avoid the conflict and to keep quiet. King Hezekiah knew that his people had done wrong and had strayed from God and His ways. He feared that God would use the evil king of Assyria to punish them. And he did not take his people's advice. He refused to keep quiet. He then prayed to God, confessing his fears, the sins of his people, their weaknesses, and their need for God's help.

In response to Hezekiah's willingness to face his fears and admit his faults, that night God sent His angels and destroyed 185,000 Assyrian soldiers camped outside Jerusalem. In fear,

Sennacherib fled to Assyria. From that day forward, Hezekiah was named Good King Hezekiah.

Unfortunately, I wasn't as brave and forthright as Hezekiah. It took a nasty bump on Frank's head to teach me about confessing and owning up to my own wrongdoing. Frank's head healed up fine, and my backside felt better in a few days too.

If you're going to have inner peace and successful relationships with others and God, you will need to do the same. Blaming others and trying to escape your uncomfortable issues won't solve anything. Until you step up and take full responsibility for your actions, God will not give you the strength and wisdom you need to face your challenges, nor will He forgive you if you do not ask. The guilt and irresponsibility will eat away, damaging your relationship to God and to others.

Take an honest look at your past and your heart right now. Is it time to say to yourself and to your heavenly Father something like this: "I'm through avoiding, blaming, hiding. and covering up. I'm ready to take full responsibility for what my actions. I'm sorry for my sins. And Your Word says, 'But if we confess our sins to him, he is faithful and just to forgive us our sins and to cleanse us from all wickedness'" (1 John 1:9 NLT).

Related Scriptures from 2 Kings

[Hezekiah] remained faithful to the LORD in everything, and he carefully obeyed all the commands the LORD had given Moses. So the LORD was with him, and Hezekiah was successful in everything he did.

(2 Kings 18:6–7 NLT)

Now, O LORD our God, rescue us from [the king of Assyria's] power; then all the kingdoms of the earth will know that you alone, O LORD, are God."

(2 Kings 19:19 NLT)

Other Related Scriptures

Whoever conceals their sins does not prosper, but the one who confesses and renounces them finds mercy.

(Proverbs 28:13 NIV)

Though your sins are like scarlet, / I will make them as white as snow. / Though they are red like crimson, / I will make them as white as wool/ . . . if you turn away and refuse to listen, / you will be devoured by the sword of your enemies.

(Isaiah 1:18–20 NLT)

What Is God Saying to You?

What are some of your failures and bad choices you have blamed others for?

If you keep avoiding doing what you know God wants you to do, what are some of the harmful consequences you might be facing?

Dear Father, the better I get to know You, the more I see that You are always with me and love me even when I admit my sins. Amen.

Get to Know God through 1 Chronicles

A Brief Overview

LIKE THE BOOKS OF SAMUEL AND KINGS, originally, 1 and 2 Chronicles were one book. If you are reading through the Bible, you will notice that 1 Chronicles mirrors parts of 2 Samuel and 1 Kings and was most likely written during the time of Ezra or Nehemiah. The Israelites were scattered throughout the Persian Empire, and some had returned to Israel.

The reason the author of the Chronicles gives so much attention to genealogies is to demonstrate the genuineness of the lineage of God's chosen people to carry out His purposes in spite of being exiled from the Promised Land. When the book was written, God's people were no longer leaders in Israel. They had lost their land and had no respect from their neighbors. They had been slaves to the Babylonians for seventy years and were discouraged. But the author challenged them never to forget that they were part of God's royal lineage and that He had not given up on them.

This book is written from a priestly perspective and emphasizes the importance of God-honoring worship and being faithful to God's Law. The author includes part of David's psalms (see 16:8–36) and the story of how David bought a threshing floor as the site for the future temple (see 21:18–30). Although David wanted to build the temple, God told him that his son Solomon would carry out that honor (see 17:1–14).

Like the books of Samuel and Kings, the Chronicles are holy books of holy history, but they have an additional purpose. Since Chronicles was written after the exile, it focuses more on the primary practices God wants His people to follow—obeying God's way of living, staying close to Him, giving God's house and His leaders respect, and carrying out God's purposes as a unique family of faith in a local house of worship.

David's magnificent prayer (see 1 Chronicles 29:10–19) gives you a glimpse of God's main message for His people. It is a prayer of thanks, promise, and worship. It reminds us of the central place gratitude must have in our lives and stresses putting God's holy purposes above our own self-centered purposes. And, like David, it asks us never to forget our high calling to be a part of God's great work.

The book also encourages us to stay faithful, for the Messiah is near. God's plans will be fulfilled. We should pray as David did: "Yours, LORD, is the greatness and the power and the glory and the majesty and the splendor, for everything in heaven and earth is yours" (1 Chronicles 29:11 NIV).

An Inspirational Theme of 1 Chronicles

I'll Pay Full Price

I was eight when I made my commitment to Jesus and was baptized as a public statement of my decision. My pastor explained that the word *baptize* meant "to put under, to immerse, or be placed under the water." It was a symbol of dying to self, being buried, raised to serve Jesus, and giving

Him everything I had out of gratitude for all He had done for me.

Mama said the Bible teaches that part of giving Jesus everything was giving him a tithe—ten percent of what I earned each week through our church. In my first week as a Christian, I messed up. That week I made one dollar mowing the lawn. Every Saturday, my buddy Bill Giles and I went to the movie. It cost seventy-five cents to get in, fifteen cents for popcorn, ten cents for a soda. So, you guessed it. I blew the whole dollar.

On Sunday morning, Mama asked if I'd put my ten-cent tithe in my church envelope. You can imagine how I hated to tell her, "No Mama, it took all I had to go to the movie. And besides, that big church will never miss my little ten cents."

I always knew I was in big trouble when Mama sat me down, took my face in her hands, and looked me in the eyes. "Bill, you're missing the whole point. Your giving your tithe to the church is not about what the church needs but about what you need." Mama then made it clearer. "Bill, Jesus gave His all for you on the cross, and you promised to give Him your all. Son, you need to decide what's going to come first in your new life as a follower of Jesus. What's most important to you—being faithful to Jesus, no matter the cost, or doing whatever feels good to you at the moment?"

That's the question we all must answer. Are we willing to pay the price? The fact is being faithful to Jesus, doing what's right, always demands sacrifice.

That's the question God asked King David. When God made him king of Israel and blessed his leadership, David promised to be faithful to serve God. But David let his successes go to his head. He forgot his commitment and promises to God.

Over time, David felt guilty and repented of his sin and asked God for forgiveness. God asked David to demonstrate his priority, to show God how much he loved Him. So David went out to find and purchase land to build God a magnificent temple. He found the perfect land, and the owner offered to give it to David free of change. David's response was one of the greatest declarations of honest sacrifice ever spoken. He responded with a big "No, never." He refused to take the land for free. He would not offer to his Lord that which cost him nothing. He paid full price. Here David disavowed all cheap, easy, apathetic, costless devotion.

Jesus required the same of His followers, saying, "If you try to hang on to your life, you will lose it. But if you give up your life for my sake and for the sake of the Good News, you will save it" (Mark 8:35 NLT).

If you take the cheap, painless way, it will ruin your faith and destroy your relationships. Pay full price. Put your Lord first. Begin every day with Paul's daily motto: "Everything else is worthless when compared with the infinite value of knowing Christ Jesus my Lord. For his sake I have discarded everything else, counting it all as garbage, so that I could gain Christ" (Philippians 3:8 NLT).

By the way, at the end of my second week as a Christian, I got back on track. I put twenty cents in my church envelope. It really felt good.

Related Scriptures from 1 Chronicles

But King David replied to Araunah, "No, I insist on paying the full price. I will not take for the LORD what is yours, or sacrifice a burnt offering that costs me nothing."

(1 Chronicles 21:24 NIV)

David built an altar to the LORD there and sacrificed burnt offerings and fellowship offerings. He called on the LORD, and the LORD answered him with fire from heaven on the altar of burnt offering.

(1 Chronicles 21:26 NIV)

Other Related Scriptures

No one can take my life from me. I sacrifice it voluntarily. For I have the authority to lay it down when I want to and also to take it up again. For this is what my Father has commanded.

(John 10:18 NLT)

I knew you before I formed you in your mother's womb. Before you were born, I set you apart and appointed you as my prophet to the nations.

(Jeremiah 1:5 NLT)

What Is God Saying to You?

What does this story of David tell you about God's character?

What are some things that tempt you to break your promises to God? What motivates you to make costly decisions for Jesus rather than doing whatever feels good?

Dear Father, the better I get to know You, the more I see how much You've done for me and how much I want to express my gratitude. Amen.

Get to Know God through 2 Chronicles

A Brief Overview

MOST BIBLE SCHOLARS BELIEVE THE PROPHET EZRA was author and editor of 1 and 2 Chronicles, which, as I previously noted, were originally one book called the Chronicles. It was written in the fifth century BC after a remnant of Israelites returned to their Promised Land from seventy years as slaves to the Babylonian Empire.

As you read 2 Chronicles, keep in mind that the recipients of the book are God's chosen people, the Israelites, who are weary from years of suffering in exile. They are a broken people but are committed to starting over in their cherished homeland. Their hearts are set on rebuilding their lives, homes, and the temple. With constant resistance from their culture and pagan religions, the Jews finally rebuild the temple but struggle for years slowly reclaiming their country.

Second Chronicles begins with King Solomon unifying his redeemed nation, confirming his position as God's chosen leader, and crushing continual attacks and rebellions. Solomon finally constructs the world-famous temple in Jerusalem, which is based on the plans God delivered to his father, David. Six of the nine chapters focus on King Solomon's construction on the temple, a task reserved for him by God before Solomon's birth (see 2 Chronicles 2–7).

The book unfolds a cycle of righteousness and corruption among Israel's leaders. Some kings were shockingly evil, ignoring God's Law and leading the people into immoral practices. Other kings, such as Solomon, started their roles as God's leaders by being holy and committed to God's law but eventually were absorbed into their pagan culture. A few kings drifted away from God's way but repented and returned to become godly leaders, such as Manasseh (see 33:1–25). And finally, only a few kings stayed true to their calling, such as Josiah, about whom the Bible says, "He did what was right in the eyes of the LORD" (2 Chronicles 34:2 NIV).

God's plans and purposes will ultimately be fulfilled no matter the resistance. Even powerful international leaders such as Tilgath-Pilneser of Assyria, Sennacherib of Assyria, and Nebuchadnezzar of Babylon were no match for Israel's great God. The basic question of this book is "Will you be faithful in following God's will and live by His law no matter the circumstances?" The two main messages of 2 Chronicles are (1) faithfulness to God is rewarded with inner peace and God's blessings, and (2) no matter who you are, unfaithfulness to God is judged seriously.

An Inspirational Theme of 2 Chronicles

Get Anything You Want

I was just a little fellow when the TV show "I Dream of Jeannie" first aired and quickly became the most viewed sitcom in America. It was about a two-thousand-year-old genie and an American astronaut named Tony.

In the pilot episode, Tony's one-man space capsule falls in the South Pacific Ocean near a deserted island. Tony makes it to the beach and finds a strange bottle. He rubs it, and smoke comes out, followed by a cute Persian-speaking genie. Jeannie and Tony cannot communicate because she speaks Persian. So Tony tells her he wishes she could speak English. Jeannie smiles and blinks. With a puff, Tony's wish comes true. From then on, every time Tony wants something, he just asks his Jeannie. She blinks, and miraculously he gets anything he wants.

Could it be that millions of viewers tuned in every week for years to witness Jeannie blink and make wishes come true because deep down inside all of us we wish we could just blink and get anything we want—that much needed money, that perfect relationship, that cure for a serious health problem, or some other wish?

You may remember that Jesus told His disciples, "You can ask for anything in my name, and I will do it" (John 14:13 NLT). Did Jesus mean if you became a believer and asked Him sincerely for anything, he would be your personal Jeannie? Look closely at what he said: "You can ask for anything *in my name,* and I will do it" (emphasis mine).

So if getting what you want depends on asking in Jesus's name, what does that mean? It simply means to ask in harmony and in agreement or in union with Jesus. Remember, Jesus often said that He and his heavenly Father were one in Spirit. They were so close that Jesus would never do anything or ask for anything unless He knew it was something His Father wanted. Sometimes, in fact, He knew what His Father wanted was going to be hard, unpopular, uncomfortable, and even painful. But what Jesus wanted most was what pleased His Father most. Jesus wanted to carry out His Father's purpose and whatever aided most in serving His Father's children. That is why when Jesus faced the horror of being crucified, He humbled himself and prayed, "Yet I want your will to be done, not mine" (Matthew 26:39 NLT).

Nearly a thousand years before, when Solomon became king and God asked him what he wanted if he could have anything, Solomon replied like Jesus. He wanted God's wisdom so he could care for God's children the way God wanted. God gave him what he wanted and more because Solomon wanted what his heavenly Father wanted.

So, can you pray and get anything you want? Of course—if, like Solomon and Jesus, you humble yourself and make sure what you want is what Jesus wants for you and His people. If what you are asking for today will bring glory to God, will help carry out God's purposes in your life, and would be what Jesus would ask for if He were praying on your behalf, then go for it. Ask for anything. God can't wait to answer your prayer.

Related Scriptures from 2 Chronicles

Then if my people who are called by my name will humble themselves and pray and seek my face and turn from their wicked ways, I will hear from heaven and will forgive their sins and restore their land.

(2 Chronicles 7:14 NLT)

That night God appeared to Solomon and said, "What do you want? Ask, and I will give it to you!"

Solomon replied to God, "You showed great and faithful love to David, my father, and now you have made me king in his place. O Lord God, please continue to keep your promise to

David my father, for you have made me king over a people as numerous as the dust of the earth! Give me the wisdom and knowledge to lead them properly, for who could possibly govern this great people of yours?"

God said to Solomon, "Because your greatest desire is to help your people, and you did not ask for wealth, riches, fame, or even the death of your enemies or a long life, but rather you asked for wisdom and knowledge to properly govern my people—I will certainly give you the wisdom and knowledge you requested. But I will also give you wealth, riches, and fame such as no other king has had before you or will ever have in the future!"

(2 Chronicles 1:7–12 NLT)

Other Related Scriptures

He went on a little farther and bowed with his face to the ground, praying, "My Father! If it is possible, let this cup of suffering be taken away from me. Yet I want your will to be done, not mine."

(Matthew 26:39 NLT)

[Jesus] humbled himself in obedience to God and died a criminal's death on a cross.

(Philippians 2:8 NLT)

What Is God Saying to You?

Why do we sometime pray, asking for things that may not be God's will for us?

What are some reasons you should pray only for what will bring honor to God and carry out His will for you and others?

Dear Father, the better I get to know You, the more I see You know best. You know what I need more than I do, and I want what You want. Amen.

Get to Know God through Ezra

A Brief Overview

IN THE HEBREW BIBLE, Ezra and Nehemiah were considered one work, though internal evidence suggests they were written separately and joined together in the Hebrew Bible. They were later separated again in English translations.

Ezra was a priest and scribe. He led a group of Jewish refugees back to Israel during Cyrus the Great's reign over the Persian Empire. Cyrus was the ruler of the largest empire in the world, including numerous international empires and the powerful Babylonian Empire.

The book records two periods following seventy years of Babylonian captivity. Ezra 1 through 6 covers the years 538 to 515 BC and reports the first return of Jews from captivity by Zerubbabel, beginning with the edict of Cyrus of Persia to free the Jews and pay for the rebuilding of their temple in Jerusalem. Ezra 7 through 10 continues the story more than sixty years later, when Ezra leads the second group of exiles to Israel in 458 BC.

Ezra's book describes the activities of the Jews rebuilding their homes and businesses in and around Jerusalem. It gives insights into God's activities among His people as they struggle to start over and survive in a pagan land. Ezra reminds them and us that Israel is still God's people and that God had not forgotten them. Ezra also tells us how many of God's children renewed their covenant with God and once again became obedient to Him.

Ezra gives us one of the greatest intercessory prayers in the Bible (see Ezra 9:5–15) and provides us with two main challenges: (1) the importance of maintaining God's house (see Ezra 1:1–6:22) and (2) the need for reformation for a country to survive (see 7:1–10:44). The main emphasis of the book is the faithfulness of God to keep His promises and that when God's people remained faithful to Him, He continued to bless them. It also reveals how God even moved the hearts of powerful political rulers such as Cyrus, Darius, and Artaxerxes to help carry out His purposes.

An Inspirational Theme of Ezra

Does What You Do Really Matters?

In a world where it seems like the only people who matter are the famous, rich, and powerful, do you ever feel like nothing you do or say matters? It's easy to be paralyzed by feeling insignificant. It's easy to just quit trying.

Don't do it. Why? Because what you do and say really does matter more than you think. God's Word tells us that God loves using the seemingly insignificant acts of love, kindness, and care of ordinary people to make life-changing differences beyond our wildest imaginations. Take those four young Jewish boys, Daniel, Shadrach, Meshach, and Abednego. They were slaves in Babylon, mere teenagers, prisoners from a tiny, powerless, conquered country. Surely what they did and said didn't matter. Who would blame them if they just shut down?

But they didn't. They kept on doing what little they could even when it seemed it made no difference. Cyrus was so moved by the faithfulness of those slave boys that he freed all Jews and financed the rebuilding of their homeland. At the time, it seemed like what they were doing didn't matter, but behind the scene, God was using their faithful acts to transform lives.

That ancient true story reminds me of a modern true story. Evangelist Billy Graham is one of the most well-known preachers in the world. Since he began preaching in 1940, the media has reported his enormous stadium events, evangelistic films, radio and television programs, counseling of presidents and kings and leading millions of people to Christ.

But what many people do not know is that all of Billy Graham's accomplishments nearly never happened. In his 1997 book, *Just As I Am*, Dr. Graham tells of the time when he first began is work as an evangelist. The crowds did not show up. No one responded to his invitations at the end of his sermons. People were questioning his beliefs. Some of the press was making fun of his style. A seminary friend challenged his theology. And Billy especially got discouraged because it seemed like all of his efforts were not making any difference.

Then one day, a friend advised him to get away from this work and get alone with God. So, Billy went to the California retreat center of Forest Home and spent time in solitary reading the Bible. He tells how he kept seeing the same phrase "Thus, sayeth the Lord... Thus, sayeth the Lord..." Then he walked out into the woods, got on his knees, and cried out, "Father, I am going to accept this as Thy Word—by faith! I'm going to allow faith to go beyond my intellectual questions and doubts, and I will believe this to be Your inspired Word!"

From that day forward Billy Graham just kept on doing what God called him to do and left the results up to God. Shortly after that experience, Dr. Graham held his now historic 1949 Los Angeles Tent Crusade. The meeting was planned to last three weeks, but it lasted eight weeks with packed crowds every night. Thousands made public decisions for Christ. When the media outlets nationwide reported how the crusade was unprecedented, Billy's ministry began to spread around the globe. Billy Graham's faithfulness and obedience paid off.

Your experiences and challenges will be different from those of Daniel, Shadrach, Meshach, and Abednego. Your doubts and difficulties will be different from Billy Graham's. But you have the same God and He will honor your faithfulness like He has throughout history. So, be faithful in the good times and bad times. Do what God directs you to do, and let His Spirit do the rest.

Related Scriptures from Ezra

In the first year of King Cyrus of Persia, the Lord . . . stirred the heart of Cyrus to put this proclamation in writing . . . "This is what King Cyrus of Persia says: 'The LORD, the God of heaven, has given me all the kingdoms of the earth. He has appointed me to build him a Temple at Jerusalem, which is in Judah. Any of you who are his people may go to Jerusalem in Judah to rebuild this Temple of the LORD.'"

(Ezra 1:1–3 NLT)

King Cyrus himself brought out the articles that King Nebuchadnezzar had taken from the LORD'S Temple in Jerusalem . . . Cyrus directed Mithredath, the treasurer of Persia, to present them to the prince of Judah, the leader of the exiles returning to Judah.

(Ezra 1:7–8 NLT)

Other Related Scriptures

Whoever is the least among you is the greatest.

(Luke 9:48 NLT)

Instead, God has deliberately chosen to use ideas the world considers foolish and of little worth in order to shame those people considered by the world as wise and great.

(1 Corinthians 1:27 TLB)

What Is God Saying to You?

What does the way God used Daniel and his young friends say about His plan and purpose?

What are some small acts of kindness, love, or helpfulness that you could do that could help carry out God's purpose in your life?

Dear Father, the better I get to know You, the more I see that You care about what I do and that these small acts may be part of Your purpose in my life. Amen.

Get to Know God through Nehemiah

A Brief Overview

EZRA WROTE BOTH NEHEMIAH AND EZRA. As I mentioned before, the two books were originally one book in the Hebrew Bible. Ezra was a priest, a representative of his Jewish heritage. In Ezra's book that carries his name, he emphasizes the rebuilding of the temple. In Nehemiah, he emphasizes the rebuilding of the walls around Jerusalem and the importance of using your job and skills to do what God calls you to do.

Nehemiah was a businessman and the cupbearer for Artaxerxes, the king of Persia. Nehemiah's job was working as an administrator in the office of the powerful king, but his heart was focused on being a servant of God and his people. Nehemiah was neither a priest nor a prophet, but God used his years of experience in business to equip him to handle the political and physical work as a leader in rebuilding God's temple and the walls around Jerusalem.

Under Nehemiah's leadership, God's people overcame many types of opposition. As governor of the new Judah, Nehemiah brought about peace between the Jews and Persian tax collectors. He and Ezra worked together as businessman and priest to accomplish God's physical and spiritual goals.

As seen in his moving prayer in chapters 1 and 9, Nehemiah was a servant-leader with a humble heart. He always gave God the credit for all that was accomplished. His life was a model of godly leadership. Nehemiah served God in nonreligious offices and led in difficult situations to help his family of faith to focus on God's goals, to develop order, and to complete the difficult tasks that were assigned.

The book of Nehemiah gives us a good example of how anyone who is committed to using their God-given skills and heart can be utilized in a great way for God. The book illustrates that God employs people with different gifts and skills to accomplish His work. It teaches us that you don't have to be a priest, prophet, or some other religious worker to be used of God.

God has a plan for every life. To Him, no one is more or less important than anyone else. Each of us is called by God, and we should view our work, jobs, or gifts in the way St. Paul described them: "And whatever you do, whether in word or deed, do it all in the name of the Lord Jesus, giving thanks to God the Father through him" (Colossians 3:17 NIV).

An Inspirational Theme of Nehemiah

Is Your Work a Necessary Evil?

Mark Twain said, "Work is a necessary evil that should be avoided." Wouldn't it be wonderful if you didn't have to work? Picture it—you get up, have no responsibilities, have nothing to do, play around all day or just do nothing. Sounds pretty good, doesn't it? Well, it may sound good for a short time. But what about the long haul?

The facts show that Mark Twain was wrong. Work can be hard and even almost unbearable at times, but work is not a necessary evil. It is a necessary blessing. Without work, people have serious troubles.

Having no work to do, no task to accomplish, no goal to reach, no one to help is a sure recipe for boredom, sickness, self-centeredness, depression, and even suicide. These are the kinds of devastating consequences we therapists see in people who are out of work or too ill to work or retired with nothing meaningful to give themselves to.

God created you to work. Work is a God-given blessing. Look at Jesus's daily life. He was always busy helping, caring, teaching, praying, serving, healing, comforting, and going about doing good. What does Jesus's view of work tell you about God?

Your God loves working and wants you to view your work the way He does. Having the wrong view of your work is about as harmful as having no work at all. You'll never have that joyful, fulfilling life you want until you look at what He has given you to do as an act of worship. When you view every task as an expression of gratitude, a demonstration of your love and service for Him, it changes your life and your relationship to God and your work. As the Bible says, "And whatever you do or say, let it be as a representative of the Lord Jesus, and come with him into the presence of God the Father to give him your thanks" (Colossians 3:17 TLB).

Howard E. Butt Jr., a wealthy groceryman from Texas, used his wealth to help break down the false ideas about work. He taught that the Bible reveals God sees all good work, no matter how mundane, as sacred and as a high calling of God. His brief messages about the value of your work went out on the radio airwaves across the country during morning drive time.

That's how Nehemiah saw his work. Although he was a Jewish slave living far from his homeland and working in the office of the king of Persia, Nehemiah viewed his work as a gift of God, as an assignment from God, and as an opportunity to be a witness for God.

When the Jews were set free to return home, God gave Nehemiah the down and dirty job of rebuilding the Jerusalem wall and leading his people to complete the task in the face of much resistance. Some did not see his job as spiritual. But Nehemiah did. He stayed focused saying, "I am engaged in a great work, so I can't come. Why should I stop working to come and meet with you?" (Nehemiah. 6:3 NLT).

How do you see your work? Do you consider it a necessary evil or a God-given blessing? I encourage you to begin each day praying this kind of prayer:

> Lord Jesus, to the best of my ability, I offer my mind, my words, my heart, and my body to you to use this day as tools in your hands. I want to be your humble servant. I thank you for choosing me to do the tasks you are giving me today. As I work for you today, help me see your Spirit working in and through me touching people's lives. In Jesus' name. Amen.

Related Scriptures from Nehemiah

The God of heaven will help us succeed. We, his servants, will start rebuilding this wall.

(Nehemiah 2:20 NLT)

"I am engaged in a great work, so I can't come. Why should I stop working to come and meet with you?"

(Nehemiah 6:3 NLT)

Other Related Scriptures

Give your bodies to God because of all he has done for you. Let them be a living and holy sacrifice—the kind he will find acceptable. This is truly the way to worship him.

(Romans 12:1 NLT)

And whatever you do or say, do it as a representative of the Lord Jesus, giving thanks through him to God the Father.

(Colossians 3:17 NLT)

What Is God Saying to You?

What does Nehemiah's purpose and leadership say about our God?

What are some things that make your work, your daily responsibilities, seem not very spiritual? What are some ways you can turn your most mundane, ordinary task into a blessing?

Dear Father, the better I get to know You, the more I see that You are a God who is busy working for Your children, and I want to do the same. Amen.

Get to Know God through Esther

A Brief Overview

ESTHER IS ONE OF THE MOST inspiring books of the Old Testament. Believers love the fascinating drama and the amazing story of God's grace, mercy, and providential care.

It is a true story that contains so many miraculous events that it would appear to unbelievers to be a fantasy. But it's not fantasy. It is the story of how our all-loving, all-powerful, all-knowing, and all-present God moves in the lives of His children in exile and especially His chosen Esther.

Esther was a young orphan slave girl raised by her cousin. Because of her outstanding beauty, she was chosen and forced by King Xerxes, the pagan leader of the Persian Empire, to become his wife. Esther hid her identity as a Jewess because she didn't want to bring shame on her godly family, nor bring possible danger to herself.

Over time, Esther found favor with everyone, including the king, and was made queen. After she gained the king's confidence, she learned there was a conspiracy to murder him, and she intervened to save his life.

Later, Esther again learned that the king's main advisor was planning genocide for all the Jews in Persia. The king did not know that his beloved Esther was a Jew. Esther had to make a choice. Would she keep quiet, stay safe, and continue to enjoy the privileges of being the queen? Or would she care more about the future of her people than she cared about protecting herself? The law of the land made it clear: if Esther were to go to the king without an invitation, telling him she was a Jew and asking him to go against his advisors, she would be executed.

While Esther was contemplating what to do, her cousin Mordecai challenged her with one of literature's most memorable questions: "Who knows but that you have come to your royal position for such a time as this?" (Esther 4:14 NIV). God spoke to Esther through her cousin, reminding her that God had been working in her life and the lives of His people all along. God let her know that He loved His people and would save them with or without her. The choice was hers.

That crucial moment was Esther's opportunity to make the most important decision in her life. God had done His part. Now the question was would Esther do her part?

Many people then, and millions for generations to come, would be affected by her decision.

An Inspirational Theme of Esther

Had an Esther Moment Lately?

William Arthur Ward was right: "Opportunities are like sunrises. If you wait too long, you miss them." And when you do, you can't get them back. It's too late. It's the same with those special spiritual opportunities God gives us that we Bible people call Esther Moments.

You have just read a synopsis of Esther's story—the story of an orphan slave girl who became a queen. Probably not in her wildest young-girl fantasies did Esther ever dare to dream of being royalty, of living in luxury, and of having such power.

Esther left much behind when she moved to the palace, but she did carry her humility with her.

Her moment of truth, her Esther Moment, comes when she must choose to save her people or herself. Will she keep quiet, do nothing, and protect herself? Or will she claim the moment and risk her own life by barging into the king's presence uninvited to try to save her people?

While she ponders what to do, time is running out. The opportunity is about to pass. It's a critical moment when her cousin asked her the question we saw above: "Who knows if perhaps you were made queen for just such a time as this?" (Esther 4:14 NLT).

Queen Esther's story could be your story too. You're probably not a queen, and maybe your decision will not affect thousands of lives. But what you do will affect someone. Perhaps you are being called to a particular task for just such a time and circumstance, an Esther Moment when someone or some family member is depending on you to step up. Your Esther Moment may last for just a minute or a day or a week. And just like seeing that sunrise, if you wait too long, you'll miss the special moment He prepared just for you.

All along your journey, God has been doing His part and offering you chances to claim your Esther Moments and witness the miracles God will do through you. And you and I may never know the impact a kind word, a simple act of kindness, a sacrifice done in Jesus's name and at just the right time will have in someone's life. Will you be on the lookout today for the Esther Moments God is planning just for you?

Related Scriptures from Esther

If you keep quiet at a time like this, deliverance and relief for the Jews will arise from some other place, but you and your relatives will die. Who knows if perhaps you were made queen for just such a time as this?

(Esther 4:14 NLT)

Then the king asked her, "What do you want, Queen Esther? What is your request? I will give it to you, even if it is half the kingdom!"

(Esther 5:3 NLT)

Other Related Scriptures

We must quickly carry out the tasks assigned us by the one who sent us. The night is coming, and then no one can work.

(John 9:4 NLT)

So you, too, must keep watch! For you don't know what day your Lord is coming.

(Matthew 24:42 NLT)

What Is God Saying to You?

What does Esther's story teach us about our God and how He works in the world? What Esther Moment can you recall that reminds you of the importance of choosing to speak up or do something God is prompting you to do?

What are some reasons you should be on the lookout, at all times, for God to give you Esther Moments?

Dear Father, the better I get to know You, the more I see You are working in my life. Amen.

HOLY WISDOM

Five Books of God's Wisdom on Dealing with Life's Problems

IN THE BIBLE, THE WORD *wisdom* does not refer to having our best way of thinking but of having God's way of thinking. It is choosing to think and value and act the way God does. In the wisdom literature, the writers use the unique Hebrew style of poetry to focus more on remembering than reporting, on picturing than explaining, and on feelings more than reasoning.

Through the books of Job, Psalms, Proverbs, Ecclesiastes, and Song of Solomon, God reveals more about Himself and His style of love. By using the power and passion of poetry, God gives us insights into His personality and His way of relating to His children when they experience suffering, pain, evil, temptation, adversaries, strained relationships, and insecurities.

Whether we witness God's grace in Job or His symbolic care for His children in the Song of Solomon, God's main message in these five books is that He is love and that His kind of love is different from the self-centered love most often seen in the lives of His fallen children. It is God's special kind of love that saves Job, leads His people to praise and prayer in the Psalms, and teaches His children how to love one another in the Proverbs.

We get to know more about God's unrelenting love when we read Solomon's highly personal words of disappointment, depression, and disillusionment in Ecclesiastes. Even when Solomon feels like all of life is meaningless, God's love remains faithful and hopeful.

And in the poetic Song of Solomon, God shows us the possibility of intimacy with Him. In this passionate story of a husband and wife who love each other more than their own lives, we get to see the intensity of God's desire to have a close relationship with us.

In the Psalms, we read the passionate poetry, songs of praise, and prayers of lament, many written by King David. They illustrate his utter dependence upon God and voice the depth of his feelings, often giving words to our own emotions. The Psalms illustrate to us that we should always be honest before God with our thoughts and feelings because He knows them anyway. We learn in the Psalms that there is nowhere we can go that God is not there to love and comfort us.

All of these poetic messages foreshadow the greatest demonstration of our Father's love, seen in the cross of our Lord Jesus.

Get to Know God through Job

A Brief Overview

JOB'S STORY IS THE FIRST of the Bible's wisdom literature. Some say Job is the most famous story of all time. It has certainly been the theme of much of literature through the ages. Job's story deals with the most important subject on the hearts of every human: the problem of evil and suffering.

The main characters in the book are Job, his three friends (Bildad, Eliphaz, and Zophar), Elihu, Satan, and God Himself. The story begins with God giving Satan permission to test Job's faith by allowing him to be afflicted by severe pain, unbearable disease, confusion, and loss of his family and everything thing dear to him. Then, through a series of arguments between Job and his friends, Job finds no comfort or help.

The more Job's friends try to explain the unexplainable, the more Job feels confused and lost. Finally, God Himself speaks, His wisdom bringing hope and meaning to Job in his suffering. Job gets to know God better than ever before.

Job's undeserved suffering touches all of us and accentuates the age-old question of evil and suffering: "Why do bad things happen to good people?" Job's response is that God allows pain for good reasons, but they are reasons we often cannot understand. For as God says in the final chapters, "Where were you when I laid the foundations of the earth? Tell me if you know so much" (Job 38:4 NLT).

Ultimately, Job's suffering did not cause him to reject God, but instead encouraged him to be drawn closer to God and have a stronger faith in Him. God never fully answered Job's questions as to *why* these things happened to him or why God allowed them. Instead, God overwhelmed Job and his friends with a new awareness of His power, love, majesty, and sovereignty.

The book ends with Job repenting and announcing that his experience with evil and suffering was worth it because it gave him a deeper and more personal sense of God's power, care, and greatness. He said, in a beautifully poetic way, "I had only heard about you before, but now I have seen you with my own eyes. I take back everything I said, and I sit in dust and ashes to show my repentance" (Job 42:5–6 NLT).

An Inspirational Theme of Job

Good News in All the Bad News

With so much evil and suffering present, do you sometimes wonder why there is so much bad happening in God's good world? Why didn't He make His world with only beauty, happiness, and love? Why didn't He create us humans so that we would always be kind, honest, thoughtful, and unselfish? If God is so loving and powerful, why does He allow so much wickedness, misery, heartache, and disasters? You would not be the first human to ask these questions.

You'll be glad to know that in all the bad news God has some really good news for you. And it may not be what you expected. For years, just like you, I've wrestled with all those hard questions about evil and suffering. It's been especially difficult when tornadoes have destroyed entire towns, tsunamis have drowned thousands, evil maniacs have murdered millions of innocent people, and as I've stood by grieving parents when an innocent baby died of cancer. When such horrors happen, *why* is almost always the first question asked. But although the most caring and smartest people from around the world have for thousands of years been trying to explain why, no one has come up with a satisfying answer. The good news is that in God's wisdom, He has something for you that's far better than any explanation.

The main message of Job's story centers around God's gifts, not his answers. Remember Job, the godly, prosperous man, who lost everything he loved—his family, his health, his home, his friends, and his peace of mind. No matter how bad things got, Job's suffering did not cause him to reject God. He never understood why he was suffering so. But by continuing to trust God through it all, Job actually found the gift of being closer to God.

I know you want to be able to rise above the misery and defeat of your personal suffering. You can by using your pain to draw you closer to God rather than withdrawing from Him. You can by beginning to view your suffering the way your heavenly Father wants you to and the way many of His children have for centuries. Can you begin to look at your suffering and say some of these things that fellow sufferers have said?

- It helped me see more clearly what really counts in my life and eternity.
- It helped me get closer to God.

- It helped me have more compassion for others who suffer.
- It helped me become stronger and more grateful.
- It helped me become more dependent on God.
- It helped me prove that my faith is genuine, not fair-weather.
- It helped me trust Jesus more and fear less.
- It helped me be more soul-conscience and less body-oriented.
- It helped me focus more on eternity and less on my earthly problems.

When suffering comes to your home, or if it is already there, the good news in all the bad news is this: God is with you. He loves you. He knows what is best for you. He has plans for you beyond your thoughts. His Spirit lives in you. For every day and every moment, He will give you enough strength and inner peace to handle anything, no matter how bad things get. And always remember, as the apostle Paul said while he suffered in prison, "What we suffer now is nothing compared to the glory [God] will reveal to us later" (Romans 8:18 NLT).

How do you view your suffering?

Related Scriptures from Job

I had only heard about you before, but now I have seen you with my own eyes.

(Job 42:5 NLT)

In all of this, Job did not sin by blaming God.

(Job 1:22 NLT)

Other Related Scriptures

So we have been greatly encouraged in the midst of our troubles and suffering, dear brothers and sisters, because you have remained strong in your faith.

(1 Thessalonians 3:7 NLT)

For God called you to do good, even if it means suffering, just as Christ suffered for you. He is your example, and you must follow in his steps.

(1 Peter 2:21 NLT)

What Is God Saying to You?

List some of the characteristics of God's personality that you see in the story of Job—God's ways that encourage you in your struggles.

What are some ways you feel like your sufferings have brought you closer to God?

Dear Father, the better I get to know You, the more I see that having You with me is more important to me than having answers to my questions. Thank You. Amen.

Get to Know God through Psalms

A Brief Overview

THE BOOK OF PSALMS HAS BEEN a favorite of Christians around the world from the first century to this day. It was certainly a favorite of the gospel writers. Of the 219 Old Testament quotations in the New Testament, 116 are from the Psalms.

Psalms is a collection of lyrical poems by several authors. David is credited with writing at least seventy-three of the 150 psalms. Other authors include Moses, Asaph, Corah, Solomon, Ethan, and Heman. A few psalms have no author's name included.

The book of Psalms includes five collections, each ending with a doxology. In this book, we find psalms focusing on Jehovah God, His creation, Israel's history, messianic overtones, and psalms for special occasions.

The Israelite used the book of Psalms as their hymnal. Many were set to music. They all express the deep feelings and thoughts of their writer and of God's heart for His children. Some convey sincere sorrow to God. Others are emotional songs of praise for who God is and gratitude for what God has done. Some songs are called pilgrim psalms because they were sung especially when God's people were on a pilgrimage, such as going up to Jerusalem for holy festivals. Other types of songs include wisdom psalms, royal psalms, victory psalms, law psalms, and songs of Zion. All of them help us get to know how God thinks and feels.

The key word in the psalms is *hallelujah,* which literally means "praise the Lord." To say or sing *hallelujah* is a statement of faith and a proclamation of praise. Psalms 50 and 150 are the most often quoted psalms. Psalm 50 may be the Bible's most comprehensive song of faith. The last psalm, 150, has been called the "Hallelujah Chorus" of the book and is referred to in other places in the Bible thirteen times. Some consider Psalm 150 the chorus of the other psalms.

The book of Psalms is primarily a guide for God's people to help them express their love and confess their hearts. The writings emphasize God's faithfulness in times of trouble and remind His people of the authority of God's Word and the abiding love of God. In this, the psalms are invaluable, God-blessed guides that you can use in praying to God and in your listening to God as He speaks to your heart.

An Inspirational Theme of Psalms

What's Your State of Mind?

According to Neale Walsch, author of the *Conversations with God* series, "The biggest problem on the planet is fear." He believes most of your problems are caused by your fears.

There's no doubt that your fears can paralyze, divide, enslave, and rob you. But God's Word disagrees with Walsch. The Bible tells us that fear is not your biggest problem.

For years, I've counseled people struggling with all types of fears—disabling phobias, devastating doubts, stressful anxieties, and self-destructive insecurities. What I've discovered is that God's Word is proven in our everyday experiences. Fears are not people's basic problem. They are only outward symptoms of a deeper problem. The parent of all problems: pride.

One of the most respected Christian writers of all times, C. S. Lewis, agreed. In his seminal book *Mere Christianity*, Lewis reminds us that "Pride leads to every other vice: it is the complete anti-God state of mind."

It was that "anti-God, I-can-handle it myself" state of mind that turned fearless David into fear-filled David. As a young, inexperienced shepherd, brave David let his family know that he was not afraid of the giant Goliath. He admitted that he would not fight Goliath in his own strength but would approach Goliath with God's strength. And when the time came, humble and fearless David looked up at that mountain of a man and said, "You come against me with sword and spear and javelin, but I come against you in the name of the Lord Almighty, the God of the armies of Israel, whom you have defied" (1 Samuel 17:45 NIV).

While he had a humble heart, David accomplished great victories. But, as often happens over time when God blesses us, the humble, successful shepherd David became the arrogant King David. God gave him many successes, but David forgot the source of his achievements. He let pride creep in and eventually take over. He lived a new state of mind that said, "Look at how capable I am. I don't need God. I can do this on my own."

As pride pushed humility out, fear slowly moved in. The Bible records that David began to fear his enemies. He even felt afraid of his family members, questioned his own abilities and, finally, doubted his every thought.

God didn't give up on David. And in time David returned to his shepherd-boy humility. Much of the book of Psalms contains David's songs and prayers of honest confessions and humble dependence on God. History remembers him as "a man after God's own heart" (see Acts 13:22). His heart and state of mind were at peace with himself and God.

You can have what David had by making the same choice David made. It's yours to make. Choose to make that difficult but necessary giant change in your state of mind. Admit your inability to handle your life and eternity by yourself. And, beginning each day, and throughout your day, ask your heavenly Father to show you even the smallest malignant cell of pride in you and to replace it with His humility. As you choose to have that godly state of mind, your fears will slowly disappear, and you too will become a child after God's own heart.

Related Scriptures from Psalms

Even when I walk / through the darkest valley, / I will not be afraid, / for you are close beside me. Your rod and your staff / protect and comfort me.

(Psalm 23:4 NLT)

I praise God for what he has promised. / I trust in God, so why should I be afraid? / What can mere mortals do to me?

(Psalm 56:4 NLT)

Other Related Scriptures

Not that we are competent in ourselves to claim anything for ourselves, but our competence comes from God.

(2 Corinthians 3:5 NIV)

So do not fear, for I am with you; / do not be dismayed, for I am your God. / I will strengthen you and help you; / I will uphold you with my righteous right hand.

(Isaiah 41:10 NIV)

What Is God Saying to You?

What do the Psalms and God's listening ear teach us about God's character?

What are some of your fears that have been with you for years and that you want to overcome?

Dear Father, the better I get to know You, the more I see that You want to and are able to replace my fears with faith and peace. Thank You, Lord. Amen

Get to Know God through Proverbs

A Brief Overview

THE PROVERBS, LIKE PSALMS, are a collection of brief sayings written by a number of authors. Solomon says that he is the author of most of the book. His name is stated at the beginning of the three main sections.

The words *wise* and *wisdom* together occur 113 times in the Proverbs. The sheer number of instances lets you know the central message of the book is clearly that God wants you to think, to value, and to act in a wise way—the way God does. Being wise is not about being smart, knowledgeable, clever, or prudent. It is about living like you were designed to live—made in His image.

Proverbs is the most practical book in the Bible. It primarily uses short statements that will help you in making wise decisions. It will assist you in living a successful and meaningful life in God's eyes.

Some who read through the Proverbs notice that the book includes some sayings that are similar to proverbs from other cultures in that part of the world. No doubt writers from other cultures used sayings from Proverbs. It is also possible that God led Solomon and the other writers of the Proverbs to use statements of truth that are true in any culture.

Solomon's message is filled with hope and encouragement. You will find the Proverbs brimming with God's wisdom for you when you cannot trust your own feelings and thoughts, when so many contradictory media and unfriendly voices cause you confusion, and when you have troubled relationships. Proverbs is a clear path to wisdom for your every decision, giving you confidence that your God not only wants you to follow the wisdom of His Word but also the leading of His Spirit.

An Inspirational Theme of Proverbs

If It Feels Good, Is It Good?

"This feels so right, it must be the right thing to do. It feels so good, it must be good. But is it good and right because it feels good and right?" Do you ever ask yourself that question? When it comes to important decisions, everyone says your wisest choice is to, "Trust your gut. Go with your heart. Follow your feelings." But should you?

Brandi was only seventeen when she attempted suicide. On her first date, she was so infatuated by the sweet words of a handsome, older boy that she quickly gave him her heart. It felt perfect. It felt so right. In a short time, he told her he loved her and wanted to marry her. But after she had given herself totally to him, he disappeared. She was brokenhearted and kept repeating to me, "How could I have been such a fool?" Sadly, our feelings often lie.

In 1960, when Elvis Presley's song "It Feels So Right," was released, it came as no surprise when it hit the top of the music charts. The repeated theme of the entire song resonated with the minds and hearts of millions. As the lyrics seem to ask, if something feels right, then how can it be wrong?

Tragically, for many like Brandi, those sugar-coated lies that feel so right and good too often end up in pain, shame, and failure. Just ask the drug addict, the bankrupt gambler, or the many others who made their initial decisions based how they felt.

If you're looking for a more confident way of making good decisions and avoiding so many dead ends, disasters, and heartaches, stop trusting your fickle feelings and start trusting in God's wisdom. God made you, so you should not be shocked that He knows what is best for you. He knows you better than you know yourself. And He knows what works and what does not. So, here is His secret to true wisdom and good decisions: "Trust in the LORD with all your heart; do not depend on your own understanding. Seek his will in all you do, and he will show you which path to take" (Proverbs 3:5–6 NLT).

To trust in the Lord means you admit, without reservations or exceptions, "I can't make good decisions on my own. I can't trust my feelings and my own thinking to do what's best." Trusting in the Lord means, depending on God's wisdom and way, not on your way.

Depending on the Lord "with all your heart," means to give the Lord control over your heart—your emotions, feelings, and desires. To trust in the Lord with all your heart is to choose to give your God-given emotions, feelings, and desires to Him, putting those God-given gifts into His hands to be used the way they were designed to be used.

God wants to protect you, through His wise instructions and guidance, from making foolish, painful mistakes. His

Word says, "The wise are glad to be instructed, / but babbling fools fall flat on their faces." (Proverbs 10:8 NLT)

You do not have to go looking for God's wisdom and personal help. Like the father in the story of the prodigal son, your heavenly Father is waiting for you with outstretched arms. You have been gone from home long enough. Now is your time to come home to feeding on His Word daily. Come home to regularly getting alone with Him and sharing your heart with Him. When you do, you'll find His wisdom and discover that your feelings, desires, and ambitions will be the same as His.

Related Scriptures from Proverbs

Start with GOD—the first step in learning is bowing down to GOD; only fools thumb their noses at such wisdom and learning.

(Proverbs 1:7 MSG)

Wisdom is more precious than rubies; nothing you desire can compare with her.

(Proverbs 3:15 NLT)

Other Related Scriptures

For the wisdom of this world is foolishness to God. As the Scriptures say, "He traps the wise in the snare of their own cleverness."

(1 Corinthians 3:19 NLT)

In him lie hidden all the treasures of wisdom and knowledge.
(Colossians 2:3 NLT)

What Is God Saying to You?

What do these wise sayings found in the Proverbs have to say about the character and nature of our God?

What is the difference between human wisdom and God's wisdom?

Dear Father, the better I get to know You, the more I see that You are wise and want to make me wise. Thank You, Lord. Amen.

Get to Know God through Ecclesiastes

A Brief Overview

Ecclesiastes is a Greek word that means "called out of the crowd." It refers to people who hear God's call and leave their old crowd to join others in following God. It's about choosing a new leader, a new family, and new purpose in life. The word *ecclesiastes* comes from the same Greek root word *ecclesia,* translated into English as *church,* and refers to someone who hears Jesus's call, accepts His invitation, leaves an old life to begin a new life with Him.

As the author of Ecclesiastes, Solomon saw himself as not only the son of David but the one who was called out, chosen to be God's spokesman: "Look, I am wiser than any of the kings who ruled in Jerusalem before me. I have greater wisdom and knowledge than any of them" (Ecclesiastes 1:16 NLT). He knew he was the one who was to build the temple of God.

This book of Solomon's is a poetic reflection of his life. As king and one of the wealthiest men that had ever lived, he had the power and resources to do and have almost anything he wanted. The sad and sorrowful tone of most of the book reveals Solomon's regrets for his selfish lifestyle, egocentric attitude, and bad choices. Ecclesiastes is a testimony of a life journey that began with other-centered values and God-given purposes that along the way were lost and replaced with selfishness and meaningless.

The main message of Ecclesiastes is summarized by Solomon in the now famous starting point of the book: "Vanity of vanities, saith the Preacher, vanity of vanities; all is vanity" (Ecclesiastes 1:2 KJV). It was Solomon's conclusion that life without a relationship with God, and without following His purpose, is a foolish and miserable existence. It's doomed to constant feelings of utter futility, complete dissatisfaction, hopeless wandering, lack of fulfillment, and depressing loneliness where nothing makes any sense.

Yet in all of Solomon's sadness, he remembered how life could be. He longed for the life he once knew in God's will. He remembered being happy and excited about life, feeling like a young man in love. He remembered how good it was following God's purpose for his life and how God provided everything he needed, even when he was young and just starting out. He recalled how God loved him through it all and never left him, even when Solomon left God.

Ecclesiastes is a warning and confession to stay true to being one who is called out of the crowd, one who stays close to God and is faithful to His purpose.

An Inspirational Theme of Ecclesiastes

Asking the Right Question?

Perhaps you have experienced something painful and unpredictable like a frightening sickness, a broken heart, the death of someone close to you, an accident, the loss of your job, or the pain of a struggling relationship. In those times, have you ever asked, "Why did this happen to me?"

If you're asking such questions and having such thoughts and feelings, you have lots of company. Since we all have so many limitations in understanding life's problems and what's best for us, questions and fears are part of our normal human response. While working as a chaplain in a metropolitan hospital emergency room, the question I heard most was, "Why? Why is this happening?"

Do you know why we almost always focus on the Why question in such hard times? I think the main reason is we forget that we are not machines. With a machine, when something goes wrong, if you can find the cause, you can get the problem fixed. But we are not machines. We are complex physical, emotional, relational, and spiritual beings made in the image of God. We don't work like robots.

If your car won't crank, you go through a list of questions: Is the cause a dead battery? Am I out of gas? Is the problem a bad spark plug? Because it's a machine, all you need to do is to figure out what caused the problem, and then fixing it is easy. So naturally you and I think that's the proper way we should handle our life troubles. We assume something or someone causes every problem. And if we can discover the cause, we can fix the issue.

That is also the thinking of most of the world's religions. They assume all suffering happens because of karma—the belief that the universe is like one big machine. If anything goes wrong, it is because someone has done wrong and someone must pay. There must be balance. You always get what you deserve. Many Bible believers have a karma-like way of handling suffering. They think to themselves, "God's Word tells us we reap what we sow. So if I am suffering, I have done wrong."

That's a mistake even the wise Solomon made. He bought into the teachings of the religions around him. In Ecclesiastes, we see Solomon constantly struggling, trying to answer the questions of why his life made no sense, why he felt so depressed even though he was so rich, what caused him to be so miserable. The more Solomon tried to figure out the Why question, the more miserable he became. Finally, as the master teacher, he came to the point where he concluded, "Everything is meaningless, says the Teacher, completely meaningless!" (Ecclesiastes 1:2 NLT).

But God never gave up on Solomon. Eventually Solomon listened to God and discovered that He still loved him just like He had in Solomon's youth and wanted to have that same kind of intimate father-son relationship with him that they'd once had. Solomon realized that what he needed most was to stop giving his attention to the endless questioning of God and blaming himself for all his miseries and start giving his full attention to rebuilding his close relationship with Him.

That is the same point Jesus made to his disciples when they saw a man who was blind from birth and asked Jesus who had sinned to cause this suffering. Jesus told them, "You're asking the wrong question. You're looking for someone to blame. There is no such cause-effect here. Look instead for what God can do" (John 9:1–3 MSG).

Jesus is saying the same to you today. When you experience evil or suffering or you feel hopeless or that your life is meaningless, Jesus wants you to ask what God's purpose is for you in all this. What can you do to honor Him and let this problem draw you closer to Him and to encourage His children who are going through similar things?

How will you respond to whatever you are facing today? Will you ask the Why question or the What question?

Related Scriptures from Ecclesiastes

As you enter the house of God, keep your ears open and your mouth shut. It is evil to make mindless offerings to God. Don't make rash promises, and don't be hasty in bringing matters before God. After all, God is in heaven, and you are here on earth.

(Ecclesiastes 5:1–2 NLT)

Remember your Creator now while you are young, before the silver cord of life snaps and the golden bowl is broken . . . For then the dust will return to the earth, and the spirit will return to God who gave it.

(Ecclesiastes 12:6–7 NLT)

Related Memorable Scriptures

"Why ask me about what is good?" Jesus replied. "There is only One who is good. But to answer your question—if you want to receive eternal life, keep the commandments."

(Matthew 19:17 NLT)

If you are wise and understand God's ways, prove it by living an honorable life, doing good works with the humility that comes from wisdom.

(James 3:13 NLT)

What Is God Saying to You?

What does the message of Ecclesiastes and the sorrowful words of Solomon tell you about the nature of our God?

When you experience hard times, what are some reasons your Lord is more interested in you asking the What questions than the Why questions?

Dear Father, the better I get to know You, the more I see that You care more for my life and my relationship with You than just answering my questions. Thank you, Lord. Amen.

Get to Know God through Song of Solomon

A Brief Overview

SONG OF SOLOMON BEGINS with these words: "This is Solomon's song of songs, more wonderful than any other" (Song of Solomon 1:1 NLT). This short book was written not as a book but as a song. The lyrics are a love story through which Solomon poetically reveals the intensity and depth of God's love for us and the security and satisfaction we, as God's children, can enjoy when we have an intimate relationship with Him. The word *love* appears more times in Song of Solomon, one of the shortest books in the Bible, than in any other book. Solomon wrote it as a testimony through which we get a glimpse into the heart of God.

There are some important things to keep in mind as you read the word *love* in the Bible and especially in the Song of Solomon. When William Tyndale published the first English Bible in 1525, he chose the English word *love* to translate the original Hebrew word *ahab* and the Greek word *agape*. In Tyndale's day, the word *love* meant something radically different from what it means today. In our culture, we use the word *love* to communicate our passionate feelings for something or someone. In Tyndale's day the word *love* meant what it meant in the Bible. It was used to communicate an act of total commitment. The words *ahab* and *agape* were not so much about feelings as they were about actions. The Bible talks about us loving (*ahab, agape*) the Lord with all our minds, bodies, hearts, and souls. Love is a wholehearted, intense giving of your total self. The closest modern equivalent to the original *ahab* and *agape* is *intimacy*. To *ahab* or *agape* God is to have an intimate relationship with Him.

The Song of Solomon focuses on the importance of intimacy and how central it is to be able to have the kind of relationship God created us to have. Often the language in Song of Solomon sounds so highly romantic and passionate that the reader who comes across it for the first time is often shocked and confused. It seems out of character from any other writing in God's Word. In fact, early Christian and Jewish historians and theologians like Origen and Jerome reported that some orthodox Jews would not even allow their young men to read the Song of Solomon until they were thirty years old. They believed its language was too suggestive and would lead to unhealthy thoughts and problems.

In spite of some reservations, the book was added to the Holy Scriptures because an overwhelming number of Jewish scholars saw it as God speaking through Solomon in a parabolic style seeking to communicate the importance of deep, meaningful love.

Song of Solomon is a passionate, storytelling song that was meant to be sung not read, celebrated not debated. It was designed to express the wonderful and unexplainable dimension of the intimate kind of relationship God wants for us and with us. It shows us that a God-designed relationship with Jesus is not so much about correct rules and perfect thinking as it is about being one with Him in our minds, hearts, and actions.

An Inspirational Theme of Song of Solomon

Finding True Love

Have you ever known someone for a long time but felt you didn't really know him or her at all? That's the way a depressed wife felt after twenty years of marriage. Her confession was one of the most heartbreaking I ever heard. "I feel like I've been married to a stranger all these years," she said.

How is that possible? Can you be married to someone and be with him virtually every day for twenty years and never feel like you know him? Unfortunately, it's not only possible, it's easy and too often the case. Too many couples live together but feel alone. On the outside they look happy, but on the inside, they feel alone and sad. It's that painful gap between a tolerable relationship and an intimate relationship. It's the difference between a relationship that merely survives and one that really thrives.

If you're not careful, the same thing can happen to you in your relationship with God. You can easily start out giving yourself wholeheartedly and enthusiastically to Jesus. But slowly, even without being aware of it, you can one day discover that your intimate relationship has become a tolerable religion.

That's what happened to so many of God's finest leaders. Take King David. He started out so close to God that he was able to slay giants and build a godly nation. But over time, David lost his close relationship with God and hit the bottom morally.

The same thing happened to Solomon. When David turned the kingship over to his son, he gave Solomon valuable fatherly advice from his life experience—advice about what should be first place in his life: "Solomon, my son, learn to know the God of your ancestors intimately" (1 Chronicles 28:9 NLT). Years later, in the Song of Solomon, King Solomon gave that same time-tested advice to his people. In his poetic and symbolic story, he told of a man and his wife who overcame great difficulties by maintaining their intimate relationship.

Centuries later, the great missionary Paul shared this timeless guidance to the struggling new Christians in Philippi. Paul's stirring testimony tells how he handled life's challenges. He said, "I count everything as loss compared to the priceless privilege *and* supreme advantage of knowing Christ Jesus my Lord [and of growing more deeply and thoroughly acquainted with Him—a joy unequaled]. For His sake I have lost everything, and I consider it all garbage, so that I may gain Christ" (Philippians 3:8 AMP).

Since you're reading this devotional, my guess is you know a lot about God. But, more important, do you really *know* Him? Are you so close to Him that you think, feel, value, and act like your mind, heart, and actions are one with Him?

Today, make Paul's challenge your prayer: "Lord, help me count everything as loss compared to knowing you more deeply and intimately."

Related Scriptures from the Song of Solomon

My beloved is mine, and I am his.

(Song of Solomon 2:16 NIV)

Many waters cannot quench love, / nor can rivers drown it. / If a man tried to buy love / with his wealth, / his offer would be utterly scorned.

(Song of Solomon 8:7 NLT)

Other Related Scriptures

I've loved you the way my Father has loved me. Make yourselves at home in my love. If you keep my commands, you'll remain intimately at home in my love.

(John 15:9–10 MSG)

Everything that goes into a life of pleasing God has been miraculously given to us by getting to know, personally and intimately, the One who invited us to God.

(2 Peter 1:3 MSG)

What Is God Saying to You?

What are some signs that your relationship with God is not as intimate as you would like it to be?

What are some actions you can take to have a more intimate relationship with God?

Dear Father, the better I get to know You, the more I see that You want to have an intimate relationship with me, and I'm so grateful. Amen.

MAJOR PROPHETS

Five Longer Books by Prophets through Whom God Spoke

FROM THE BEGINNING, our heavenly Father created us in His image and gave us a free will. Since He made us and knows everything about us, He knew we would exercise our free will to make good and bad choices. So He had a plan to help us.

The Hebrew the word *prophet* means "one who speaks for God." Part of God's plan to help us was to continually speak to us through His chosen prophets. Just like God's children in the Old Testament, you can get to know God more by listening to Him speak through His seventeen special prophets. Five of the prophets wrote longer books and are called the Major Prophets. The twelve who wrote shorter books are called Minor Prophets.

God's common message through all of them is clear. If you remain faithful to the image of God in you, you will have a close relationship with Him and life at its best. Choose to turn your back on Him, and you will bring serious consequences on yourself, your family, and others.

The stories in the Major Prophets show how so many of God's chosen children repeatedly choose a self-centered, self-destructive, no-need-for-God way over a God-centered, God-blessed relationship. Their choices brought them confusion, discord, and misery. For their Father, their wrong choices brought Him pain but also hope.

Even with all the stories of the people's sins and their consequences, the Major Prophets also continually reveal God's hope for His children. His love and hopefulness are noticeable in every book because God's forgiveness and presence are real and never ending. He knew some of His children would choose Him over self and choose eternity over temporary pleasure.

Therefore, through His prophets, you see God's pain and hope, His justice and mercy.

Finally, in the Major Prophets you see God as the "foreteller of the future." Our God always respects our free wills, yet He is able to see what is coming. God's mysterious ability to do both is beyond our human minds, but both His judgments and deliverances are always present. The most astounding and hope-filled foretelling in the Major Prophets is related to the events about the coming of our Lord Jesus and His kingdom.

Get to Know God through Isaiah

A Brief Overview

THE BOOK OF ISAIAH is a prophetic piece written around 700 BC. It is the first book of the Major Prophets. Isaiah is called the Prince of Prophets, a poetic genius. And his book is both the most quoted Old Testament book in the Gospels and the Bible's most messianic document.

Over the centuries, people have been in awe over the mystery that the Bible has sixty-six books and Isaiah has sixty-six chapters. There are thirty-nine books in the Old Testament and thirty-nine chapters of judgement in Isaiah. And the New Testament has twenty-seven books, and Isaiah has twenty-seven chapters of hope.

Isaiah presents some of the most remarkable prophecies of any book in the Bible. It has amazing details about the coming and the life of the Messiah, Jesus, God's son.

The main message of the book of Isaiah is that God's people must return to the Lord and that if they do not, there will be judgment. But, like the other Major Prophets, Isaiah reminds us that even with judgment God offers mercy and hope. The key verse in the book summarizes Isaiah's theme: "We all, like sheep, have gone astray, each of us has turned to our own way; and the Lord has laid on him [Jesus] the iniquity of us all" (Isaiah 53:6 NIV).

The first section of Isaiah, verses 1 through 39, describes the rebellion of both the northern and southern kingdoms of Israel.

He begins by urging them to "Wash and make yourselves clean. Take your evil deeds out of my sight; stop doing wrong" (Isaiah 1:16 NIV). He reminds them that He is a God of hope and forgiveness, saying, "Therefore, the Lord himself will give you a sign: The virgin will conceive and give birth to a son and will call him Immanuel" (Isaiah 7:14 NIV). This passage was fulfilled in Matthew 1:22–24 in the New Testament.

The second section is chapters 40 through 55, which prophesy the return and restoration of God's people from their exile in Babylon. Isaiah continues to remind his countrymen of God's truth: "I am the first and I am the last; apart from me there is no God" (Isaiah 44:6 NIV). It also foretells the wonderful coming of Jesus to bring forgiveness of our sins through His cross: "He was oppressed and afflicted, yet he did not open his mouth; he was led like a lamb to the slaughter, and as a sheep before its shearers is silent, so he did not open his mouth" (Isaiah 53:7 NIV).

The final section of the book is chapters 56 through 66. Here Isaiah tells about God's promise of His new heaven and new earth for those who commit their lives to Him and accept His grace. He reveals the long-awaited hope for people who have been abused and afflicted. He also describes God's responsible judgment for all those who rejected His gift of Jesus: "See, I will create new heavens and a new earth. The former things will not be remembered, nor will they come to mind" (Isaiah 65:17 NIV).

Chapter 53 is one of the most incredible chapters in the Bible. Seven hundred years before God's incarnation in Jesus, Isaiah tells about the scandal of the cross (verses 1–3), the benefits of his passion (verses 4–9) and the success of his sacrificial suffering (verses 10–12).

Isaiah provide us with a thoughtful, emotional, and accurate prophesy of our God's mind and heart.

An Inspirational Theme of Isaiah

In a World of Phony Phone Calls

Have you ever felt like things will never get better? That there's nothing anybody can do? There's just no hope? Most of us feel that way at times: when our test results are discouraging, our money runs out, we're abandoned or turned down again or our hearts get broken, or our lives are threatened by a devastating virus. It can get very discouraging. Writers and artists through the centuries have given us painful stories and images of hopelessness.

Without Hope is a self-portrait of Surrealism artist Frida Kahlo. Her life had been plagued by illness and surgeries. The medical options available to her in the mid-twentieth century now seem brutal and tortuous. Only a few days before she died, lying in a hospital bed barely able to move, the artist painted this now world-famous portrayal of life without hope. It is a grotesque depiction of how bad things can be when one has no hope.

As a minister and chaplain, I've seen it too often: when people lose hope, they give up. They don't want to live any longer. It's easy to lose hope living in a culture where there's so much false hope—dishonest guarantees, slick scams, deceptive advertising, bogus medical cures, phony phone calls, and fraudulent get-rich schemes. You begin to wonder if there is no place and no one in whom you can find real hope.

The prophet Isaiah, whose name means "God is my salvation or hope," saw the hopeless condition of his countrymen. They had abandoned God, putting their hope only in their wealth, their armies, their leaders and in themselves. It was a foolish and empty dream. A plague more devasting than they could have imagined was coming. The world's most powerful empire was on its way to conqueror and enslave them.

God warned His people to stop putting their hope in themselves: "Doom to you who think you're so smart, who hold such a high opinion of yourselves!" (Isaiah 5:21 MSG). But God's warning was also an invitation of hope: "Listen to me, all who hope for deliverance, who seek the Lord! Consider the quarry from which you were mined, the rock from which you were cut!" (Isaiah 51:1 TLB).

God offered hope to the people in Isaiah's day, and He offers us the same hope today. It is a belief built on the solid rock of His character. When everything else is unstable, He is not. He was and is our temporal and eternal solid foundation. No matter the circumstances, you can rest on your one and only dependable hope for now and eternity. God wants to raise you up and help you rebuild.

That was the message Pastor John Rippon shared in his inspiring lyrics of hope. In 1787, following the horrible plague that struck England and took thousands of lives, Pastor Rippon wrote the favorite old hymn "How Firm a Foundation."

When through fiery trials thy pathway shall lie,
My grace, all-sufficient, shall be thy supply.
The flame shall not harm thee; I only design
Thy dross to consume and thy gold to refine.

Fear not, I am with thee, oh, be not dismayed,
For I am thy God and will still give thee aid.
I'll strengthen thee, help thee, and cause thee to stand,
Upheld by My gracious, omnipotent hand.

How firm a foundation is our God. Rest on that!

Related Scriptures from Isaiah

All of us, like sheep, have strayed away. We have left God's paths to follow our own. Yet the LORD laid on him the sins of us all.

(Isaiah 53:6 NLT)

Those who trust in the LORD will find new strength. They will soar high on wings like eagles. They will run and not grow weary. They will walk and not faint.

(Isaiah 40:31 NLT)

Other Related Scriptures

I pray that God, the source of hope, will fill you completely with joy and peace because you trust in him. Then you will overflow with confident hope through the power of the Holy Spirit.

(Romans 15:13 NLT)

Let us hold tightly without wavering to the hope we affirm, for God can be trusted to keep his promise.

(Hebrews 10:23 NLT)

What Is God Saying to You?

What does Isaiah's message say about the character of God?

What is the hardest thing for you about having hope in difficult days? Where do you look for hope when you feel your conditions seem hopeless?

Dear Father, the better I get to know You, the more I see that You are the solid foundation of my hope. Amen.

Get to Know God through Jeremiah

A Brief Overview

THE BOOK OF JEREMIAH is prophetic and dramatic. It is a history but is not presented in a chronological order. It was written during the ministry of Jeremiah around 626 to 586 BC. The main rulers of Judah during that period were the kings Baruch, Ebed-Melech, and Nebuchadnezzar.

The main message of the book is that God's destruction is certain unless His rebellious children repent and again become His grateful people. Jeremiah was a priest who preached mostly about the seriousness of sin and the shortness of time left to change. Chapters 1 through 10 give God's call to Jeremiah: "The Lord reached out and touched my mouth and said, 'Look, I have put my words in your mouth!'" (Jeremiah 1:9 NLT). In this section, Jeremiah points out and condemns Judah's rebellion, faithlessness, hatred, and various forms of immoral behavior. Chapters 11 through 28 describe Jeremiah's warning about God's holy and just anger about people's false idols and sacrifices to strange gods.

Chapters 29 through 38 focus on God's New Covenant and the hope of a new day of deliverance. Yet King Zedekiah refuses to accept God's warning and throws Jeremiah into prison. Chapters 39 through 52 then present the painful story of the fall of Jerusalem in 586 BC—something many prophets prophesied. Jeremiah tells about the captivity by the Babylonian Empire and how King Zedekiah's son was murdered and the king was seized, blinded, and taken away as a slave in Babylon.

Chapter 50 is a key chapter. It tells of God's promises to set His nation free from captivity. God describes the Israelites as sheep that have been scattered by lions. First the king of Assyria ate them up. Then King Nebuchadnezzar of Babylon cracked their bones. Therefore, the God of Israel tells all the people that He will punish the king of Babylon and his land just as He punished the king of Assyria. Later we learn that the capital of Assyria was so devastated that it went undiscovered until nineteenth century AD.

Jeremiah's prophesies give a unique insight into the mind and heart of Jeremiah and God. The book includes many personal expressions of emotional commitment. It presents Jeremiah not only as the weeping prophet brought onto the scene to deliver God's message but also as a compassionate human being who sincerely cares for his people.

The book also provides a good glimpse of the new way God plans to transform His people once the Lord Jesus comes to earth. God's new promise would be the way of putting His law in His people, writing it on their hearts rather than on tablets of stone. Jeremiah promises that God will have a personal relationship with His children through His Son, Jesus.

An Inspirational Theme of Jeremiah

Another Gift Nobody Wants

The world-renowned deaf-blind author Helen Keller wrote what we all know: "The best and most beautiful things in the world cannot be seen or even touched. They must be felt with the heart." The Bible uses the word *heart* to refer to those God-created, built-in emotions we call feelings. The heart is the house of our feelings, desires, and will. It's the part of us that we see in God, who fully expresses His feelings of love, joy, peace, as well as anger, disappointment, and sadness.

That's why Jeremiah talked so much about the heart. He told God's people that God had put His desires, His hopes, His laws for a godly life not just their heads but in their hearts. Jeremiah called God's people to love God with all their hearts and not just with obedience to the written laws.

How we use our feelings reveals who we are and what counts most in our lives. We're grateful for those wonderful feelings like love, joy, and peace. We all thank God for such cherished good feelings. But sometimes we forget about those other God-gifted feelings that nobody seems to want. Did you know that pain, fear, and sorrow can be gifts of God too?

The famous surgeon and pioneer in leprosy research Dr. Paul Brand wrote an historic book, *The Gift Nobody Wants: Pain*. In it he said that pain, which most people avoid at all cost, is what people with leprosy want most. Why? Because when lepers lose their ability to feel pain, they hurt themselves without even knowing it. Their wounds lead to infections, amputations, and even death. Dr. Brand explained that none of us may see it at first, but we all need pain to protect us from hurting ourselves and others.

Not only in Jeremiah but throughout the Bible we can see that every feeling we have is a gift of God that can be used to honor Him and draw us closer to Him and one another. It is all about how we use our feelings.

When the elder missionary Paul sent young Timothy to an extremely difficult and depressing challenge, Timothy was afraid and worried that he would fail. Paul urged Timothy to stir up all of his gifts and use their flame to energize himself to be more passionate about his work—to use his feelings like fear, anger, and pain to invigorate and motivate himself.

I was six when a hurricane swept across South Florida and threw a palm tree through my bedroom wall. I was so afraid that I leaped out of my bed, ran to my parents' bedroom, and jumped into their bed. What do you suppose they did? Tell me to stop being a frightened child? Of course not. They hugged me and told me I was safe.

When storms come crashing into your life and you're that frightened child, be assured your heavenly Father wants you to use your fears to cause you to jump into His loving arms. Picture yourself there. And try repeating this simple prayer: "Thank You, Father, for all of Your gifts. I give You my feelings of fear and worry. Help me use them to make me a more grateful, sympathetic, humble, and better servant of Yours. Amen."

Related Scriptures from Jeremiah

I, God, search the heart and examine the mind. I get to the heart of the human. I get to the root of things. I treat them as they really are, not as they pretend to be.

(Jeremiah 17:10 MSG)

Do not fear the king of Babylon anymore, says the LORD. For I am with you and will save you and rescue you from his power.

(Jeremiah 42:11 NLT)

Other Related Scriptures

Then Jesus wept.

(John 11:35 NLT)

Wherever your treasure is, there the desires of your heart will also be.

(Matthew 6:21 NLT)

What Is God Saying to You?

What kinds of things cause you the most fear and anxiety, and how can you use them to honor God and draw you closer to Him?

What are some feelings Jesus expressed that give you a better picture of the heart of God?

Dear Father, the better I get to know You, the more I see how understanding You are of my fears and worries. Amen.

Get to Know God through Lamentations

A Brief Overview

LAMENTATIONS, ANOTHER BOOK OF JEREMIAH'S, is a prophetic and dramatic story. It naturally follows the book of Jeremiah and reveals the heart and soul of the young prophet whose heart is broken over the plight of his people.

In his *Dictionary of Bible Characters*, Dr. Alexander Whyte, one the most gifted Bible scholars of all times said, "There is nothing like the Lamentations of Jeremiah in the whole world. There has been plenty of sorrow in every age, and in every land, but never such a preacher and author, with such a heart for sorrow has ever again been born."

Jeremiah's ministry took place while Good King Josiah led Israel. Both he and Josiah were young men who were leaders in the great Jewish revival prior to the nation's downfall. The revival was short lived since God's people again loved God's blessings more than the One who blessed them.

King Josiah died in the strategic battle at Megiddo against Pharaoh–Nechoh. But Jeremiah continued his work as God's prophet during the reign of the four other kings whose leadership was marked by unfaithfulness to God and rampant immorality. Jeremiah tried as earnestly and passionately as he could to call his people back to God, but he never saw any sign of repentance. One of the most memorable parts of this book is his remembrance of the destruction and burning of his beloved Jerusalem. He wept as he witnessed the city burn to the ground and as his friends, family members, and countrymen were slaughtered.

Jeremiah's weeping over the fall of Jerusalem reminds us of Jesus, who sat weeping over Jerusalem six centuries later. Jeremiah wept over the ashes of what had already been done. Jesus wept over what he knew was going to take place.

Lamentations painfully pictures a man of God who mourns a needless tragedy that could have easily been avoided. Although his people brought the judgment of the holy God on themselves, Jeremiah still grieved as a mother kneeling at the graveside of her wayward child. Yet at the heart of this message of tears stand a few significant words of hope for those who choose to give God control of their lives:

> Because of the LORD'S great love we are not consumed, / for his compassions never fail. / They are new every morning; / great is your faithfulness. / I say to myself, "The LORD is my portion; / therefore, I will wait for him." / The LORD is good to those whose hope is in him, / to the one who seeks him.
>
> (Lamentations 3:22–25 NIV)

The book of Lamentations gives us light in the midst of any darkness.

An Inspirational Theme of Lamentations

Regaining Life Out of Control

Joni Eareckson Tada was only seventeen when she dove into shallow waters of the Chesapeake Bay and her life was totally changed in seconds. The accident left her a quadriplegic, paralyzed from her shoulders down. She lost her desire to live and almost committed suicide. For years, she suffered more than most of us can imagine. She felt like her life was out of control.

Today, over half a century later, Joni still lives without the use of her limbs, but she likes to tell audiences around the world that she's gained far more than she's lost. She is now an internationally known mouth artist, talented vocalist, radio host, author of forty books, and a producer of movies and music albums. Joni's life proves that when you feel like your life is completely out of control, you can get it back under control. But how?

The Bible is full of true-life stories of people like Joni. Take Jeremiah, who told part of his story in the book of Lamentations. If there were ever a man who felt like his life was out of control, it was Jeremiah. His circumstances were so chaotic and heartbreaking that in his compassion he wept over the plight his people.

Known as the Weeping Prophet, Jeremiah had plenty of reasons to cry. He wept over the way his family turned their backs on God. He wept over the destruction of his beloved temple in Jerusalem. He wept as he watched his people being herded off like cattle to become slaves in a foreign country. It was not after the chaos, but in the middle of it, when Jeremiah made a decision that brought him inner peace and a renewed feeling that his life was no longer out of control. What was that decision?

It is the same decision Job made when he lost all his possessions, health, and family. It is the same decision Paul made when he lost everything he owned and ended up in a Roman prison facing death. It is the identical decision Moses made when he lost his royal position in Egypt and ended up in the desert being asked by God to set his people free. They all decided the same thing: when you have no control over the circumstances or the people around you, give God command of what counts most. There is always something or someone who will seek to take control of everything in your life on earth, but you alone get to choose to what or to whom you will give control of your heart, your mind, and your eternity.

In the middle of all his helpless and hopeless feelings, that truth came to Jeremiah's mind: "I call to mind … I have hope: Because of the Lord's great love we are not consumed, for his compassions never fails. They are new every morning; great is your faithfulness" (Jeremiah 3:21–24 NIV). Jeremiah found inner peace and courage by giving the Lord control of his heart and destiny.

The Lord is aware that in times of great loss, chaos, and fear His children will grieve and feel confused, angry, worried, and afraid. But He gives you a way to move beyond those feelings. You can choose to let the Spirit of the Living God, who lives in you, control (influence) your mind, heart, and actions. You can turn over the reins of your feelings, life, and eternity to Him who has, as Jeremiah said, great love, great compassion, great faithfulness, and great hope for you.

Joni and Jeremiah made that choice. Will you make that choice and accept His gifts that are "new every morning"?

Related Scriptures from Lamentations

Yet this I call to mind, / and therefore I have hope: / Because of the LORD'S great love we are not consumed, / for his compassions never fail. / They are new every morning; / great is your faithfulness. / I say to myself, The LORD is my portion; therefore I will wait for him.

(Lamentations 3:21–24 NIV)

The LORD is good to those whose hope is in him, to the one who seeks him.

(Lamentations 3:25 NIV)

Other Related Scriptures

The LORD is my strength and shield. / I trust him with all my heart. / He helps me, and my heart is filled with joy. / I burst out in songs of thanksgiving.

(Psalm 28:7 NLT)

Be on guard. Stand firm in the faith. Be courageous. Be strong.

(1 Corinthians 16:13 NLT)

What Is God Saying to You?

What does God's choice of Jeremiah as His prophet say about the heart and mind of God?

What parts of your life do feel are often controlled by other people? What are some ways you can give God's Spirit control (influence over) your life?

Dear Father, the better I get to know You, the more I see that You want the best for me, which is giving You control of my mind, heart, and behavior. Amen.

Get to Know God through Ezekiel

A Brief Overview

Ezekiel's name literally means "God will strengthen" or "God will give courage." Ezekiel certainly lived up to his name. He was trained and ordained in Jerusalem to be a priest but never got the chance to serve in the Holy City. Instead, along with his family and fellow Jews, in 597 BC he was taken captive to a refugee camp in a foreign land.

Ezekiel was a contemporary of Jeremiah and Daniel. But unlike his fellow prophets, Ezekiel did not live in Babylon. He was forced to make his new home and parish where God placed him, several miles from Babylon in a crude settlement near the Kebar River, a branch of the grand Euphrates River. He was there along with about ten thousand Jewish slaves.

The priest, whom God called to be His voice for His children in exile, started right out announcing hope for a new day. While his people still grieved over their plight, thinking they were living in the last days and feeling lower than they had ever imagined, Ezekiel looked up, anticipating God's vision for him. And God did give him that vision—one that became known worldwide: "While I was with the Judean exiles beside the Kebar River in Babylon, the heavens were opened, and I saw visions of God" (Ezekiel 1:1 NLT).

Ezekiel's prophecy began early in the exile and continued for some twenty-two years. Most of God's message to Ezekiel's rebellious family members focused on God's judgment for their unrepentant sins, but Ezekiel also brought them God's message of hope and restoration. In chapter 37 he provides a dramatic vision of the rebuilding of the temple and the restoring of God's people.

The book of Ezekiel also provides a reminder to all of us that God did not allow the exile only for the purpose of punishing His children. It lets us know that God kept His word as He had always done. He used their suffering to help them see Him for who He was and to see how foolish and futile it was to try to live as though He doesn't matter.

Ezekiel's most memorable vision was that of a valley of dry bones. God asked Ezekiel if bones in that hopeless condition could live again. The prophet replied, "'O Sovereign LORD,'" I replied, "'you alone know the answer to that'" (Ezekiel 37:3 NLT). Then God told Ezekiel what we all need to hear when we are faced with "dry-bone" situations. He told Ezekiel to say, "Speak a prophetic message to these bones and say, 'Dry bones, listen to the word of the LORD!'" (Ezekiel 37:4 NLT).

The main message of the book of Ezekiel is that God's people should remember God is able to do anything He chooses to do, and He wants to give His people life at its best. God is all-loving and all-powerful.

An Inspirational Theme of Ezekiel

First, Check His Track Record

Since I was ten, I've loved sharing beautiful parts of God's creation that come to my eyes and out through my paint brushes. Painting has been my hobby for all these years, and I still I love it. So you can imagine how nervous I was when I discovered I had a congenital eye disease that will eventually require a corneal transplant, a delicate surgery.

After considerable research and discussions with my ophthalmologist, I learned the national success rate of this procedure is about 90 percent which is good. But then I thought, *What if I'm part of that unsuccessful 10 percent?* Research also indicated that some actually lost their sight. I didn't want to risk it.

Just before deciding not to do it and instead hope for the best, I visited my potential surgeon. I knew the national success rate was 90 percent, but when I asked her about her personal rate, she humbly replied, "I've done hundreds of these, and so far, my success rate is 100 percent." You guessed it—I've changed my mind, and when my 100-percent-of-the-time doctor says it's time, I will let her do the surgery based on her excellent track record.

Anytime we're faced with a dangerous health issue, a difficult decision, a situation that looks highly risky or even impossible, and we're looking for someone we can trust, the first question we need to ask is clearly, "What is his or her track record over a long period of time?" One of the best examples of this truth is found in the Bible story of the prophet Ezekiel. He and his countrymen were captured and taken captive to Babylon and forced to live as slaves in a filthy makeshift settlement. After years of suffering as a result of their bad choices and with no prospect of going home, most of them had given up hope. But then one night in a vision, God gave Ezekiel a breathtaking glimpse of the future.

God stood the prophet before a valley full of dry bones and asked him if he thought old, dry, bleached out, scattered bones like those could possibly live again. Ezekiel answered that God was the only one who knew the answer to that question. Then God asked Ezekiel to do the same thing God asks of each of us to do when we face our dry-bone situations: he asked Ezekiel to take Him at His word.

God told Ezekiel that He was going to blow His breath into those dry bones and bring them back to life. It sounded strange and didn't make any sense to Ezekiel, but he did what may seem to you and me like something extremely risky: he took God at His word so wholeheartedly that the very next day he went out and told everyone God was going to rescue them and give them a new start in their homeland.

Why would Ezekiel believe something that seemed so unbelievable? Was it blind faith or just a whole lot of I-hope-so? Neither. Ezekiel trusted God because he knew God's track record. He knew this was not God's first miracle. He knew God had been doing miracles of all kinds for thousands of years—dividing the Red Sea; healing blind, deaf and diseased people; transforming lives; and even raising people from the dead. Ezekiel remembered, considered the evidence, and moved ahead.

No doubt on occasion you will be faced with your own valley of dry bones. When that happens, God will ask you what He asked Ezekiel twenty-five hundred years ago: "Do you believe I can make these dead, dry bones live again?" Before you answer, before you decide whom you will trust with your life and eternity, remember God's track record and don't forget, His success rate is 100 percent.

Related Scriptures from Ezekiel

I will put my Spirit in you and you will live, and I will settle you in your own land. Then you will know that I the Lord have spoken, and I have done it, declares the Lord.

(Ezekiel 37:14 NIV)

I will save them from all their sinful backsliding, and I will cleanse them. They will be my people, and I will be their God.

(Ezekiel 37:23 NIV)

Other Related Scriptures

The Lord is trustworthy in all he promises and faithful in all he does.

(Psalm 145:13 NIV)

God will do this, for he is faithful to do what he says, and he has invited you into partnership with his Son, Jesus Christ our Lord.

(1 Corinthians 1:9 NLT)

What Is God Saying to You?

What are some areas of your life that feel like a valley of dry bones?

As you think about the way God related to Ezekiel, what are some reasons you believe you can trust God for handling the dry-bones items in your life?

Dear Father, the better I get to know You, the more I see that You can be trusted when all seems impossible because You have an amazing track record of taking care of Your people. Amen.

Get to Know God through Daniel

A Brief Overview

WHILE STILL A YOUNG MAN, Daniel was exiled to Babylon with other youthful Israelites whom their conquerors believed were exceptionally talented (see Daniel 1:3–4). Daniel's Babylonian masters renamed him Belteshazzar to identify him as one of their promising servants. Daniel remained as a servant in Babylon during the entire seventy-year Jewish captivity (see Daniel 1:21; 9:2). However, he rose in respect, influence, and prestige becoming a leader throughout the kingdom (see Daniel 6:1).

The book of Daniel is a record of his experiences and prophecies. Even while in captivity, Daniel was such a young man of integrity and responsibility that the king gave him unusual privileges of the highest levels of society. Daniel and his three young friends, Shadrach, Meshach, and Abednego are well known by Bible readers because of their miraculous experience in the fiery furnace and because of their faithfulness to God in the face of a strongly polytheistic religious culture.

The book of Daniel emphasizes the biblical theme that our God is the sovereign Creator and ruler over heaven and earth, even when everything seems to be going wrong and the anti-powers of this world seem overwhelming. The book is also unique in Daniel's detail on the timeline of the coming of God's promised Messiah. The themes of God's sovereignty and faithfulness occur several times in the book, including Daniel's deliverance from the lions' den, his friends' rescue from the fiery furnace, and the future salvation of God's people from the forces of evil (see Daniel 6:19–23; 3:23–30; 7:9–22).

An Inspirational Theme of Daniel

Does Being Honest Really Pay?

We all know that we should not lie. Or said in the positive, we all know we should tell the truth and be honest. This is one of God's Ten Commandments. But did you know God made honesty so important to your DNA that you can never have a peaceful inner life or a loving relationship without it? That is the way God made you. You cannot escape it.

Unfortunately, sometimes we don't act like this commandment is all that important. As Dan Ariely said in his book *The Honest Truth About Dishonesty*, most of us see ourselves as honest while regularly keeping secrets, lying, and cheating in what we consider small matters.

Recently my brother Frank sent me an article from the *Harvard Business Review* entitled "Why Be Honest If Honesty Doesn't Pay." The writer's research on multiple major corporations revealed that in our super-competitive business world, honest guys actually finish last most of the time, while liars and deceivers more often win. The hidden thesis of some businesses is that lying pays off and honesty doesn't, leading us to believe you just cannot tell the truth and survive in the real world.

Although that is often true, it is only partially true. Facts show that the salesperson or the business that wins over the competition with extraordinary but dishonest claims over time loses. People eventually feel cheated, used, and deceived.

God has a different thesis: honesty always pays off. Solomon put it this way: "Better to be poor and honest than to be dishonest and rich" (Proverbs 28:6 NLT). You know why that's true? It is because honesty is part of how you're built. God made you in His image, and He always tells the truth, avoids deceit, and is absolutely trustworthy.

Honesty is like gravity. Gravity is one of God's physical laws. If you ignore it, you'll hurt yourself. Honesty is also one of God's relational laws. If you ignore it, you'll hurt your relationships with God and others.

At first glance, being honest may not seem all that important, and we often attempt to explain why we tell lies. But God's Word demonstrates that honesty is part of every God-given value. For example, humility is a product of being honest about ourselves. Intimate love deepens when a couple is honest and practices humility. Honesty produces personal joy, patience, and inner peace. When we're honest about where we got everything, we become more grateful, generous, and kind. Integrity and faithfulness are other names for honesty in action. If you want God's best, you will take honesty seriously.

A good example of how honesty pays off is the famous story of Daniel and the lions' den. King Nebuchadnezzar threatened to throw Daniel into a den of hungry lions because Daniel would not worship the king. To avoid death, Daniel could have secretly acted like he worshipped Nebuchadnezzar. He could have lied. But he knew it would destroy his witness, his integrity, his relationship with God, and his own sense of inner peace. So Daniel chose the lions' den over dishonesty.

When the king witnessed Daniel's honesty and courage and how His God delivered him, the king became a believer and made Daniel a national leader. In time Daniel used his position to help set his people free from slavery and return them to their homeland.

Our God doesn't always deliver us *from* our lions' dens. Sometimes He chooses to deliver us *in* or *through* our trials. Regardless, His rewards are always worth far more than our costs for being honest.

If you're facing a lions' den in your life, you may feel that it will cost you to do what is right, what is honest. But remember, it will bring you God's best.

Related Scriptures from Daniel

[Daniel said,] "My God sent his angel to shut the lions' mouths so that they would not hurt me, for I have been found innocent in his sight. And I have not wronged you, Your Majesty." The king was overjoyed and ordered that Daniel be lifted from the den. Not a scratch was found on him, for he had trusted in his God.

(Daniel 6:22–23 NLT)

Shadrach, Meshach, and Abednego replied, "O Nebuchadnezzar, we do not need to defend ourselves before you. If we are thrown into the blazing furnace, the God whom we serve is able to save us. He will rescue us from your power, Your Majesty. But even if he doesn't, we want to make it clear to you, Your Majesty, that we will never serve your gods or worship the gold statue you have set up."

(Daniel 3:16–18 NLT)

Other Related Scriptures

The godly are directed by honesty; the wicked fall beneath their load of sin.

(Proverbs 11:5 NLT)

We reject all shameful deeds and underhanded methods. We don't try to trick anyone or distort the word of God. We tell the truth before God, and all who are honest know this.

(2 Corinthians 4:2 NLT)

What Is God Saying to You?

What do these stories about Daniel and his friends in the furnace say about the God they served?

List some ways dishonesty damages relationships with people we love.

Dear Father, the better I get to know You, the more I see how honest You are with me. Help me always be honest. Amen.

MINOR PROPHETS

Twelve Shorter Books by Prophets through Whom God Spoke

IN THIS FOURTH SECTION OF THE BIBLE, God chooses twelve men to speak for Him to His children and to us. These spokesmen of God are not called minor prophets because their messages are of less importance but because their books are shorter than the major prophets. Through the writings of Hosea, Joel, Amos, Obadiah, Jonah, Micah, Nahum, Habakkuk, Zephaniah, Haggai, Zechariah, and Malachi, you will gain additional insights into God's character. You will learn more about His main interests and His ways of relating to His children. You will read verses that were favorites of Jesus and His followers. You will see prophecies about Jesus that were all fulfilled.

Your heavenly Father will also provide you with five similar themes through each of these twelve men's unique personalities. As you continue to get to know your God better through the Minor Prophets, be sure to keep an eye out for these characteristics of God's personality.

- His fairness and mercy for His rebellious children and His warnings
- His honesty by telling them the truth about sin and its consequences
- His integrity by reminding them of judgment's heartbreaking reality
- His earnest desire for His children to turn from their sins to Him
- His gift of forgiveness and hope of renewal and restoration

Get to Know God through Hosea

A Brief Overview

HOSEA'S NAME MEANS "SALVATION," a reference to his position in Israel as the one who brought hope to those who returned to God and listened to the prophet's message. Hosea was a minister, and God instructed him to marry Gomer, who was a prostitute before their marriage. Hosea and Gomer had three children—two sons and a daughter. The prophet gave symbolic names to his children and Gomer to represent God's children and their unfaithfulness.

The book of Hosea begins with the prophet identifying the kings that ruled during his prophetic ministry. The first four—Uzziah, Jotham, Ahaz, and Hezekiah—governed over the southern kingdom of Judah from 790 BC to 686 BC, while Jeroboam II reigned the northern kingdom of Israel from 782 BC to 753 BC. This indicates that Hosea lived in the middle to late eighth century BC (755–715 BC) and was a contemporary of Isaiah and Micah.

Although the story of Hosea's personal life was real, his book was unique in the way he used his painful personal life as a testimony and symbol of God's message to the children of Israel. He loved and married Gomer, knowing she would break his heart and lose his trust. Yet Hosea still loved Gomer and sought to woo her back, which was symbolic of God's faithful and merciful love for his wayward children. The cycle of rejection, repentance, redemption, and restoration was clear in

Hosea's personal life and in God's relationship with all of His children. It's a pattern also seen in the messages of the other minor prophet's books.

The main message and theme of this heart-wrenching true story is obvious. Although God is just in faithfully bringing judgment on sin, He is also faithful in His earnest attempts to bring His people back to Him. Sprinkled throughout the book, Hosea pictures God's children as rebellious, self-centered people turning their hearts away from God to other so-called gods. Yet even with their ungrateful spirit and behavior, God still makes plans and provisions to get them back.

In Hosea's story, he tells how he eventually finds a way to rekindle his relationship with Gomer. She has fallen so low that she is about to be sold as a slave on the public square. So Hosea buys her back to save her from slavery. With his expression of forgiving love, they start over as in the days of their youth. With this story, Hosea uses intimate and personal language to describe God's amazing forgiveness and mercy—the kind of mercy that led God to send His son to give His blood in payment for our sins and bring us back into a right and intimate relationship with Him.

An Inspirational Theme of Hosea

Learning to Swim Can be Scary

If you wanted to learn how to swim, would you prefer to go it alone, jumping into the deep end of the pool and taking your chances on drowning as you figure out how to swim for yourself? Or would you rather have an experienced swimming instructor get in the pool with you and help you learn how to swim? No-brainer, right?

As early as I could walk, I played on the white-sand beaches of my hometown, Pompano Beach, Florida. But I didn't know how to swim. So, early one morning, my daddy said, "Bill, it's time for you to learn how to swim." When we got to beach, Daddy told me how his daddy had taught him to swim. Without any help or instructions, Granddad had tossed my father into deep water, saying, "It's up to you, son. Swim or drown." But my daddy didn't do that. He held my hand and said, "You have nothing to fear. I'm going into the water with you. You'll be fine." In no time I was swimming like a fish.

As frightening as life is sometimes, the good news of Jesus is that you don't ever have to jump into life's unfamiliar waters alone. The Bible says it, and Christians over the centuries have experienced it—your loving, knowledgeable, and strong Father always goes ahead of you and will be with you in every situation.

Even when God's children were sinking in the rough waters of their own sin, the prophet Hosea reminded them that their God was able and wanted to rescue them. Hosea tells the story of his wife, Gomer—how she left him and their children to fend for themselves while she decided to return to her life of prostitution. Eventually, she was to be sold like an animal on an auction block in the public square. But out of his faithful love, Hosea bought her back and they started their relationship over.

Hosea used his own true-life story to remind his wayward Israelite family that they had been Gomers. Hosea told the rebellious Israelites that God still loved them and wanted them back so much that he would do whatever it cost Him to show His love and forgiveness: "I will heal their waywardness. I will love them lavishly. My anger is played out. I will make a fresh start with Israel" (Hosea 14:4 MSG).

Sadly, some only think of God as an impersonal cosmic force. They believe they live in a sink-or-swim world where they must face the deep waters of life alone. They haven't yet come to know Jesus in the way I and so many other Christians have. Years ago, when I was lost and reached out to Jesus, He pulled me out of my own sins and became my Savior. But that is not all. He also became my daily guide and personal friend. He has never left me and has been with me through every storm in my life, from a serious car accident to fighting a life-threatening cancer.

That's what Jesus wants for you. He wants to get into the scary waters with you, give you His expert guidance, help you learn how to swim, and stay with you every step of your life. As you face all of your deep-water decisions and experiences today, will you ask Him to lead you? Or will you dive in head first, taking your chances? One of my favorite hymns, entitled "God Leads His Dear Children Along," says it beautifully.

> Sometimes on the mount where the sun shines so bright,
> God leads His dear children along.
> Sometimes in the valley in the darkest of night,
> God leads His dear children along.
> Some through the water, some through the flood,
> Some through the fire, but all through the blood,
> Some through great sorrow, but God gives a song,
> In the night season and all the day long.

Related Scriptures from Hosea

I will win her back once again. I will lead her into the desert and speak tenderly to her there. I will return her vineyards to her and transform the Valley of Trouble into a gateway of hope.

(Hosea 2:14–15 NLT)

I will show love to those I called 'Not loved.' And to those I called 'Not my people,' I will say, 'Now you are my people.' And they will reply, 'You are our God!'

(Hosea 2:23 NLT)

Other Related Scriptures

His sheep recognize his voice and come to him. He calls his own sheep by name and leads them out.

(John 10:3 NLT)

Do not be afraid or discouraged, for the LORD will personally go ahead of you. He will be with you; he will neither fail you nor abandon you.

(Deuteronomy 31:8 NLT)

What Is God Saying to You?

Since Hosea's story parallels God's story, what does it say about God's heart?

What are some important decisions you need make and want God's direction on?

Dear Father, the better I get to know You, the more I see that You love me and want to lead me in making my decisions. Amen.

Get to Know God through Joel

A Brief Overview

JOEL MEANS "JEHOVAH IS GOD." Although God's children were surrounded by many people who had superstitions and erroneous beliefs about gods, the prophet's name is a bold declaration of singularity. Likewise, the book of Joel is a reminder to everyone that the God of Abraham, Isaac, and Jacob is the only true God. All other supposed gods are imaginary, manmade ideas. The God Joel told the people about is the true Creator of everything and is all-powerful, all-loving, all-knowing, and all-present.

Around 800 BC, Joel warned his family members living in Judah about a crucial day coming. He called it "the day of the Lord" (see Joel 2:1–11). Prior to his preaching, the region had experienced a devastating plague of locusts. To make matters worse, a severe famine followed the locusts. God used those dreadful events to convey words of warning to get His people's minds and hearts refocused.

Joel leaves no question about what is about to happen. He repeatedly pleads with the people to wake up and turn from doing wrong to avoid the consequences—nations around them attacking and destroying everything like the locust and famine had done before. Joel urges his fellow countrymen to stop ignoring God, to ask for God's forgiveness, and to turn back to Him. He offers hope by telling them of God's desire to forgive and restore them and promises safety for them on that terrible day. He assures them that their possessions will be restored and their relationship with God will be renewed. But he also reminds them the day of the Lord is coming one way or the other.

The phrase "the day of the Lord" is a common theme in the Bible and is always used as a reminder of God's character. He has great care for His children, with a freeing love that allows us to make their own choices. He did not create and program us to be robots, and He will not violate His gift of a free will for each of us. Yet He is a holy God who takes sin seriously. And although things may *seem* out of control, ultimately He is in control of His creation.

The book of Joel is a powerful message of fear and love, wrath and hope, judgment and forgiveness. God gave Joel the ability to see more than his present situation. And Joel's message is a God-alarm, an emergency call for His people in all ages to wake up and decide whom they will follow before their terrible day comes. But Joel was also aware of the presence of our invisible God and of a coming new and glorious day for those who turned to Him.

An Inspirational Theme of Joel

Tears and Smiles

Do you sometimes cry when you lose someone you love even when you know they are going to heaven? My wife, Phyllis, likes to say, "Tears are good for you. If your eyes leak, your head won't swell."

Over the years, I have served as the preacher for many memorial services. And after a while, I started noticing a common and fascinating thing about the faces of most Christians at funerals. Their faces are covered with both tears and smiles at the same time.

I remember such a January morning when those Texas chilling winter winds felt colder than usual as I stood at the graveside of my old friend, Simon. Simon was chairman of deacons at a church where I had served as pastor. He was not only my best friend, he was everything a pastor could want in a church leader and everything a family could want in a godly husband and dad.

On that gray winter day in that old family graveyard, with its rows of sun-bleached tombstones and weather-washed artificial flowers, I stood beside Simon's casket and glanced at the open grave as I had done so many times. The whole place appeared lifeless and seemed to whisper, "This is the end."

As was my custom at interment services, I began by saying:

> Everything around us says, "This is the end." But we who know our resurrected Lord Jesus know this is not the end. It only appears that way. Our physical eyes only see death, but our spiritual eyes see beyond death to eternal life. Like God's Word tells us, we do not get so fixated on what we see around us that we miss out on the whole reality beyond the physical—that spiritual world where Jesus went before us to prepare a place for us and Simon.

That's when it happened. That fascinating thing so many Christian do at funerals. There were tears, lots of tears. After all, Simon was dearly loved. But more noticeable than the tears were the smiles—big smiles, beaming through the tears—

proclaiming, "He is not here. He is fully alive now. He's home with God. And it won't be long before we'll see him and Jesus and all the family." They all had that look of inner peace and anticipation.

The prophet Joel had that same way of looking at things. He lived in a dark day when most of God's children ignored God and lived self-centered, present-only lives. Joel looked at things differently. He kept one eye on the present and one on God's future. He foresaw a terrible day coming for those who ignored God and a wonderful day coming for those who faithfully served Him. He wept for the single-focused and rejoiced with those who looked beyond the present to the great day of the Lord.

Like our Savior and Lord, Jesus, Christians over the centuries under pressure have demonstrated the same relentless, faith-focused approach to life and eternity. When our culture and emotions shout, "It's the end of the road. You've lost. There's no way out," we Jesus followers quietly respond differently. We say, "No it's not. You just can't see what we see. Like our Lord, we see beyond our suffering, our crosses, our graves, our cloudy days." We are not surprised by heartaches, disappointments, plagues, unfair or unexplainable circumstances. Jesus had all of them and told us we would too. And, yes, at times we shed tears, lots of tears. But through it all, and more important, we smile inside and stay focused on eternity.

If you're one of those Christians who has tears and smiles at the same time, pause right now, close your eyes, think about God's future for you, put a big smile on your face, and whisper to Him, "Thank you, Lord."

Related Scriptures from Joel

The LORD says, "Turn to me now, while there is time. Give me your hearts. Come with fasting, weeping, and mourning. Don't tear your clothing in your grief but tear your hearts instead." Return to the LORD your God, for he is merciful and compassionate, slow to get angry and filled with unfailing love. He is eager to relent and not punish.

(Joel 2:12–13 NLT)

Everyone who calls on the name of the LORD will be saved.

(Joel 2:32 NLT)

Other Related Scriptures

Those who love their life in this world will lose it. Those who care nothing for their life in this world will keep it for eternity.

(John 12:25 NLT)

From eternity to eternity I am God. No one can snatch anyone out of my hand. No one can undo what I have done.

(Isaiah 43:13 NLT)

What Is God Saying to You?

When you think about eternity, what feelings come to your mind and heart?

How do Jesus's promises about taking you and your loved ones to heaven influence your thoughts about God?

Dear Father, as I get to know You, I realize there is so much more than I can see, so much more than what I can touch. Help me, like You, to have an eternal perspective. Amen.

Get to Know God through Amos

A Brief Overview

AMOS STARTED OUT AS a small-town shepherd and fruit farmer but became a nationally famous preacher. He was from Tekoa, a village ten miles south of Jerusalem. Amos let everyone know he did not come from a family of priests or prophets and didn't set out to speak out for God. His life changed when God called him to do what seemed impossible. He was to confront the king of Israel face to face and deliver him a personal warning from God.

History tells us that Amos preached two years before the great earthquake, which Greek historians say was around 550 BC. It was a time of great prosperity for Israel. By God's power, they had won many battles and controlled most of the key trade routes in the region, but they let their wealth and power go to their heads. Craving the pleasures and the immoral practices of their pagan neighbors more than they loved God, they began to act self-centered and behave shamefully toward those in their country who were less fortunate.

Amos held them responsible and repeatedly pointed out their lack of justice and compassion. They stooped so low in their search for self-gratification that they sold needy people in their own neighborhoods for extra money. They took advantage of the helpless and oppressed the poor by making them work harder for less pay.

Amos also described how the Israeli men brought shame to God and their families by using women and young girls in immoral ways. Intoxicated by their own success and power, they had lost their God-given call to care for one another in purity and to make the family a sacred union of love and respect.

With the Israelite people enjoying an almost unparalleled time of success, God recognized that they did not see His gifts as resources to help others but as power to make their lives more comfortable and pleasurable. Their outer lives were gleaming with success, but their inner lives were filled with moral decay.

Through Amos, God warns His people of the disease of ease and the perils of privilege. He clearly communicates God's anger and displeasure with their hypocritical lives and their lack of stewardship of His gifts. Amos's prophecy ends with a brief picture of hope for those who change their ways in time.

An Inspirational Theme of Amos

Fix Your Eyes. Don't Get Distracted.

Can you guess the first and most important of the Ten Commandments of working in a woodshop? It's simple: "Thou shalt not get distracted." It's all about keeping your eyes on what you're doing. And by the way, the other nine don't matter if you break big number one.

Ask my friend, Chris. He's a master woodcrafter, and he'll tell you from personal experience just how critical it is to never get distracted when using a table saw. Chris is so experienced and comfortable using all of his power tools he could almost use them without thinking. But that was the problem a while back. He got too comfortable and wasn't thinking, at least not about what he was doing. And it took less than a second for that razor-sharp, ten-inch saw blade to severely injure his finger and hand.

Far too often, that's what happens not only to people who work in woodcrafter shops but to people like us who work in our life-crafter shops. If you're not careful, you get comfortable and take your eyes off what counts most to you and to your Lord. You can easily get pulled away from God and all He has for you by the world's good and evil magnets. The media, the marketers, and even your friends constantly battle for your brains and tug at your heart. And if you break the first commandment of working in your life-crafter shop, injury is certain.

That was the main message the prophet Amos had for his comfortable and highly successful family members. God had so richly blessed them that they got distracted. They started loving the gifts God gave them more than the Gift Giver and His purpose for granting so much to them. So when they took their eyes off God, He warned them in a series of woes.

In our day, Amos would be saying on God's behalf, "Watch out," especially if these attitudes and actions describe you:

- Watch out if you live in luxury and expect everyone else to serve you.
- Watch out if you live only for today, indifferent to the fate of others.
- Watch out if you think life is a party held just for you.
- Watch out if you are addicted to feeling good and living a life without pain or discomfort.

- Watch out if you are body fussy and are obsessed with looking good.

God's message was clear: Don't get distracted by such things. Stay focused on your relationship with Me and My purpose for your lives or get ready for serious trouble.

And, by the way, over time Chris's hand healed, and he's now back in his woodshop making beautiful pieces. Recently while we were talking woodshop and remembering his accident, we agreed there's a good reason the first commandment of the woodshop is first.

Related Scriptures from Amos

Woe to you who think you live on easy street in Zion, who think Mount Samaria is the good life. You assume you're at the top of the heap. You're voted the number-one best place to live. Well, wake up and look around. Get off your pedestal.

(Amos 6:1 MSG)

Seek God and live! You don't want to end up with nothing to show for your life.

(Amos 5:6 MSG)

Other Related Scriptures

Look straight ahead and fix your eyes on what lies before you. Mark out a straight path for your feet; stay on the safe path. Don't get sidetracked; keep your feet from following evil.

(Proverbs 4:25–27 NLT)

Let us run with endurance the race God has set before us. We do this by keeping our eyes on Jesus, the champion who initiates and perfects our faith.

(Hebrews 12:1–2 NLT)

What Is God Saying to You?

List some things in your life that try to distract you from doing what's most important to you and your Lord.

What are some habits you can use to help you keep the eyes of your heart on Jesus and His plans for you?

Dear Father, the better I get to know You, the more I see how You stay focused on Your plan for my life. Help me do the same. Amen.

Get to Know God through Obadiah

A Brief Overview

OBADIAH MEANS "GOD'S SERVANT" or "One who bows low before God." Obadiah's name was a continual reminder of his book's theme: God demands that His people be grateful, humble servants. Although the book is only one brief chapter, making it the shortest in the Old Testament, its main message is profound: Pride destroys. Humility builds.

Through His servant Obadiah, God warned Israel's neighbor nation Edom that its people were in serious trouble with God because of their prideful attitude. Edom took pleasure in the destruction of their neighbor, Jerusalem, by the Babylonians and during the invasion even plundered the homes and businesses of their family members.

The Edomites were descendants of Abraham, Isaac, and Jacob's brother, Esau. For generations they'd fought with Israel, their relatives located southeast of the Dead Sea. They lived in homes carved out of solid stone cliffs on top of the Seir Mountain range. Archaeologists have studied the Edomite culture and found that the Edomites took great pride in their strongholds and believed they were impregnable.

Obadiah predicted that the Edomite nation would be wiped off the face of the earth. That prophecy came true when the Babylonians invaded in 582 BC. It was during that same invasion that Edom helped in the siege of Jerusalem. According to Obadiah, when the Babylonians took Jerusalem and obliterated God's temple, the Edomites were there cheering on the Babylonians. Obadiah warned the Edomites that their lack of humility would be their downfall. And so it was. They took pride in their strength and security, but it was their pride that brought God's judgment. By AD 70 Edom disappeared from history.

Obadiah warned the Edomites about their pride:

> You have been deceived by your own pride / because you live in a rock fortress / and make your home high in the mountains. / "Who can ever reach us way up here?" / you ask boastfully. / But even if you soar as high as eagles / and build your nest among the stars, / I will bring you crashing down, / says the LORD.
>
> (Obadiah 1:3–4 NLT)

An Inspirational Theme of Obadiah

An Unforgettable Picture

In his article "Why Being Humble Is Stupid," Josh Bocanegra promotes a popular idea: "Humility is not a virtue. It's an imperfection. It doesn't make you better. It makes you weaker and ineffective."

The Bible and experience prove the opposite—above all, the one quality essential to building an effective life and successful relationship with God and others is humility. Why? Because being humble doesn't mean you become weaker and less effective. It means you become stronger and more effective by doing things God's way rather than the world's way. It's not about putting yourself down. Rather, it's about lifting others up. As C. S. Lewis put it in *Mere Christianity,* "Humility is not thinking less of yourself, but thinking of yourself less."

Thinking too much of yourself or about yourself is the root of most failures in life. The prophet Obadiah told his countrymen that they were about to be destroyed not because they were weak but because they prided themselves in their supposed impenetrable mountain fortress. They were about to go down as a nation not because of their poverty; they were wealthy and enjoying the comforts of life. No, they were going to be punished because of an internal disease, the worst kind of all: pride. Obadiah said it this way: "You have been deceived by your own pride" (Obadiah 1:3 NLT).

I'm reminded of an experience I had. It was the morning after major abdominal surgery and three miserable nights in the ICU. The doctors wanted me to try to stand up beside the bed. As my wife, Phyllis, carefully maneuvered me out of the bed to stand up, the bulb on my drain tube came off and fell to the floor and began spraying body fluids seemingly everywhere. At that moment my surgeon walked in wearing a suit and tie like he was going to an important meeting. He took one look at the situation, hurriedly put on gloves, spoke calmly to us as he got on his knees, and proceeded to clean my feet, legs, and the floor around me.

Why did he do what he did? He could have called on the team of interns and nurses standing behind him. He did it not because he was a nationally distinguished surgeon, which he was. It was not because he was head of his department in the medical school. It was because he was a humble man of God.

Remembering how he bathed my feet brings to mind a similar scene. More than anything, Jesus wanted His disciples to be humble. So rather than give them a verbal definition of humility, He gave them an unforgettable picture. The Son of the Creator of the universe got down on His knees and washed their feet. Now that's a definition you'll never forget. It's no surprise that the Hebrew word for *humble* literally means "to get low or bow down."

As you begin your day, test your humility. Can you make these statements?

- I'm no know-it-all. I'm open and honest about my weaknesses and failures.
- I'm no show-off. I always seek to put others and God in front of me.
- I'm no spoiled brat. I'm grateful in all circumstances.
- I'm no hurtful critic. I'm understanding, not critical, of others' weaknesses.
- I'm no pompous braggart. I give God credit for everything I have.
- I'm no talkative interrupter. I listen carefully to others.
- I'm no boastful egotist. I seek God's will before I do anything.

Related Scriptures from Obadiah

You should not have rejoiced when the people of Judah suffered such misfortune. You should not have spoken arrogantly in that terrible time of trouble.

(Obadiah 1:12 NLT)

The day is near when I, the Lord will judge all godless nations! . . . Those who have been rescued will go up to Mount Zion in Jerusalem to rule over the mountains of Edom. And the Lord himself will be king!

(Obadiah 1:15, 21 NLT)

Other Related Scriptures

God gives strength to the humble but sets himself against the proud and haughty. So give yourselves humbly to God.

(James 4:6–7 TLB)

Do nothing out of selfish ambition or vain conceit. Rather, in humility value others above yourselves, not looking to your own interests but each of you to the interests of the others.

(Philippians 2:3–4 NIV)

What Is God Saying to You?

What does God's displeasure with pride say about His character?

God is all-powerful, but He is also humble. In what ways do see humility in the acts of God?

Dear Father, the better I get to know You, the more I see that You are humble and want me to be humble like Your Son, my Lord. Help me be so. Amen.

Get to Know God through Jonah

A Brief Overview

THE BOOK OF JONAH is a true story about a man's struggle between doing what he wanted and what God wanted. His Hebrew name meant "dove." Some say he was given this name because he was a messenger of peace and hope. (As an aside, Jonah was one of only four writing prophets in the Bible that Jesus mentioned by name during His earthly ministry. Isaiah, Daniel, and Zechariah were the others.)

Jonah is acknowledged in the first verse of the book as the son of Amittai, who was from the small town called Gath-hepher, which was near Nazareth on the Sea of Galilee (see 2 Kings 14:25). God wanted Jonah to carry His saving message to His wayward children in Nineveh, the capital of the Assyrian Empire. Jonah didn't want to go. He was prejudiced and hated Nineveh's people, who were his country's enemies.

During Jonah's time as a prophet, Jonah was proud Israel was at peace and prosperous among the nations in the region in a political sense. But Israel was not as successful in the spiritual sense. Since the days of Solomon, Israel had done well materially—but by taking advantage of the poor. It was the same message we read about in Jonah's fellow prophet Amos.

Jonah heard God call him, but he turned his back on God. He got in a boat headed in the opposite direction of Nineveh. When God sent a storm, the boat's crew figured Jonah was the problem and tossed Jonah overboard. The minute he left the boast, miraculously the storm stopped.

Although Jonah turned his back on God, God didn't turn His back on Jonah. He brought a big fish to swallow Jonah and save him from drowning. During his three days in the fish's belly, Jonah realized his problem and cried out to God, and God forgave him. When the fish spat Jonah on Nineveh's shore, Jonah faithfully delivered God's warning to Nineveh and His invitation to come back to Him. To Jonah's surprise, the people repented, and God showed them mercy.

Jonah got so angry that he left town and sat alone under a tree pouting. He forgot God's grace to him and returned to his egocentric ways, He cared more about his own comforts and prejudices than the lives and destinies of the 120,000 people who lived in Nineveh.

An Inspirational Theme of Jonah

Habits for Finding and Following God's Will

Sometimes I just can't figure out what God wants me to do. Other times I know exactly what He wants, but I still do what I want. I can imagine you feel the same way sometimes. But in our hearts we know finding God's will and doing it is by far the best thing for us and others.

One summer my country cousin, David, came to visit me in Ft. Lauderdale Beach. He had never seen the ocean and could hardly wait to jump in. Mama knew David was anxious to get in that water, so she promised to take us to the beach later. In the meantime, she warned us not to go swimming in the nearby canal because it wasn't safe.

Of course, David ignored Mama's warning and leaped into the canal and into those razor-sharp barnacles waiting at the bottom. David spent the rest of his vacation sitting on the beach with his feet wrapped in bandages watching everyone else swim.

That's the essence of Jonah's story. Jonah knew what God wanted him to do, but Jonah did what he wanted. Doing things his way got Jonah into serious trouble, including spending time in the belly of a large fish.

There's a little of Jonah in all of us. But thankfully, there are some disciplines we can use to help us to discover what God wants us to do and then to stay on the path of doing it. Here are five transforming habits Jesus practiced that can help you discover and do God's will for you:

1. Start each day feeding on God's Word and listening for him. Don't focus on your prejudices.
2. Pause throughout your day and talk intimately with God. Don't just talk with God in hard times.
3. Choose God's friends for your friends and get their advice. Don't count on the advice of unbelievers.
4. Stay aware of His presence by thanking Him throughout your day. Don't just thank Him at meals.
5. Watch for places God is working and join Him. Don't just ask Him to support your plans.

Related Scriptures from Jonah

Then Jonah prayed to the Lord his God from inside the fish.

(Jonah 2:1 NLT)

Then the word of the LORD came to Jonah a second time: "Go to the great city of Nineveh and proclaim to it the message I give you." Jonah obeyed the word of the LORD and went to Nineveh.

(Jonah 3:1–3 NIV)

Other Related Scriptures

[Jesus] went on a little farther and bowed with his face to the ground, praying, "My Father! If it is possible, let this cup of suffering be taken away from me. Yet I want your will to be done, not mine."

(Matthew 26:39 NLT)

I have discovered this principle of life—that when I want to do what is right, I inevitably do what is wrong . . . Thank God! The answer is in Jesus Christ our Lord.

(Romans 7:21–25 NLT)

What Is God Saying to You?

What does the story of the big fish that swallowed Jonah say to you about the extreme measures your Lord will go to help you come back to him?

God gave Jonah a second chance. What does that tell you about God's character and your hope?

Dear Father, the better I get to know You, the more I see the value of Your way for my life and believe it is by far the best way. Amen.

Get to Know God through Micah

A Brief Overview

AROUND THE TIME Isaiah, Amos, and Hosea were delivering similar messages for the Lord, God chose Micah to speak for Him to His self-centered and rebellious children. Micah lived in an agricultural part of Israel and was not a part of the governmental centers of his nation. His simple lifestyle may have helped in giving him compassion for the poor and less fortunate of his country, the physically infirm, those who were considered outcasts, and those who lived in pain. It's not surprising that Micah directed much of his prophecy toward the coldhearted and impassionate leaders of Samaria and Jerusalem, the capital cities of Israel and Judah.

The name *Micah* means "Who is like the Lord?" Micah worked diligently to live like his Lord wanted him to live and not like his wicked culture. He labored passionately in trying to convince God's children to do the same. God sent Micah on a difficult mission to deliver some highly disturbing and demanding news not only to strangers but to his own family, friends, and community. Fully committed to their own ideas and habits, they refused to listen and were not interested in what God wanted.

Micah's primary message had two edges. It was clear and critical for his people in that day, but it is just as valuable for us in our day: God is a good and patient and generous and merciful God who loves us and wants only what's best for us.

But also, God is a fair and responsible God who will not ignore selfish violators of His laws and purposes.

Micah concludes his book with a call to the Lord as his only foundation for salvation and mercy, pointing the people to the coming of the Messiah and an everlasting hope in their faithful God.

An Inspirational Theme of Micah

Encouraging Truths for Discouraging Times

Usain Bolt, the world's fastest man at the writing of this book, holds many trophies including nine Olympic golds, but he didn't have it easy. His hardships would have caused most people to give up—childhood scoliosis resulting in a curved spine and various track injuries. But Bolt kept going. He detailed his determination in his music video, reminding us that every time someone pushes him around or puts him down, they're doing him a favor because it just makes him stronger.

Troubles make some people more determined, kinder, and more grateful while they make others weaker, bitter, and more self-centered. You may be facing some difficult situation right now. God has always provided His children what they needed in such times. Will you let your troubles help make you stronger or bitter?

In Micah's day, God's children are about to experience suffering like they've never known. They are discouraged and afraid. Through Micah, God tells them He requires more than religious talk and temple attendance: "The LORD has told you what is good, / and this is what he requires of you: / to do what is right, to love mercy, / and to walk humbly with your God" (Micah 6:8 NLT).

Micah offers his sinful family hope. But he tells them that they must return to God soon. He also discloses that the Messiah is coming to save them. He also gives them and us one of the most specific prophecies in the Old Testament when he names the very town where Jesus will be born 750 years later: "But you, O Bethlehem Ephrathah, are only a small village among all the people of Judah. Yet a ruler of Israel, whose origins are in the distant past, will come from you on my behalf" (Micah 5:2 NLT).

Throughout his message, Micah gives believers reasons to be encouraged in the middle of their troubles even when unbelievers are discouraged. He gives them at least four promising truths to help them for their seemingly hopeless days. These same great pillars of truth will help you become better and not bitter when hard times come. Remember:

1. *His invisible plan*. When hard times hit, it may appear that God has disappeared. But remember this truth: your God is just as much alive and at work behind the scene in your hard times as He is in your good times.
2. *His unshakeable peace*. When all seems chaotic, nothing makes sense, and you feel worried and afraid, remember this truth: your God is your peace. He who calms storms can be your inner peace in your storm.
3. *His special purpose*. While you're hurting, remember this truth: your God has a purpose for you during this time. He hurts with you and will be with you through it all.
4. *His amazing payday*. Right now, life may seem ridiculously unfair. But remember this truth: your God

has a wonderful payday coming. With Him, no suffering goes unnoticed. No act of faith goes unrewarded. Today's misery will fade in comparison to God's amazing tomorrow and what God has in store for you.

Related Scriptures from Micah

But you, O Bethlehem Ephrathah, are only a small village among all the people of Judah. Yet a ruler of Israel, whose origins are in the distant past, will come from you on my behalf.

(Micah 5:2 NLT)

[The Messiah] will stand to lead his flock with the LORD'S strength, in the majesty of the name of the LORD his God. Then his people will live there undisturbed, for he will be highly honored around the world. And he will be the source of peace.

(Micah 5:4–5 NLT)

Other Related Scriptures

Because we are united with Christ, we have received an inheritance from God, for he chose us in advance, and he makes everything work out according to his plan.

(Ephesians 1:11 NLT)

Don't worry about anything; instead, pray about everything. Tell God what you need and thank him for all he has done. Then you will experience God's peace, which exceeds anything we can understand. His peace will guard your hearts and minds as you live in Christ Jesus.

(Philippians 4:6–7 NLT)

What Is God Saying to You?

Hundreds of years before Jesus was born, through Micah, God said Jesus would be born in Bethlehem. What are some things that prophecy tells you about your God?

What is it about God that helps you most when you are having hard times?

Dear Father, the better I get to know You, the more I see You as my wonderfully encouraging Father even during my most difficult days. I am grateful You care so much for me. Amen.

Get to Know God through Nahum

A Brief Overview

THE BOOK OF NAHUM BEGINS with the vision of the prophet given him by God. His name means "one who comforts or has compassion." God had compassion for his children in Judah, and to the surprise of many, God had compassion for their Assyrian enemies. But the Assyrians were so vile and stubborn they would not accept the Lord's invitations, and judgment followed.

The Assyrian armies had already destroyed Samaria, the capital of the northern kingdom of Israel, around 722 to 721 BC. The army was poised and ready to take the southern kingdom of Judah. The Assyrians were some of the most brutally destructive warriors in the ancient world. Their leaders gloated over gruesome forms of torture and horribly mutilated their captives.

The major content of Nahum's message is the Lord's judgment on Nineveh, the capital of the Assyrian Empire, for her tyranny, cruelty, and wickedness. The book ends with the destruction of the city and Nahum's emphasis on God's compassionate nature.

There is a bright yet tiny jewel in the book that should not be missed. Compared to the rest of the story, it is so short that it could go unnoticed. Nahum speaks for God and tells God's children not to trust in their own strength but to let God be their Savior God. He reminds them, "The Lord is good, a refuge in times of trouble. He cares for those who trust in him" (Nahum 1:7 NIV). This is a message that rings throughout the Old and New Testament and still today.

An Inspirational Theme of Nahum

God Is Your Refuge

Do you sometimes feel like life is just too hard, too much? I do. Over the years, I've noticed that all of us, even those close to God, occasionally go through dark valleys.

Even Henri Nouwen, recognized internationally as one of the most famous and sensitive spiritual leaders of our generation, had his periods of what he called "extreme anguish." He wrote thirty-nine books on being close to God. Yet at times, he felt he couldn't keep going. In his book *Dark Night of the Soul,* Nouwen explained what helped him most was turning to and knowing Him as his refuge.

The Bible writers use the word *refuge* often. What does it mean? A refuge is a safe place or protective shelter. In Bible days, it was where you could go to find caring, knowledgeable, and strong people to help you if you were frightened and hurting. In our day, we refer to a refuge as a life-saving shelter where abused people go for protection, comfort, and guidance.

In the prophet Nahum's day, God's people were beaten down and facing devastating threats on every side. God told them not to try to fight the forces of evil on their own strength but to let Him be their personal refuge in times of trouble.

That's what God wants for you today. He is ready and eager not only to be your refuge in times of trouble but in all times. And since Jesus is your living Savior, you don't have to go looking for a refuge. When you give him your life, He comes to lives in you and becomes your ever-present inner refuge.

When you feel like life is getting too hard, don't be discouraged. Remember what God's Word promises you: "Don't you realize that your body is the temple of the Holy Spirit, who lives in you and was given to you by God?" (1 Corinthians 6:19 NLT).

He is your indwelling refuge.

Related Scriptures from Nahum

The LORD is good, / a strong refuge when trouble comes. / He is close to those who trust in him.

(Nahum 1:7 NLT)

The LORD is slow to get angry, but his power is great, and he never lets the guilty go unpunished.

(Nahum 1:3 NLT)

Other Related Scriptures

God is our refuge and strength, / an ever-present help in trouble. / Therefore, we will not fear, though the earth give way / and the mountains fall into the heart of the sea, / though its waters roar and foam / and the mountains quake with their surging / . . . The LORD Almighty is with us; / the God of Jacob is our fortress.

(Psalm 46:1–3, 7 NIV)

LORD, you are my strength and fortress, / my refuge in the day of trouble!

(Jeremiah 16:19 NLT)

What Is God Saying to You?

In what ways is God your refuge in times of trouble? What does that tell you about His character?

When you think about the Spirit of God living in you, being your inner refuge, how does it make you feel?

Dear Father, the better I get to know You, the more I see You as my inner refuge, giving me a deep sense of being safe, loved, and guided no matter what's happening on the outside. Thank You. Amen.

Get to Know God through Habakkuk

A Brief Overview

HABAKKUK'S NAME MEANS "EMBRACE." His message reveals how the prophet passionately embraced God's call to warn his fellow Israelites before it was too late for them. His fellow Jews in the northern kingdom had been captured and taken as slaves to Assyria. Unfortunately, his family in the southern kingdom had not learned from the fall of the northern kingdom nearly one hundred years before. They remained self-centered and ignored God.

Most of Habakkuk's short, three-chapter book is a series of his complaints and challenges to God about the way God is treating them and dealing with their enemies. Habakkuk and his people feel like God is being too tolerant of evil, allowing sinners to prosper, letting good people suffer, and ignoring Habakkuk's prayers. The Lord reminds Habakkuk that He has been and still is mercifully patient, but judgment is coming. God tells Habakkuk He will use the powerful Babylonian Empire to overpower the evil Assyrians and punish not only the evil empire but also his rebellious children.

Habakkuk's book contains one of the most famous verses in the Bible, which became the apostle Paul's main message and a much-repeated biblical theme: "The just shall live by his faith" (Habakkuk 2:4 KJV). That same theme runs throughout the other prophets' words and speaks to God's core message that there is nothing we sinners can do to save ourselves except to choose to turn to God and receive His grace through faith.

Habakkuk embraces God in the closing remarks of his book by praising God. And like us, he puts his faith in God though he still does not understand God's ways.

An Inspirational Theme of Habakkuk

What Kind of Faith Pleases God?

You wouldn't be reading this devotional if you didn't want to please God. But how *can* you please God? The Bible says that the first step to pleasing Him is to live by faith. In another version of his famous words, Habakkuk the prophet says, "But the righteous will live by their faithfulness to God" (Habakkuk 2:4 NLT). That is a concise way of saying a simple but significant truth told throughout the scriptures: the way to please God is not to just believe there is a God or talk about God but to actively live out your faith.

But exactly what is faith? Ask ten people, and you'll probably get ten different answers. If you want a simple, clear definition, look in God's Word: "Now faith is the substance of things hoped for, the evidence of things not seen" (Hebrews 11:1 KJV).

Notice, God-pleasing faith is based on something with substance, something real. Habakkuk spoke for God to His rebellious children, who had repeatedly ignored Him and embraced evil. So God warned them that the powerful Babylonian Empire was coming to conquer Israel and make them slaves. He told them that their only hope was not to depend on their weapons, wealth, or human abilities but to embrace Him, to emotionally wrap their arms around Him.

Many Americans who are deaf use American Sign Language (ASL) to communicate. ASL has a clear, graphic sign for the word *faith* that is an accurate picture of biblical faith. You position your hands like you're holding on to a rope for dear life. It is a symbol of complete dependence on that rope. You won't dare let go because you will fall to your death.

Like the ASL sign for faith, your faith pleases God when it means:

- You depend on God above everything else.
- You trust God with everything although you can't understand everything.
- You think through your options and choose God.
- You do your best to follow His Word, His Spirit, and Jesus's example in all you do.

Related Scriptures from Habakkuk

[God's] brilliant splendor fills the heavens, and the earth is filled with his praise.

(Habakkuk 3:3 NLT)

I will be joyful in the God of my salvation! The Sovereign LORD is my strength!

(Habakkuk 3:18–19 NLT)

Other Related Scriptures

It is impossible to please God without faith. Anyone who wants to come to him must believe that God exists and that he rewards those who sincerely seek him.

(Hebrews 11:6 NLT)

We live by faith, not by sight.

(2 Corinthians 5:7 NIV)

What Is God Saying to You?

What does it say about our God that He wants us to trust Him?

What does it mean to you to please God?

Dear Father, the better I get to know You, the more I see You as the one rope that I can completely count on. Thank You for being the One I can hold onto and Who is holding me. Amen.

Get to Know God through Zephaniah

A Brief Overview

ZEPHANIAH'S NAME IS A HEBREW WORD that means "hiding place," a secret place providing protection and peace in the middle of chaos. Through Zephaniah, God warns His children to turn to Him as their "hiding place" before it's too late. His message was delivered shortly before Zephaniah's Hebrew family and friends would be invaded and exiled into slavery by the brutal Assyrian army.

Like the other prophets, Zephaniah's main message is God's two-edged promise of judgment and reward. The first two chapters repeat a familiar prophetic theme—a terrible "day of the Lord" (see Zephaniah 1:7, 8, 14) is coming soon. It describes how God is long-suffering but responsible. His patience does run out. Judgment will come when He knows the time is right. Zephaniah describes the types of constant sins that generate God's ultimate wrath: rebellion, disrespect, self-centeredness, and rudeness.

The third chapter describes the hope God promises for those who return to Him. He promises a new kind of Jerusalem and new kind of great day. His poetic depiction of this new day reveals an unshakeable inner peace for all who open their hearts to God. It's the kind of peace about which Jeremiah prophesied that resides in our hearts, not in buildings, personal strength, or armies. It is the presence of the great Peacemaker.

The last three verses of Zephaniah provide a joyful picture for the faithful who will be a small remnant of the suffering captives. All the misery will fade in comparison, and their faithfulness will be worth it all. In God's timing, the faithful will no longer have any tears, weakness, loneliness, oppression, shame, rejection, sadness, or feelings of being separated from Him. They will be free to live in God's peace.

An Inspirational Theme of Zephaniah

Your Hiding Place

Help! I want out of all this stress. Do you ever feel like screaming those words? Sometimes, don't you want to just get out from under it all, run away, and hide? But you can't. You have responsibilities. People are counting on you. So what should you do? Maybe hiding is exactly what you should do.

As a spiritual leader of a nation under attack and a God-called spokesman to family members who wouldn't listen, Zephaniah felt extreme stress. I imagine there were times when he felt like screaming, "What's the matter with you people? Why don't you straighten up?"

Sometimes you probably feel like Zephaniah. You're trying to do the right thing. You're doing the best you can. And still, everything seems to be working against you. Like you, Zephaniah wanted to just run and hide. But he didn't. What did he do?

Zephaniah humbled himself and turned inward to find his own peace. And he challenged his family to "Seek the Lord, all you humble of the land . . . perhaps you may be hidden on the day of the wrath of the Lord" (Zephaniah 2:3 RSV). He did what

King David did when he felt the devastating pressures of the outside world. David turned to what he called his hiding place. He said, "You [God] are my hiding place" (Psalm 32:7 NLT).

Christians of all generations and circumstances who have found peace under pressure have done the same thing. When World War II broke out, Corrie ten Boom and her Christian family provided a hiding place in their home for Jews and others to escape the Nazi Holocaust. Eventually, the Nazi police caught them. Corrie and her beloved sister, Betsie, were imprisoned in the Ravensbrück concentration camp until Betsie died and Corrie was freed.

With her dying breath, Betsie assured Corrie of inner peace in the face of her imminent death, reminding Corrie that there is no pit so deep that Jesus will not be deeper still. While Corrie experienced horrific, daily torture from the guards in the notorious Ravensbrück camp, she found inner peace in what she called her hiding place.

Eventually, Corrie was miraculously released. In her best-selling book *The Hiding Place*, she said, "Jesus is Victor, and He will never let us down. With Jesus, even in our darkest moments, the best remains. And the very best is yet to be."

So, when your pressures are great and you feel like hiding from it all, do just that. But don't run far away to look for peace. Peace is as near as your heart. Turn inward. For Jesus is your peace, and He's waiting for you.

Related Scriptures from Zephaniah

Seek the Lord, all you humble of the land . . . perhaps you may be hidden on the day of the wrath of the Lord.

(Zephaniah 2:3 RSV)

Jerusalem will be told: "Don't be afraid. Don't despair. Your God is present among you."

(Zephaniah 3:16–17 MSG)

Other Related Scriptures

For you are my hiding place; you protect me from trouble.

(Psalms 32:7 NLT)

The Lord is my fortress; my God is the mighty rock where I hide.

(Psalms 94:22 NLT)

What Is God Saying to You?

What are some things in your life that are causing you the greatest stress these days? Make a list and tell your heavenly Father about each of them.

What are some reasons you need God as your "hiding place" rather than trying to handle things on your own?

Dear Father, the better I get to know You, the more I see You as my hiding place. Thank You. Amen.

Get to Know God through Haggai

A Brief Overview

HAGGAI'S NAME MEANS "one who celebrates." And if anyone had good reason to celebrate, it was the prophet and spiritual leader Haggai and his fellow Israelites. For just a short time before he wrote this book, God had miraculously delivered them from seventy years of slavery to their Babylonian conquerors.

While holding the Israelites in exile, Babylonia was conquered by the Persian Empire under King Cyrus the Great. During Cyrus's reign, God told Cyrus to set the Israelites free. God chose Zerubbabel, the leader of the Israelites, to persuade the king to fund the costs for the Israelites' return home and the expenses needed to rebuild the Temple. Shortly after Zerubbabel led Israel back to the Promised Land, they began to celebrate God's gracious provisions and to enjoy their lives as free people. They went to work cleaning up the ruins and rebuilding a new temple, new homes, new businesses, and their communities.

Unfortunately, it wasn't long before they did not have enough time or funds to finish God's house because they were using all their resources to build their own houses and businesses. God said through Haggai, "Why are you living in luxurious houses while my house lies in ruins?" (Haggai 1:4 NLT).

Their Savior God was disappointed and angry. How could His newly rescued children once again put Him at the bottom of their priorities? How could they be so ungrateful and foolish as to try to rebuild their lives on a self-centered foundation? God reprimanded the newly redeemed Israelites for not honoring Him and keeping their commitment to rebuilding His temple. But the real issue was not about buildings at all; it was about God's greatest desire. What He wanted most from Israel was not a beautiful building but a grateful heart.

Haggai closes his book by writing about Zerubbabel, the leader, who set God's people free and led them back to God's Promised Land. Haggai uses Zerubbabel's name as a symbol of the coming Messiah, Jesus, who will set all people free. Through Haggai God declares, "Tell Zerubbabel governor of Judah that I am going to shake the heavens and the earth . . . 'I will take you, my servant Zerubbabel son of Shealtiel,' declares the LORD, 'and I will make you like my signet ring, for I have chosen you,' declares the LORD Almighty" (Haggai 2:21–23 NIV).

An Inspirational Theme of Haggai

What's at the Top of Your To-Do List?

Do you make to-do lists? I do. We make them so we don't forget things that are important to us. What's on your to-do list today? We all have so many things to do that it's easy to leave off important things that are not emergencies. For example, are those things you plan to do to help keep you close to God somewhere on your list for today?

Remember, the quality of your life and your relationship with your Lord will not only be determined by how you prioritize the things on your to-do list, but by what you put on that list.

Charles Monroe Sheldon's *In His Steps*, one of the bestselling books of all times, tells the story of a homeless man who comes to a church for help. The pastor and parishioners are good people but are too busy with other priorities. They ignore the man, and shockingly, he dies. Under conviction, the pastor challenges the church to commit the next full year to making one new practice their priority. Before making any decision, they are to ask this question: "What would Jesus do?" The results are surprising and far reaching.

In the book of Haggai, the prophet also challenged his people to reevaluate their misplaced priorities. God had recently rescued them from seventy years of slavery. He has brought them back home and told them to begin rebuilding His house of worship, but they were too busy building their own houses. He wanted them to put rebuilding His house in first place on their to-do list. That would be a symbol of making their relationship with Him their number one priority.

Rick Warren, author of *The Purpose Driven Life*, put it this way: "You're never going to become a friend of God in your spare time. You have to make knowing God your number one priority in life."

Would you consider taking a second look at your to-do list? Maybe even rewriting it? If so, first ask, "What would Jesus do?" You may want to add some of Jesus's daily practices that helped Him daily stay close to His Father:

- He *listened* for His Father's voice.
- He *thanked* His Father constantly.
- He *touched* hurting people everywhere He went.

- He *simplified* His life, making time for His Father.

I don't imagine Jesus had a physical to-do list, but if He had, these reminders may have been at the top.

Related Scriptures from Haggai

Why are you living in luxurious houses while my house lies in ruins?

(Haggai 1:4 NLT)

My Spirit remains among you, just as I promised when you came out of Egypt. So, do not be afraid.

(Haggai 2:5 NLT)

Other Related Scriptures

Seek the Kingdom of God above all else, and live righteously, and he will give you everything you need.

(Matthew 6:33 NLT)

Where your treasure is, there your heart will be also.

(Luke 12:34 NLT)

What Is God Saying to You?

When you make a to-do list, what are the kinds of things you put at the top? What are a few things your Lord might want you to put at the top?

What factors influence you most in putting certain tasks closer to the top of your to-do list?

Dear Father, the better I get to know You, the more I see the value of putting You as my priority. Amen.

Get to Know God through Zechariah

A Brief Overview

ZECHARIAH MEANS "THE LORD REMEMBERS." Observe what God had Zechariah write in this book so people of all ages would remember what God did in the lives of Zechariah and His people. As the prophet leader of the first group of liberated Israelites from exile in Babylon, Zechariah had good reason to shout with his people, "The Lord remembers." Their merciful and powerful God had kept His promise. He rescued them and brought them home.

Born to enslaved parents in exile, Zechariah had never experienced life as a free man. He grew up as a contemporary of the prophets Ezra, Nehemiah, and Malachi. Like the others, Zechariah told his newly freed Israelite family that the Lord remembered their unrepentant sins that brought judgment and that the Lord remembered the promise He made to Abraham and his descendants. So the Lord forgave them and gave them another chance.

Although the weary and broken slaves returned to an unrecognizable mass of ruins, what was once their majestic Jerusalem, Zechariah had good news for them. He reminded them of a series of visions he'd received from the Lord. The visions pictured a prosperous Jerusalem, a restored temple, and a people living in freedom and harmony with each other and God.

Second to Isaiah, Zechariah has more references than any other Old Testament book to Jesus's first and second comings to earth. Many New Testament passages point to fulfilled prophesies in Zechariah such as Jesus being:

- the Branch (see Zechariah 3:8, 6:12; Matthew 27:29)
- the lowly king riding on a donkey (see Zechariah. 9:9–10, Mathew 21:4–5)
- the Savior betrayed for thirty pieces of silver (see Zechariah 11:12–13; Matthew 27:6–10)
- the crucified Savior with pierced hands (see Zechariah 12:10; John 19:37)
- the Shepherd (see Zechariah 13:7–9; Matthew 26:31)
- the returning king in His second coming (see Zechariah 14:4–9; Matthew 16:27–28)

An Inspirational Theme of Zechariah

Follow the Facts

While I attended Florida State University, I enjoyed spelunking. It is classified as an extreme sport because you risk your life climbing, crawling, and squeezing through small passageways under the earth's surface. With all that twisting and turning in the unmapped dark, it's easy to get disoriented and even lost. So experienced spelunkers spray-paint arrows on the rock walls of uncharted caverns. To be sure we were going in the right direction to get back to the opening of the cave, we simply followed the arrows, not our best hunch.

Jesus didn't expect people to follow Him because He was persuasive or charismatic. He gave them solid evidence to let them know He was worthy of being followed. Before Peter left being a fisherman to follow Jesus, Jesus first performed a fisherman's miracle. On a day when fish were not biting, Jesus helped Peter catch so many that they broke Peter's nets.

God did the same throughout the Old Testament. He never expected people to risk their lives following His call or orders without first giving hard evidence proving He was worthy of obedience. For example, before Moses left his safe, desert hideaway to take on Egypt, God miraculously spoke to him from a burning bush.

In Zechariah, God called His people to follow His leadership and stop following the popular practices of their culture. And, as always, God expected them to follow Him not just because He said to but because of what He had already done. The evidence, the factual acts of His miracles, gave them and their family members an evidence-based faith.

That's still our God's way of leading you and me in everything we do. As emphasized in Josh McDowell's book *Evidence That Demands a Verdict*, God is and always has been the God who gives us real evidence that must be taken seriously. He is the God who acts. He is more than a good idea or the best philosophy going around. He is a real, personal being, who speaks to people, heals the sick, parts seas, calms storms, raises people from the dead, and comes to earth to give Himself for us.

How do we know all that? Because He gave us a good mind to examine the evidence, analyze the facts, and come to the most responsible conclusion. He does not want us to follow Him or His way of life because someone talks us into it or because we think His teachings are better than other teachings.

The God of the Bible, the God of our risen Lord Jesus, wants us to follow the facts and then step out wholeheartedly on faith.

As you go through your day with all of its twists and turns, sometimes with dark and disorienting circumstance to handle, often with conflicting voices pulling at you, and with so much at stake, try this—follow the arrows in God's Word. He put them there to show you the true way home.

Related Scriptures from Zechariah

Everything I said through my servants the prophets happened to your ancestors, just as I said.

(Zechariah 1:6 NLT)

Rejoice, O people of Zion! / in triumph, O people of Jerusalem! / Look, your king is coming to you. / He is righteous and victorious, / yet he is humble, riding on a donkey— / riding on a donkey's colt.

(Zechariah 9:9 NLT)

Other Related Scriptures

If I do his [God's] work, believe in the evidence of the miraculous works I [Jesus] have done, even if you don't believe me. Then you will know and understand that the Father is in me, and I am in the Father.

(John 10:38 NLT)

When [Barnabas] arrived and saw this evidence of God's blessing, he was filled with joy, and he encouraged the believers to stay true to the Lord.

(Acts 11:23 NLT)

What Is God Saying to You?

What are some ways in the Bible that you can see God has demonstrated He does what He says?

What evidence do you have that God is involved in your life?

Dear Father, the better I get to know You, the more I see You do what You say. Amen.

Get to Know God through Malachi

A Brief Overview

MALACHI'S NAME MEANS "messenger of God." His book is the last in the Old Testament. Genesis was the first and pictures God's beginnings where all is beautiful and good, but Malachi ends the Old Testament with a radically different picture. God's beautiful and good creation has changed dramatically. It is now filled with chaos, disfunction, and disharmony. People are not holding hands and walking through a perfect garden like Adam and Eve were. They are struggling with runaway evil, waywardness, wars, and separation from God. It is an ugly picture of people overcome by anger and fear, far from God's desired design. It is a pitiful place where people are slaves and slave owners, far from God's creation where people were free and helping each other.

God created humans in His image. He gave humans a free will—the ability and right to make choices in harmony with or in rebellion against Him. Malachi's warnings are the same basic messages God delivered through His other prophets: His people must choose to repent of their sins and return to Him, bringing honor to His name, or face certain punishment.

Malachi's message for his day focused on the familiar problems occurring around 500 BC when Israel was disheartened about the future of their nation. God's children were doubting they would ever see God's promised restoration. They were discouraged and complaining to God that He was not keeping

His promises to them and their forefathers. In their minds, it was all God's fault.

The main content of the book is a series of interchanges between our gracious Lord and His angry people. He answers their accusations with examples of how their complaints are false and misleading. He reminds them that they have been dishonoring Him by bringing Him worthless gifts, by ignoring the holy covenant they made with Him, and by being selfishly unfaithful to their spouses and families.

In short, their dishonorable decisions to do things their own way and not God's way damaged their relationships with one another and with God. They needed God. They needed a Savior.

An Inspirational Theme of Malachi

Big Little Decisions

Will the many, ordinary, little, seemingly unimportant decisions you make today turn out to be that unimportant after all? Here's a God-truth you can bank on: one of those little decisions you'll make today could, in God's plans for you, become a life-transforming decision.

That's exactly what happened to Doris Taylor. She was seven when a spinal injury left her unable to sit up, turn her head, or feed herself. For twenty years, she had to use a wheelchair and spend many of her days in hospitals and rehab facilities. Then one day, during her normal rebab activities, Doris learned that some of her friends with disabilities didn't have enough to eat at home.

With Doris's severe physical limitations, no one would have blamed Doris if she had decided to do nothing. Instead, on that ordinary day, she listened to God and made a seemingly insignificant decision. She decided to recruit some friends, cook a hot meal, and deliver it to a few homebound friends.

Doris had no idea God had a much bigger plan in mind. She had no idea that when she decided to follow God's call, Meals on Wheels would be born. She had no idea that years later her little, God-honoring decision would turn into a ministry that helps millions of people every year in five thousand Meals on Wheels chapters in America alone and thousands more around the world.

The prophet Malachi tries to drive this same truth home to the people of Israel. He warns them of the serious, long-term, and horrible consequences that come to those who make their everyday decisions using the I'll-do-it-my-way method instead of the I'll-do-it-God's-way approach. C. S. Lewis said in *Mere Christianity*, "Good and evil increase at compound interest. That's why the little decisions we make every day are of infinite importance."

Never forget. You were made in God's image. He gave you the right to make your own decisions, good or bad, helpful or harmful. He has wonderful, long range plans for your relationships, work, health, and so much more. He wants to lead you in making God-honoring decisions that will open doors to His plans for you. But He will not force you to make the best decisions.

God's Word, His family, and His Spirit are available to guide you. How will you make your seemingly insignificant decisions today? Plan now to see them as big little decisions that will bring honor to His name as part of His beautiful plans for you.

Related Scriptures from Malachi

Listen to me and make up your minds to honor my name.

(Malachi 2:2 NLT)

They passed on to the people the truth of the instructions they received from me. They did not lie or cheat; they walked with me, living good and righteous lives, and they turned many from lives of sin.

(Malachi 2:6 NLT)

Other Related Scriptures

In all your ways submit to him, and he will make your paths straight.

(Proverbs 3:6 NIV)

There is a way that appears to be right, but in the end, it leads to death.

(Proverbs 14:12 NIV)

What Is God Saying to You?

What are some decisions you've made that seemed insignificant at the time but turned out to be important to your life?

Why are there no little decisions when it comes to doing God's will?

Dear Father, the better I get to know You, the more I see that You can make important events out of my seemingly insignificant decisions and acts. Amen.

THE FOUR GOSPELS

Accounts of the Life and Words of Jesus

AN EXCELLENT WAY to get to know God better is to examine the life of His Son, Jesus, to hear the stories Jesus tells and the stories others tell about Him in the Gospels.

The most accurate, untainted way for you to observe your unseen God is to observe Jesus, His very real flesh-and-blood Son. The clearest way for you to hear God is to listen to Jesus and listen to what Jesus's faithful friends observed as they followed Him about. The truest way for you to understand God's way of thinking is to examine Jesus's decisions and insights. And the deepest way for you to know the way God feels and what He values is to watch Jesus relate to His Father's children.

Jesus said, "If you really know me, you will know my Father as well" (John 14:7 NIV). The Greek word for *gospel* literally means "Good News." These four initial books of the New Testament are known as the Gospels because they are God's message of good news to you and all of His children. Our Father chose four of Jesus's closest friends to speak for Him as He tells you about the birth, life, ministry, death, resurrection, and return of our Lord. Through the personalities of Matthew, Mark, Luke, and John, your God gives you glimpses of His expanded way of helping you and all His children get back to Him and stay close to Him.

Each gospel writer shares many of the same stories and narratives. But do not miss some of the common threads in each of them that will help you get to know God better. Here are eight such common threads:

- God's reminder that Jesus is the God-Man, the incarnation of God in human form
- God's revelation of the fulfillment of His plan for His children
- God's humility and example seen in Jesus's public baptism
- God's ability to do anything, as seen in Jesus's miracles and teachings
- God's demonstration of His love through Jesus's betrayal, trial, suffering, and death
- God's power over sin and death revealed in Jesus's resurrection
- God's hope, encouragement, and mission for Jesus's followers
- God's promise of His heaven for all Jesus's followers

Get to Know God through Matthew

A Brief Overview

MATTHEW IS THE MOST JEWISH-ORIENTED BOOK in the New Testament. A Jew himself, Matthew cited fifty-seven Old Testament passages revealing that Jesus was the long-awaited Messiah, the Son of God, the incarnation of God.

Matthew comes first in the New Testament because when the order of books to be included in the New Testament was being decided, the committee believed Matthew had written his gospel before Mark, Luke, and John. Most scholars today readily believe that Mark was written first and Matthew most likely second. Several factors indicate that Matthew wrote his gospel around AD 60 to 65 but certainly before AD 70 since he does not mention the destruction of Jerusalem, which was a significant event in the lives of all Jews.

Matthew's main purpose in writing his gospel was to help his readers be confident that Jesus was Immanuel, God-in-flesh, the Messiah, the savior, a humble servant, a friend of sinners, and Israel's King of a new kind of kingdom. He also focused on the main reason God Himself came to earth and took on flesh and chose the name Jesus, meaning "one who sets free." God's purpose was to set all people free through the sacrifice of His son on the cross and His triumphant resurrection.

As a tax collector for the Romans, Matthew was hated by his fellow Jews for the heavy-handed burden he put on them. But after Matthew's conversion, his life was transformed, and he became one of Jesus's twelve chosen apostles. As one of Jesus's inner circle, Matthew wrote as an eyewitness to the work, miracles, suffering, and resurrection of our Lord.

He also had another reason for writing his gospel. He wanted to prepare the followers of Jesus for the escalating international Roman persecution of Christians as the Romans attempted to eliminate Christians from the Empire. After waiting for hundreds of years for God's promised messiah, God's people wondered if He had abandoned them or given up on them. Matthew reminded them that God had not forgotten them and would never give up on them. Jesus was God's fulfillment of all of His promises.

Matthews helps us see that Jesus was God in human form, revealing that He is all-knowing, able to help us make the best choices and overcome seemingly impossible circumstances. He is all-loving, even willing to die for us. He is all-powerful, performing more and greater miracles than anyone in history. And He is all-present, with us all the time and everywhere.

An Inspirational Theme of Matthew

God's Timing or Your Timing?

When my wife, Phyllis, and I take our morning walk each day, we usually see cardinals, blue birds, vermillion flycatchers, and all sorts of other feathered friends enjoying the sunrise and their spectacular view of the Texas Hill Country. It must be wonderful to be able to fly. Wouldn't it be fabulous to be able to fly as free as a bird?

We humans have been wishing and trying to soar like birds for thousands of years. King David wanted to fly. Twenty-seven hundred years ago, he was so tired of his personal problems he wrote, "Oh, that I had wings like a dove; then I would fly away and rest!" (Psalm 55:6 NLT). Even the ancient Greeks made up characters like Icarus and his father, Daedalus, who attempted to fly away from their difficulties by making themselves wings from bird feathers, strings, and wax. (By the way, it didn't work.) And Leonardo da Vinci, the brilliant artist and mathematician, drew plans for a mechanical-winged machine known as an ornithopter. (His ingenious gadget didn't work either.)

We still long to fly like birds, not inside an aluminum bus with wings propelled by jet engines. No, what we want is to leap into the sky and glide effortlessly through the air like one of our sweet birds. That profound, inner, human longing to take to the air may be the source of the popular idiom "as free as a bird."

Deep within all of us lies our basic desire to be free, to be able to do and be all God intended. The reason our hunger for personal and spiritual freedom is so intense is because God created us that way. And He has made it possible for us to be free through Jesus.

Matthew's account of Jesus life and words helps us see that Jesus was God in human form come to set us free. The Bible word *salvation* literally means to be "set free." It's a picture word. Imagine a bird with its wings tied to its body. The bird is alive, but it can't fly. It can't do or be what it was designed to do and be. It needs a savior, someone who will cut it loose.

We are that bird. It's easy to slowly, subtly, and subconsciously get all wrapped up and tangled up in unhealthy habits. Then one day we wake up and realize our wings are tied down. We want to be free to reach our dreams and God's plans for our lives, but we tried to do it on our own and failed. And we realize we need help.

Maybe this is the time in your life when you are ready to make a change. You're ready to get cut loose from something that has tied you up or held you down for years. The Bible says, "The truth will set you free" (see John 8:32). And Jesus said, "I am the truth" (see John 14:6). Truth is simply that which you can count on. If you're ready to be set free from whatever is holding you back, reach out to Jesus. With His forgiveness, guidance, and indwelling power, you *can* fly to new heights and be free as a bird.

Related Scriptures from Matthew

She will have a son, and you are to name him Jesus, for he will save his people from their sins.

(Matthew 1:21 NLT)

Simon Peter answered, "You are the Messiah, the Son of the living God."

(Matthew 16:16 NLT)

Other Related Scriptures

But now you are free from the power of sin and have become slaves of God. Now you do those things that lead to holiness and result in eternal life.

(Romans 6:22 NLT)

So, Christ has truly set us free. Now make sure that you stay free, and don't get tied up again in slavery to the law.

(Galatians 5:1 NLT)

What Is God Saying to You?

Since God loves you enough to send Jesus to die for you so that you can be free from your sins and free to be all He intended, what does that tell you about the way He thinks?

List some things in your life that you wish you could be free from.

Dear Father, the better I get to know You, the more I see that You are the only source of freedom. Help me to be free of anything that entangles me and keeps me from being all that You want me to be and do. Thank You. Amen.

Get to Know God through Mark

A Brief Overview

THE GOSPEL OF MARK is the second book in the New Testament, and it is the most concise. It was probably written from Rome prior to AD 60. Mark's full name was John Mark. He was Barnabas's nephew and Simon Peter's spiritual son (see Colossians 4:10), and his mother was a wealthy and highly respected Christian in the Jerusalem church. He was a close friend of the other three gospel writers and the apostle Paul. He traveled with Paul on Paul's first missionary journey.

In AD 64 Rome burned and the crazed emperor Nero blamed Christians. This began the empire-wide Christian persecution. One of Mark's purposes in writing his account of Jesus's life and teachings was to prepare Christians for the persecution.

As you read Mark, you'll notice what many Bible students have recognized over the centuries. There is no account of Jesus's genealogy or birth in this gospel. That is because Mark is written primarily not for Jews but for Gentiles—non-Jews. Mark focuses on what Jesus did and who he was, not on his lineage or background. Another thing that's clear is that the other three gospel writers used much of Mark's book when they wrote their books. For example, Matthew repeated 601 of the 678 verses in Mark.

Mark's gospel is action packed. It uses the word *immediately* forty-two times. It's a fast-pace, get-it-done book that has great appeal to contemporary Christians. Forty percent of the book gives the details of the final week of Jesus life.

Mark emphasizes Jesus's role as the Servant King who is unlike any king in history. Mark describes King Jesus by quoting Jesus's description of himself: "The Son of Man came not to be served but to serve others and to give his life as a ransom for many" (Mark 10:45 NLT).

An Inspirational Theme of Mark

Fifty-Seven-Cent Faith

Everyone has faith. But do you have enough faith? Enough to please God, to get you into heaven, to see your prayers answered? If you're like many, you may wonder just how much faith you need? Is your not having enough faith the reason things don't go right for you?

Jesus gave us a clear answer that the size of your faith is not what counts. He said it this way: "I tell you the truth, if you had faith even as small as a mustard seed, you could say to this mountain, 'Move from here to there,' and it would move. Nothing would be impossible" (Matthew 17:20 NLT).

It's not the size of your faith but the object of your faith that makes all the difference. That means even if you have just a little, weak, child-like faith, but it depends on God, He says that's enough. With that tiny amount, God is willing and able do great things in your life.

Mark's account of Jesus's life and words focuses on Him as the long-awaited Messiah and the Savior for all who put their small, immature, childlike faith in Him. Jesus said, "I tell you the truth, anyone who doesn't receive the Kingdom of God like a child will never enter it" (Mark 10:15 NLT). Jesus constantly rejected the commonly held belief in His day—and in our day too—that only those who have a knowledgeable, grown-up faith can make it with God.

Jesus gave us a real-life example of His way of looking at faith. It is the story of the Widow's Mite. When He saw a poor widow make a small donation of only two small coins compared to the large donations of some rich people, "Jesus called his disciples to him and said, 'I tell you the truth, this poor widow has given more than all the others making contributions'" (Mark 12:43 NLT).

That poor widow's story reminds me of another unforgettable true story of the faith of a little girl from Philadelphia. Pastor Russell H. Conwell's sermon in the church's Temple Review Magazine on December 19, 1912, tells us that one Sunday morning, Hattie May Wiatt tried to go to church for the first time but was turned away because it was too crowded. When young pastor Conwell noticed she was crying, he comforted her and found her a corner in the children's Sunday school class where she could stand. Hattie gave him a big hug and smile, which left a lasting memory.

Shortly after, Hattie got sick and died, and Pastor Conwell preached at her funeral. Before the service, Hattie's mother gave him Hattie's small, crumpled purse that contained fifty-seven cents. Her mother told the pastor Hattie had been saving her pennies for some time. She also left a note in her purse, "This is to help build the little church bigger so more children can go to Sunday school."

Later, Pastor Conwell told that story to his congregation. The newspaper picked up the story. Before long, people from far and wide were so inspired that large amounts of money poured in. Soon the church formed Wiatt's Mite Society, whose members dedicated themselves to making Hattie's fifty-seven pennies multiply. Today, if you visit the campus of the Temple Baptist Church in Philadelphia, you'll see a mega church with a sanctuary that seats thirty-three hundred and Temple University where hundreds of students are trained every year. You'll admire the Good Samaritan Hospital and a Sunday school building housing hundreds of children so that no child in the area will ever be left outside.

In a special room in that Sunday school building, you can view a picture of Hattie, the little girl who so sacrificially and faithfully saved fifty-seven cents. Pastor Conwell now says that Hattie had a faith only the size of a mustard seed, but it was put in God's hands and moved mountains.

So, how much faith do you need to please God, to see miracles in your life? In God's hands, fifty-seven pennies worth is plenty.

Related Scriptures from Mark

And Jesus said to him, "Go, for your faith has healed you." Instantly the man could see, and he followed Jesus down the road.

(Mark 10:52 NLT

Anything is possible if you have faith.

(Mark 9:23 TLB)

Other Related Scriptures

Now faith is confidence in what we hope for and assurance about what we do not see . . . By faith we understand that the universe was formed at God's command, so that what is seen was not made out of what was visible.

(Hebrews 11:1, 3 NIV)

We are made right with God by placing our faith in Jesus Christ. And this is true for everyone who believes, no matter who we are.

(Romans 3:22 NLT)

What Is God Saying to You?

What does God's faith requirement say about His nature and character?

What are some faith decisions you've made that seemed insignificant at the time but turned out to be important to your life?

Dear Father, the better I get to know You, the more I see that You are a big God who can do big things with my little faith. Thank You. Amen.

Get to Know God through Luke

A Brief Overview

UNLIKE THE OTHER GOSPEL WRITERS, Luke's introduction to his gospel indicates that he composed his book providing a careful rendering of the events of Christ's life in chronological order. It was written around AD 80 during the reign of the Roman emperor Domitian. Those were difficult times for persecuted Christians.

As a physician, Luke would have been trained as a careful observer, a quality that was invaluable in his writing about Jesus's ministry and words. He is also the author of Acts, and Acts 21:17 reports that he journeyed with the apostle Paul on his final visit to Jerusalem sometime in AD 57 to 58. When the Jewish leaders had Paul arrested and imprisoned in Caesarea, Luke used that time to gather information for writing his gospel. His main source was firsthand witnesses such as people who personally witnessed the life, teaching, ministry, death, and resurrection of our Lord.

Luke had a compassionate heart for people who were sick, poor, or marginalized. He primarily directed his gospel toward Greeks, who represented people searching for truth. Like Matthew and Mark, Luke recorded the true story of the woman who poured perfume on Jesus's feet. But only Luke tells us that she was an immoral woman (see Luke 7:37). And Luke alone gives us the conversation between the thieves who were crucified alongside Jesus and noted that the one who defended

Jesus received the promise, "Today you will be with me in Paradise" (see Luke 23:33–43). No other gospel writer gives us the stories of the Prodigal Son, the Good Samaritan, the Lost Sheep, or the conversion of Zacchaeus.

Matthew primarily views Jesus as King. Mark emphasizes Him as our Suffering Servant. But Luke focuses on Jesus as the Son of Man. This phrase, "Son of Man," was Jesus's favorite way to refer to Himself, pointing out He was one of them. He was tempted and struggled in every way they did while God in flesh.

Luke's gospel will help you see the heart of God. It reveals God's sincere and sacrificial care for people regardless of their position in society. It will give you a clearer understanding of what it means to truly know God and not just know about Him. It will inspire you to follow the example of our Lord.

An Inspirational Theme of Luke

Ever Been Burned?

Do you know someone who finds something wrong about everyone and speaks critically about them? Robert acted that way, and nobody wanted to be around him. I met Robert when he was a patient in the hospital. All the staff tried their best to avoid going to his room. Know why? It was simple. He was hateful and abusive and made everyone around him miserable, cursing his doctors and shouting profanity at his nurses. He complained about the food, criticized the hospital, grumbled about the poor service, whined about the hard bed, and griped about the room temperature.

When they had had all they could take, the head nurse called on the new intern hospital chaplain assigned to that floor to see what he could do. I was that chaplain. When I entered Robert's room and told him I was the chaplain, he shouted, "Get the *bleep-bleep* out of here. I don't want to hear about your God. Where was he when I was almost burned alive? I don't want to talk about him now." Robert had been in an accident and had severe burns over most of his body. He was in excruciating pain and was spreading his pain onto everyone around him.

We sometimes forget that hurting people often hurt others and that their pain may not be from fires, diseases, or broken bones. They could have been seriously hurt from critical words or someone else's actions, and the venom they spew is an outward expression of what is going on inside them. They have not learned to deal with their own pain, anger, weaknesses, and failures.

Sometimes we think people are critical and mean spirited because they're not smart or were born mean or had it tough growing up. But some of the most hateful, cynical, and hurtful people can be highly gifted and had every positive advantage growing up. And some of the gentlest, most gracious people have been knocked around bitterly by life's circumstances. It becomes a matter of the heart, of choosing how we respond.

A critical heart will always poison every part of your life and cause others to avoid you or strike back. But a gracious and forgiving heart will enrich every part of your life and positively influence your relationship with others. Without your giving grace, forgiveness, acceptance and patience, your relationships have no chance of thriving as healthy, fulfilling relationships—

the kind God wants for you. The gospel of Luke reveals that same truth in story after story—the Prodigal Son, the Good Samaritan, the Lost Sheep, the Hated Tax Collector, the Wayward Woman, and many more.

This theme of grace and redemption is the golden thread throughout the Bible and is the core message of your gracious God. John, Luke's fellow disciple, tells us the most important truth about God's nature and purpose in giving us Jesus: "God sent his Son into the world not to judge the world, but to save the world through him" (John 3:17 NLT).

No matter what you've done in your past, know this: your heavenly Father is not critical of you. He's not avoiding you. He hasn't turned His back on you. He is reaching out to you, even if you've turned your back on Him or fallen into a moral ditch or made bad choices. Your God has not given up on you.

Accept His grace today and join Him in giving grace and forgiveness to everyone you know. Remember, more than likely they, too, have experienced the cruel and painful fires of life.

Related Scriptures from Luke

Love your enemies! Do good to them. Lend to them without expecting to be repaid. Then your reward from heaven will be very great, and you will truly be acting as children of the Most High, for he is kind to those who are unthankful and wicked.

(Luke 6:35 NLT)

Do not judge others, and you will not be judged. Do not condemn others, or it will all come back against you. Forgive others, and you will be forgiven.

(Luke 6:37 NLT)

Other Related Scriptures

If you forgive those who sin against you, your heavenly Father will forgive you.

(Matthew 6:14 NLT)

You have heard the law that says, 'Love your neighbor' and hate your enemy. But I say, love your enemies! Pray for those who persecute you!

(Matthew 5:43–44 NLT)

What Is God Saying to You?

What do the stories in Luke tell us about God's nature?

What are some things you can do to become more merciful and forgiving, rather than returning criticism to those who criticize you?

Dear Father, the better I get to know You, the more I see how merciful and accepting You are. Help me to be grace giving like You. Amen.

Get to Know God through John

A Brief Overview

FOR MANY CHRISTIANS, the gospel of John is the most loved book in the Bible. It contains the most beloved verse in the Bible: "For God so loved the world that He gave His only begotten son" (John 3:16 KJV). Like no other, the gospel reveals the depth of God's love, His unparalleled sacrifice, His unimaginable power, and His remarkable compassion. Although John is not named as the author of this famous gospel, his authorship was without question among first-century Christians. He was clearly the disciple who rested his head on Jesus's shoulder, the one described as the disciple "whom Jesus loved" (see John 13:23).

As one of the three inner-circle friends of Jesus (along with Peter and James), John wrote five books of the Bible—the gospel of John; the three letters of 1, 2, and 3 John; and also the Revelation. He was the highly respected elder of the church in Ephesus, which was an outstanding church in the first century throughout that part of Europe.

As I noted before, the other three gospels picture our Lord as the Messiah King (Matthew), the Suffering Servant (Mark), and the Son of Man (Luke), but John portrays Jesus as the Son of God—God in flesh. He tells us that his gospel is for those who "believe that Jesus is the Christ, the Son of God" so they may have eternal life (see John 20:31).

The gospel of John focuses on Jesus as being the God-Man, God in flesh, the Word who existed from the beginning. The book starts by introducing the reader to Jesus as the Word: "In the beginning was the Word, and the Word was with God, and the Word was God" (John 1:1 NIV). John does not begin with the birth of Jesus but announces in the first verse of the book that Jesus lived before the world was created. John uses the second half of his book to tell us about the final week in Jesus's suffering, death, and resurrection. This emphasis on the deity of Jesus is the most unique element in John's gospel.

John uses various literary approaches to help you better understand who Jesus is. For example, he gives you Jesus's seven "I am" statements.

- I am the bread of life (see John 6:35)
- I am the Light of the world (see John 8:12)
- Before Abraham was even born, I AM (see John 8:58)
- I am the good shepherd (see John 10:11)
- I am the resurrection and the life (see John 11:25)
- I am the way, and the truth, and the life (see John 14:6)
- I am the true vine (see John 15:1)

John makes it clear what his practical purpose is in writing his good news about Jesus: "These are written that you may believe that Jesus is the Messiah, the Son of God, and that by believing you may have life his name" (John 20:31 NIV). John does not want anyone to miss the critical truth that only our supernatural God can give us supernatural eternal life.

An Inspirational Theme of John

Know Is Not Knowing

Knowing is not knowing. I know it sounds a bit crazy, but it's true. I agree with Richard Rohr, the globally recognized Christian writer who teaches that there are more meaningful ways of knowing and understanding than just the intellectual approach. Let me explain.

Getting to know someone deeply is different than just knowing about them. Saying "I know" can mean different things at different times. For example, if you say, "I know two plus two equals four," you mean I understand it, I get it, and it makes sense to me. But, if you say, "I know my husband loves me, and I know I love him," you mean something different, something more than an intellectual understanding. Your knowing is experiential and deeper and can defy explanation.

Knowing someone through love is something experienced on a higher plane and deeper level and is different than knowing facts and figures. It means you have a close, two-way relationship that is more meaningful. That's why the apostle John says many will never come to know God—because they keep trying to know God on that important but lower level. They will not risk stepping out in faith, having to depend on Him without full understanding. John says of Jesus, "The world cannot accept him, because it neither sees him nor knows him" (John 14:17 NIV).

Getting to know God is much like falling in love. That's what happened to me as I got to know my wife, Phyllis. The more we honestly and openly gave ourselves to each other, the more we experienced a deep, unexplainable love, a knowing that went beyond information.

Everyone is born with a God-hunger. Billy Graham, the evangelist, called it a God-void. It is like a special piece of the puzzle of our lives and purpose is missing, and nothing will fit that space except God's Spirit. Nothing will satisfy that hunger but God Himself. You can try all the substitutes, but none will work.

John tells us the story of Nicodemus who was searching for that missing piece. Nicodemus was a Jewish leader, an extremely moral man, a Bible scholar, and a member of the Supreme Court of the Jewish nation (the Sanhedrin in Jerusalem). Nicodemus had sought all his life to obey God's rules. He tried to fill his God-void by educating himself and doing everything he knew to do and thought was right, but nothing worked. The void was still there. He was left desperately wanting to know God and to know what would happen to him when he died.

So, in the middle of the night, while no one was watching, Nicodemus sought out Jesus. Without hesitation, Jesus explained that knowing God and knowing you're going to heaven will never happen because of your education, your good works, or because you figure it out. Jesus told Nicodemus, and He tells you, that truly knowing God is like being born again. It's God's gift. You can't earn it or make it happen. It's something that happens *to* you and *for* you when you accept His gift of love and open your mind and heart to let God's Spirit inside. Jesus closed his talk with Nicodemus by telling him that God so loved him that He gave his only Son for Nicodemus so he could have everlasting life (see John 3:1–16).

In the same way, God is reaching out to you. He already knows who you are and everything about you. But He wants to know you in a deeper, two-way loving relationship. Will you open up to Him, reach out to Him, pray to receive Him? That's when you will know what you cannot know.

Related Scriptures from John

Now we believe, not just because of what you told us, but because we have heard him ourselves. Now we know that he is indeed the Savior of the world.

(John 4:42 NLT)

Since you don't know who I [Jesus] am, you don't know who my Father is. If you knew me, you would also know my Father.

(John 8:19 NLT)

Other Related Scriptures

I have written to you who are God's children because you know the Father. I have written to you who are mature in the faith because you know Christ, who existed from the beginning.

(1 John 2:14 NLT)

When the master of the house has locked the door, it will be too late. You will stand outside knocking and pleading, "Lord, open the door for us!" But he will reply, "I don't know you or where you come from."

(Luke 13:25 NLT)

What Is God Saying to You?

What does the writing of John reveal about the eternal nature of God?

What are some synonyms you would use for the word *know* in trying to describe your relationship to Jesus?

Dear Father, the better I get to know You, the more I see You as my personal, caring Father who knows me deeply. Lord, thank You for allowing me to know You and for coming to fill that void in my life. Amen.

THE LETTERS

Accounts of God's Activities among Early Christians

DURING THE TIME when the New Testament was being written, letter writing was a common form of corresponding with organizations and individuals. An *epistle,* the Greek word for "letter," was often used for official pronouncements and for personal communications. As you study the New Testament letters, you need to keep both of these facts in mind. The letters of the apostles were sometimes addressed to specific needs among specific churches, groups, or individuals, but they were also designed to be an official document for a much larger audience.

You will notice that the New Testament letters generally begin with a mention of the author and the recipients: Who is writing to whom? Next come words of appreciation, blessing, and salutation such as "Grace and peace to you in the name of our Lord Jesus." Following those common elements comes the purpose of the letter. Usually, the letters end with a personal greeting, some words of thanks, and a formal benediction.

The final letters chosen to be included in our New Testament were written by only a few apostles, believers who had actually been with Jesus throughout His ministry. Although the authorship of a few of Paul's letters is not mentioned in the letter, it is commonly accepted that Paul wrote fourteen of the missives. Other authors include Peter, John, and two brothers of Jesus, namely James and Jude.

The dating of the New Testament letters is not exact, but the dates given in the overview of each letter are close enough to give you a sense of what was happening at that time. More than likely James was written around AD 50, making it the first letter. The three letters by John were probably written between AD 90 and 95, making them the last letters.

As your read the letters, study the overviews, consider the messages in the devotionals, reflect on the related scriptures and questions, keep in the mind that these letters are packed full of God's descriptions of what He was doing in the lives of the first-century Christians. They contain God's heart and mind. They provide comfort, instruction, testimony, assurance, security, support, warnings, encouragement, and, most of all, insights into the heart of God and the way He moves in our lives. The challenges the early Christians faced are not all the same as what you face today, but the questions and problems they had then have the same solutions, answers, and practical helps God has for you.

Look at these holy letters as God's love letters to you. See them as God's way of helping you get to know Him better through examining how He got involved in the lives and churches of the first century and how the letters helped them develop a more intimate relationship with Him.

Get to Know God through Acts

A Brief Overview

THE WORD *ACTS*, the title of the fifth book in the New Testament, comes from the Greek word *praxis* which means "activities." The book of Acts is a record of the true accounts of God's activities between Jesus's last meeting with His disciples and Paul's imprisonment in Rome.

Written by Luke, Acts provides Christians with memorable events of the Spirit of God living in and working through His people in times of great persecution and great joy. Acts is not an exhaustive account of the acts of God during the birth of the church and His global rebirth of God's plan for His people. But in Acts we get to know more about God through some of the most exciting and memorable stories in Christian history.

In Luke's account, you can visualize God's presence in remarkable events such as:

- the supernatural ascension of Jesus (see Acts 1:9)
- God's replacement of Judas (see Acts 1:21–26)
- God's miraculous revelation at Pentecost (see Acts 2:1–12)
- God's miracle during Peter's and John's imprisonment (see Acts 4:13–22)
- God's witness through Stephen's death by stoning (see Acts 7:54–60)

- the conversion of the Ethiopian during Philip's providential desert-road meeting (see Acts 8:26–40)
- Jesus's dramatic appearance to Paul on the road to Damascus (see Acts 9:1–19)
- God's expanded mission through the missionary journeys of Paul and Peter

In short, Acts is God's high drama on the human stage. The book is the only one of its kind in the New Testament in that it records the history of the rapid growth of the Christian movement from Jerusalem into the rest of the Roman Empire. It is an amazing, unprecedented story. In just thirty years, a small band of ordinary men and women from the tiny nation of Israel wholeheartedly gave themselves to Jesus and his mission. By the power of the Holy Spirit and through their unwavering commitment, they carried the gospel of Jesus to the highest level of government in the world—the emperor of Rome.

Through this significant record, you will get to know your God better as you read how He worked in the lives of people like Peter and Paul. You will be moved by the way God used common working people like you to transform lives and their culture. It will become obvious to you that the faith the early Christians had in the death and resurrection of our Lord transformed their lives. It gave them a zeal to keep on spreading the good news no matter the hardships.

It is also clear that Luke wrote the book of Acts not only to record the activities of God working in the lives of His people but to encourage future Christians to make it a priority to carry on the work of our Lord and His sacrificial people.

An Inspirational Theme of Acts

When the Unremarkable Is Remarkable

There's something inside us, perhaps pride, that makes us recoil when someone tells us that we're unremarkable. Who wants to be unremarkable? We all want to be uniquely remarkable.

That happened to me recently when I received the results of my cancer surveillance reports. The radiologist listed all my organs and then described them as "unremarkable." At first, I was taken aback. Then I discovered "unremarkable" was a medical description indicating the radiologist did not see anything that was abnormal or unusual. As I listened carefully to my oncologist's report on the same tests, I have never been so grateful to be described as unremarkable.

I am weary of words that end in *-est*. All advertisers claim that their product is the largest or the greatest or the biggest in the world. Not everything worthy of attention has to be the best or the worst.

Like me, perhaps you're tired of our superlative-driven culture where we're told if you're not the most extreme, radical, or remarkable, or the expert at something, then you're nothing. You're a nobody, a zero. Columbia professor Tim Wu wrote a book entitled *The Curse of Bigness* and described our culture as one living under this curse.

We're not the first culture to be so judgmental and status oriented. Jesus lived in such a culture, where even He, the Son of God, was looked down upon. Luke tells us that the rulers and ecclesiastical hierarchy looked upon Him with contempt and with hatred (see Luke 23:11).

There is something that happens with any organized religion that stays around a long time. And this had happened with the Jewish leaders in Jesus's day. They overemphasized intellectual achievement, academic debate, and outward appearance. These emphases morphed into an arrogant, smug elitism and sense of superiority among religious leaders. They paraded before the "common" folk, puffed up with the pride of their knowledge, dressed themselves in lavish robes, and gave themselves to extravagant rituals, all the while losing their real heart for God.

In Acts 4:13 we're told that when those Jewish rulers and the leaders of the hierarchy looked at Jesus's choices for disciples, they demeaned them as *agrammatoi kai idiotai*, the Greek words meaning "not learned" and "ignorant." They made fun of Jesus's followers, referring to them as uneducated, stupid, unremarkable common folk. And, even worse, they called them *idiotai* as though they were incapable of understanding. You would recognize we get our English word *idiot* from the Greek.

But Mark reports, "And the common people heard Him gladly" (Mark 12:37 KJV). The learned elite had looked at Jesus as a threat to their status, power, and income, but the ordinary folk looked at Him as their Savior. Jesus rebuked the prideful leaders and turned to fishermen and a tax collector and other common, ordinary folk and made them His leaders and teachers.

Jesus sees us all as valuable persons with purposes. After all, He saw enough worth in us common people to become one of us, and He even died for us. And all those unremarkable men and women who accepted His invitation to follow Him and live life His way remarkably changed the world. And Jesus is still calling out the unremarkable to do the remarkable.

Related Scriptures from Acts

When they saw the boldness of Peter and John . . . they could see that they were ordinary men with no special training in the Scriptures. They also recognized them as men who had been with Jesus.

(Acts 4:13 NLT)

As they stoned him, Stephen prayed, "Lord Jesus, receive my spirit."

(Acts 7:59 NLT)

Other Related Scriptures

The Spirit of God, who raised Jesus from the dead, lives in you. And just as God raised Christ Jesus from the dead, he will give life to your mortal bodies by this same Spirit living within you.

(Romans 8:11 NLT)

Don't let anyone capture you with empty philosophies and high-sounding nonsense that come from human thinking and from the spiritual powers of this world, rather than from Christ.

(Colossians 2:8 NLT)

What Is God Saying to You?

What are some reason people do not pray and ask the Spirit of Jesus into their lives?

What are some things in Peter's and Paul's lives that remind you of your life?

Dear Father, the better I get to know You, the more I see Your activity in human history. Sometimes Your activity comes like a whisper as inner calm, and sometimes it comes like Your mighty acts recorded in Your Scripture. Thank You for being involved in my life. Amen.

Getting to Know God through Romans

A Brief Overview

THE APOSTLE PAUL had wanted to go to Rome for a long time. But he was still waiting for God to give him the opportunity. He wrote this letter to the Christians in Rome while he was in Corinth in AD 57 (see Acts 19:21; Romans 1:10–12). When Paul wrote it, he was aware that for three years the unstable teenage Roman emperor Nero had begun his international reign of persecution and massacre of Christians. Paul wasted no time warning his fellow Roman Christians of the natural wickedness of humankind, the wrath of Nero, the prominence of sexual immorality and idol worship, and the dangerous consequences of being conformed to their culture. But his primary focus was on helping them to choose God's grace by faith and to be transformed by the power of His indwelling Spirit.

This most important Pauline letter is unquestionably the clearest and most systematic presentation in all the Scriptures of the basic beliefs of Christians. Paul's goal in writing the letter was to help people find salvation—freedom from sin and freedom to live as God designed—and to help us learn how to share and maintain the Christlike life. Paul made it clear that no one can have eternal life with God by working for it. He also repeatedly proclaimed that every human being is separated from God and is condemned to a life of sin, fear, and separation from God because we choose to rebel against Him.

For many Romans, Paul's message was too simple, too broad, and too good to be true. But for Paul, his message was not his message at all. It was God's message. Paul was simply sharing the truth that God Himself gave Paul. He was giving testimony to what had personally happened to him and to what Jesus had said. His message was about a spiritual transformation and not just another set of rules.

Paul explained the difference between a Christian, one who is controlled by the Spirit, and one who is controlled by one's sinful nature and what that difference means in the end.

> You are not controlled by your sinful nature. You are controlled by the Spirit if you have the Spirit of God living in you. (And remember that those who do not have the Spirit of Christ living in them do not belong to him at all.) And Christ lives within you, so even though your body will die because of sin, the Spirit gives you life because you have been made right with God.
>
> (Romans 8:9–10 NLT)

What are the main reasons this letter is considered by some the most important writing in the Bible?

- Next to Jesus, Paul is the most influential person in the Christian faith.
- Romans was chosen by Bible scholars to be the first letter in the New Testament.
- Many consider Romans the most quoted and influential letter in the Bible.
- Romans gives the most concise answers to life's most important questions.

- Paul considered Romans his most important letter to the world's most important city.

An Inspirational Theme of Romans

She Knows She's Going to Heaven

A few days ago, I prayed with my dear friend whose wife was within days of going to heaven. After my prayer, my friend said something I'll never forget. "Bill. As hard as this is, we're at peace because she says she knows she'll soon be in heaven with Jesus." Tonight, as I write this, we got the call. Jesus reached out, took her hand, and carried her home.

"In heaven with Jesus." How did she know that? Or was it just wishful thinking?

Saul did not believe in heaven or in Jesus. He was a highly respected legal expert and a Roman citizen who spoke five languages and taught at the University of Tarsus. He knew about Jesus but considered what he had heard absurd. Who could believe that the God of the entire universe could come to earth, be born of a virgin, and die for the sins of the world? It made no sense to him.

When Jesus's followers started spreading the message that Jesus had risen from the dead and was alive in spirit, Roman officials asked Saul to put this fire out before it got too big. Gladly obeying his assignment, Saul started rounding up Christians and throwing them in prison. But one day on his way to Damascus to arrest more Christians, the risen Jesus stopped him and spoke to him. Saul was shocked, and everything in his life changed that day. He discovered all he had heard about Jesus was true (see Acts 9:1–6).

Saul's life was so radically transformed that day that he changed his name to Paul, saying he was born again. He had "become a new person. The old life is gone; a new life has begun!" (2 Corinthians 5:17 NLT). He wrote his friend Titus that all who choose to receive the Spirit of Jesus into their lives could have "confidence that they have eternal life, which God—who does not lie—promised them" (Titus 1:2 NLT). Throughout Paul's writings, he echoed this same eternal promise: "Just as God raised Christ Jesus from the dead, he will give life to your mortal bodies by this same Spirit living within you" (Romans 8:11 NLT).

If you haven't yet received Jesus, do you know what to do? Here's what Paul says: if you confess with your mouth (ask Him in prayer) and believe with your heart (sincerely ask Him), you will be saved (see Romans 10:9). Is there any reason you can't pray this prayer right now?

> Dear Lord, You already know it, but I admit to You that I am a sinner, and I am sorry for my sins. You are so great, Lord. I don't understand much about You, but I understand that Your Bible says You know me and love me even with all my failures. And it says You sent Your Son, Jesus, to die on the Cross for my sins. And after three days Jesus rose from the dead so He could live in the Spirit and be able to come into my life. He will forgive me of all my sins and give me eternal life. I know I don't deserve it, Lord Jesus, but I ask You right now as humbly and gratefully as I know how: come into my life. I give You every part of me. I'm Yours for whatever You want. Thank You, Lord Jesus. Amen.

Now that you've done your part, you can count on Jesus to do His part. You have eternal life. He has forgiven you of every sin and will take you to heaven when your physical body dies. And until it's your time, Jesus will also keep on empowering you to live for Him.

Related Scriptures from Romans

We are sure of this because Christ was raised from the dead, and he will never die again. Death no longer has any power over him.

(Romans 6:9 NLT)

I pray that God, the source of hope, will fill you completely with joy and peace because you trust in him. Then you will overflow with confident hope through the power of the Holy Spirit.

(Romans 15:13 NLT)

Other Related Scriptures

This is the secret: Christ lives in you. This gives you assurance of sharing his glory.

(Colossians 1:27 NLT)

I have written this to you who believe in the name of the Son of God, so that you may know you have eternal life.

(1 John 5:13 NLT)

What Is God Saying to You?

What does Paul's conversion experience say about our living God?

Describe your own conversion experience and how it was different from Paul's.

Dear Father, the better I get to know You, the more I see You as my Redeemer who wants me to live a fruitful life on earth and live with You eternally in heaven. Thank You for making that possible through Jesus Christ. Amen.

Get to Know God through 1 Corinthians

A Brief Overview

IT WAS NOT LONG AFTER PAUL founded the church in Corinth when he learned that they were experiencing deep divisions. The congregation's leaders sent a letter to Paul listing some of their most difficult problems. The letter to the Corinthians was Paul's answer to their questions.

Corinth was the second largest city in the Roman Empire, an international metropolis with people from many different cultural backgrounds. The city contained numerous temples, all under the umbrella of the Temple to Aphrodite (Venus for the Romans). Venus was the goddess of sex, fertility, and love. The city and religious leaders supported prostitution as a major business. Salesmen and sailors from around the world came to Corinth to let their hair down and feel free to engage in unrestrained Roman-style love.

No doubt the culture clearly had a devastating influence on the church members' view of love and family. Paul did not encourage the new Jesus followers to leave the city but to stay and transform their corrupt and destructive view of love the Jesus way. He expected them to be light in the darkness.

Paul spoke directly to them and gave them clear models on how Jesus followers in a local fellowship should address their differences. Paul took his normal approach—he faced their divisions and immoral behavior with tough, straight talk, contrasting the difference between the Roman way and the

Jesus way that had transformed his life. The letter covered various problems related to both life and doctrine, splits and squabbles, carnal immorality, litigations among believers, being married versus being single, freedom in Christ, worship practices, the value of the Lord's Supper, teachings on the resurrection, and how to view spiritual gifts.

For Paul, the Corinthians' underlying problem was their misunderstanding of what real love is. As usual, like Jesus, Paul made things simple. He reminded them that Jesus said the most important thing was to love the Lord God with all their hearts and their neighbors as themselves (see Luke 10:27). He told them that all their problems were caused by one big problem: not loving God and each other properly.

An Inspirational Theme of 1 Corinthians

Not All That Glitters Is Gold

Our ten-year-old daughter, Kim, wanted a watch. I figured she would likely lose it or break it, so I decided to by her a toy one. But while I was in Manhattan on business, I saw a fellow selling watches out of his suitcase on the sidewalk. I was curious and stopped to look. He proclaimed he had a girl's Rolex gold bracelet watch that normally sold for fifteen thousand dollars. But he told me that since it was used he would take twenty-five dollars.

I took a chance, thinking it was about the same price as a toy watch and it was beautiful and kept perfect time. That is, for three weeks. Then her arm turned green and the watch stopped. I took it to a jeweler and asked if it was worth fixing.

He looked inside it and said, "If you paid more than ten dollars, you got ripped off."

Frankly, I was not surprised when I learned the truth. That experience reminded me of the now famous statement, "Everything that glitters is not gold." Shakespeare said it 550 years ago in his *Merchant of Venice*. Mark Twain later repeated it. Now it's in multiple songs and books, reminding us of how easy it is to be deceived and heartbroken by appearances, imitations, and sincere-sounding words about love.

How can you discern the difference between real, transforming love and imitations? Not long after Paul started the new congregation in Corinth, they sent him a letter listing questions about their problems—broken relationships, differing beliefs, and conflicting cultural influences. Paul recognized that they had one over-arching problem causing all the others—their misunderstanding of real love. Paul summarized his solution with Jesus's words, "Let love be your highest goal!" (1 Corinthians 14:1 NLT).

But how could they tell if their love or someone else's love was real or an imitation? After all, the popular and accepted view of love where they lived was the opposite of the Jesus way. Their city was second only to Rome in size and fame, but it proudly took first place as the most immoral city in the empire. Welcoming visitors to Corinth was the Temple to Aphrodite. It was the community's way of saying, "Welcome to the city of love." This imaginary goddess of sex, fertility, and love was conceived and propagated by wealthy, ruling-class men who wanted someone to divinely approve of their unfaithful, animal-like behavior. Supported by the business and religious leaders, over one thousand temple-based prostitutes lined the streets of the city offering so-called love for contributions.

In his famous thirteenth chapter of the letter, Paul presents possibly the clearest and certainly the most famous description of the differences between real love—the Jesus way—and imitation love—the Roman (Pop-American) way.

- Real love puts the other's needs first. Fake love puts personal desires first.
- Real love takes less so the other has more. Fake love takes all it can.
- Real love respects and encourages. Fake love is about present pleasures.
- Real love is faithful and honest. Fake love is deceitful and disloyal.

Today, as you seek to give and receive love, ask the Lord to help you remember "Not all that glitters is gold" and choose the Jesus way of loving, which is better than pure gold.

Related Scriptures from 1 Corinthians

Be on guard. Stand firm in the faith. Be courageous. Be strong. And do everything with love.

(1 Corinthians 16:13–14 NLT)

Three things will last forever—faith, hope, and love—and the greatest of these is love.

(1 Corinthians 13:13 NLT)

Other Related Scriptures

Those who wish to boast should boast in this alone: that they truly know me and understand that I am the LORD who demonstrates unfailing love and who brings justice and righteousness to the earth, and that I delight in these things. I, the LORD, have spoken!

(Jeremiah 9:24 NLT)

You must love the LORD your God with all your heart, all your soul, and all your mind. And . . . Love your neighbor as yourself.

(Matthew 22:37–39 NLT)

What Is God Saying to You?

What two experiences in Jesus's life come to your mind when you hear the word *love*? What does this say about God's nature?

What two experiences in your life come to your mind when you hear the word *love*?

Dear Father, the better I get to know You, the more I see why the Bible says You are love. Help me to love You sincerely and to be known for loving others the way You do. Amen.

Get to Know God through 2 Corinthians

A Brief Overview

AFTER PAUL'S FIRST LETTER to the Corinthian church, he wrote a second letter to them that was never preserved yet is referenced (see 2 Corinthians 2:1–11; 7:8). Paul later got a positive report from Titus about the improved conduct of the Corinthians (see 2 Corinthians 7:13), which motivated him to write yet another letter to them. It is this letter that is called 2 Corinthians in the Bible.

In this highly personal second letter to the new church in Corinth, Paul opens up more than ever before about his emotional struggles, failures, and disappointments. He also shares his feelings about the lavish example of the Macedonian churches, especially the non-Jewish members, who financially supported their Jewish Christian brothers and sisters in Jerusalem. He also gives encouraging yet challenging words about the importance of making donations to help other Christians across racial and national lines.

Although the young church had experience dealing with disagreements and personal squabbles, by the time Paul wrote 2 Corinthians they had worked through their differences and were in unity. They had taken Paul's earlier directives seriously and put loving each other ahead of their own desires. They repented of their un-Christlike behaviors and were a living example to the unbelieving majority in Corinth.

Because Paul felt it was important for the strategically located church to be clear about the apostles' authority in all matters, he rearticulates his position on his apostleship and how it was from God, not just man. Paul knew the church members needed reminding that what he and the apostles taught were God's teachings, not their own.

A major emphasis in this second letter to the Corinthians is Paul's confession of his weaknesses and his suffering in the name of Christ. He focuses on how the power and grace of God in these experiences gave him new insights and revelations into the character of God (see 2 Corinthians 11:1–12:13).

An Inspirational Theme of 2 Corinthians

When Boasting Is Good

Which do you like talking about more, your mistakes or your accomplishments? Most of us would rather never mention our mistakes and hardships and would frankly prefer that everyone forget our failures. We've convinced ourselves that bringing up our successes makes us look good, but sharing our sins and blunders hurts our reputation.

That's not the way God sees it. And in his second letter to the Christians in Corinth, Paul corrects the young Christians' faulty thinking on this important subject. While he was trying to reassure them that he had credibility, he told them more about his mistakes, miseries, and personal problems than his successes. And he instructed them to do the same.

Paul was grateful to God that when he had suffered or sinned in the past, the Lord Jesus continually reminded him, "My grace is sufficient for you, for my power is made perfect in weakness" (2 Corinthians 12:9a NIV). Paul went on to challenge his Corinthian friends not to boast of their own successes and accomplishments but to uncover their mistakes and use them to let people see God's glory. "Therefore I will boast all the more gladly about my weaknesses, so that Christ's power may rest on me," he said (2 Corinthians 12:9b NIV).

Paul echoed the words of Solomon: "People who conceal their sins will not prosper, but if they confess and turn from them, they will receive mercy" (Proverbs 28:13 NLT).

God has a way of using his weakest children to be his greatest witnesses. That's exactly the way it was with the heroes and heroines in the Bible. Look at Noah. Such a courageous man. Yet after God saved him from the flood, Noah got drunk and performed unspeakable acts of sin (see Genesis 9:18–23). Take Moses. Next to Jesus, possibly God's great leader. Yet he lost his temper and killed a man (see Exodus 2:11–14). And there is Mary Magdalene, a woman with an immoral reputation whom Jesus later chose to be a leader in the early church (see Matthew 27:55–56). God knew their imperfections and weaknesses but chose them anyway.

So remember, your Lord is completely familiar with your every imperfection and yet does not give up on you. The amazing way He forgives you and chooses to use even your weaknesses are a witness to the greatness of His love and faithfulness. He will not let you go because you, at one time, let go of Him. The best way you can show your gratitude for His love and encourage others is not by sharing all the good things you have done for God. Rather, it's by sharing how God in His mercy dealt with you.

Paul said it this way: "Praise be to the God and Father of our Lord Jesus Christ, the Father of compassion and the God of all comfort, who comforts us in all our troubles, so that we can comfort those in any trouble with the comfort we ourselves receive from God" (2 Corinthians 1:3–4 NIV).

George Matheson had failing eyesight from birth but totally lost his sight later while in seminary to become a pastor. As a young pastor, he was engaged to marry the love of his life. But just before their wedding, his fiancée broke his heart saying she could not go through life married to a blind man.

Matheson never married. For years, he never told anyone about his secret pain, keeping it hidden. Then one day he thought about how he'd lost his sight and how his fiancée left him, yet how Jesus never had. He was so inspired that he wrote the famous hymn, "O Love that Wilt Not Let Me Go." It is an emotional confession in which he boasts, "O Love that will not let me go . . . Light that follows all my way . . . Joy that seekest me through pain."

Later in his life, Matheson said that his hymn was actually the fruit of his suffering. It was a witness to God's power and love. By sharing his pain, his heartbreaks, his wounds, and losses, he found personal comfort and a way to comfort others.

What will you do with your past mistakes and failures? Will you boast of your goodness or of God's goodness? Will you keep your mistakes hidden? Or will you seek to find ways every day to share with others God's love that will not let you go?

Related Scriptures from 2 Corinthians

Each time [Jesus] said, "My grace is all you need. My power works best in weakness." So now I am glad to boast about my weaknesses, so that the power of Christ can work through me.

(2 Corinthians 12:9 NLT)

That's why I take pleasure in my weaknesses, and in the insults, hardships, persecutions, and troubles that I suffer for Christ. For when I am weak, then I am strong.

(2 Corinthians 12:10 NLT)

Other Related Scriptures

This High Priest of ours understands our weaknesses, for he faced all of the same testings we do, yet he did not sin.

(Hebrews 4:15 NLT)

He remembered us in our weakness. His faithful love endures forever.

(Psalm 136:23 NLT)

What Is God Saying to You?

When Paul reveals how God worked in and through him and his weakness, what is revealed about God's character?

What are some reasons that you find it difficult to talk about your weaknesses and past failures?

What are some ways that boasting of God's blessings can be helpful to others?

Dear Father, the more I get to know You, the more I see my weaknesses and failures are opportunities for You to reveal Your love and power to me. Thank You, Father. Amen.

Get to Know God through Galatians

A Brief Overview

WHILE REVISITING THE NEW CHRISTIANS in the church in Corinth around AD 53, the apostle Paul wrote this letter to be circulated to all the churches he had started earlier in the central part of Asia Minor called Galatia, which is modern-day Turkey. Eighteen months after starting those churches, Paul learned that a group of legalistic Jews called Judaizers had been following him from city to city undermining his message. They despised Paul for teaching that everyone, including Jews, needed Jesus as their Savior. They were infuriated with Paul for claiming that Jesus was the Messiah, God's Son, and that people could receive God's grace by faith in Jesus alone.

Paul was heartbroken and angry when he discovered that the relatively new Galatian Christians had so quickly allowed themselves to be misled by the false teachings of his enemies. So Paul began his letter with a series of arguments on what God had revealed to him about the relationship between grace and God's Law.

Unlike Paul's other letters, this one had no words of praise, compliment, or thanksgiving. He did not ask for prayer or spend time telling how much he missed them. Paul got right down to business. As one commentator says, Paul put on his war-paint before he started writing. He simply had no room for making God appear to approve of a graceless law or lawless grace.

For example, he told them that God blessed Abraham not because he'd kept the laws given by Moses. After all, God had not even given those laws until centuries after Abraham died. It was clear that God forgave Abraham and made him righteous by His grace through faith, not by Abraham's keeping the Law.

The letter has a serious tone because Paul believed a most serious subject was under attack—the very foundation of the Galatians' relationship with God and society's future. The heart of the gospel of Jesus was at stake.

Paul's focus was on Jesus's counterculture, two-sided message: anyone can be saved (that is, set free from the penalty of their sins and set free for abundant living now and for eternity) by accepting God's free grace through faith. The bottom-line message was grace is the only way to life and the only way of life that works.

Paul cleared up the confusion caused by his legalistic critics. He helped the Galatians see that obeying God's law and living by grace were not ideas at odds but actually two sides of God's loving personality. Paul said it is wrong to think that the Old Testament presents a God of law and order but the God of Jesus is nothing more than a God of sentimental lawlessness.

From the time Paul wrote the letter to the Galatians until today, Christians have struggled with the proper relationship between living by God's grace and obeying God's law. How can we affirm one without diminishing the other? How can we avoid a narcissistic, lawless, do-whatever-I-want life and also avoid a cold-hearted, legalistic, unsympathetic attitude?

How does Paul resolve this seemingly unresolvable problem? He points us to Jesus, the embodiment of grace and law in complete harmony. Through Jesus's character, thinking, attitude, speaking and behavior, Paul sees a perfect balance of grace and obedience. He challenges all Christians to let the life, words, and Spirit of Jesus be our inner guide.

An Inspirational Theme of Galatians

When It's Hard to Give Grace to Some

Do you find it difficult to give grace to some people? I'll admit it up front: I do. I know Jesus said to love even your enemies, but He didn't say it would be easy. What about that mean-spirited neighbor? And then there's that dishonest, irritable coworker. How about that self-centered in-law who finds something wrong with everything? And what about that egotistical and abusive bully? Need I go on? I think you would agree it is really hard to give grace to some folks.

The good news of the Bible is that God knows how hard it is for you to give grace to those folks, especially those who have repeatedly done hurtful things. But do not get discouraged. You can do it. Grace is your heavenly Father's business. It has been since the beginning, and He's ready to help you do the same.

The reason He finds it easy give grace to the most undeserving is because He is the source of all grace. He never runs out. No matter what His children do, He still loves us, never gives up on us, and doesn't do like we do, giving grace only to those we deem deserving or who might give us something in return. God's grace is real—a free gift with no strings attached.

If I had to summarize the Bible in one sentence, it would be something like this: the God of grace made you, knows you inside and out, loves you regardless of your past, sacrificed His

Son for you, and will keep on giving you His free grace if you reach out to Him in faith.

You are God's custom-made child. He made you one of a kind. And your Creator Father's love for you is not based on how good you are but on how good He is. His grace is not performance based. It is Spirit based. That means giving grace is not just what He does, it's who He is.

It hard for us to give grace to difficult people because we're not properly connected to the source of all grace. We're so immersed in the payback, tit-for-tat world around us we can't think God's way. You may have grown up in an environment where grace was conditional, dependent on how you performed. If you did well in academics, athletics, or social activities, you were loved. But if you fell short, you were criticized and made to feel ashamed. When life experiences teach you that love and grace are rewards for doing good, is it no wonder you find it hard to understand and practice God's kind of grace?

The apostle Paul wrote his letter to the Galatians to help them correct this same false view about God's grace. Paul's enemies had been following him from city to city confusing his new converts. The legalistic Jewish teachers told the new Christians that Paul was wrong. They taught that God's grace was only available to people in proportion to how they kept God's laws. Paul explained that trying to gain God's love by doing good and keeping His laws was not the way God operated. He explained that Jesus had shown him grace not because he was good but in spite of how bad he was.

Not knowing how to handle free grace makes it hard for us to give grace and receive grace. Our self-made, independent egos have been taught from birth that we have to work for what we get. We spend most of our time with people who think that, in some way, every gift is a quid-pro-quo deal. Nothing is ever really free.

Until you personally experience God's undeserved grace and know you would be lost without it, you will never believe it is real. Otherwise it will be just another interesting religious concept, a noble ideal. More than likely, you will keep on living by your lifelong ego-driven system and good-works approach to relating to God and others.

I still don't always find it easy to give grace to everyone, especially those difficult people. But when I recognize God's amazing grace to me and find myself spending more time talking with Him and thanking Him for His free, life-giving grace, I find it easier and actually even enjoyable to give grace to those who are the most difficult for me to love.

Related Scriptures from Galatians

For if you are trying to make yourselves right with God by keeping the law, you have been cut off from Christ! You have fallen away from God's grace.

(Galatians 5:4 NLT)

I do not treat the grace of God as meaningless. For if keeping the law could make us right with God, then there was no need for Christ to die.

(Galatians 2:21 NLT)

Other Related Scriptures

So just as sin ruled over all people and brought them to death, now God's wonderful grace rules instead, giving us right standing with God and resulting in eternal life through Jesus Christ our Lord.

(Romans 5:21 NLT)

God saved you by his grace when you believed. And you can't take credit for this; it is a gift from God. Salvation is not a reward for the good things we have done, so none of us can boast about it.

(Ephesians 2:8–9 NLT)

What Is God Saying to You?

What does the idea of grace say about God's heart and His desire for you?

To what kinds of people is it most difficult for you to extend grace? Why do you feel that way?

Dear Father, the more I get to know You, the more I see that Your grace is my only hope, and it makes me love You with all that is in me. I praise You for being the loving, grace-giving Father You are. Amen.

Get to Know God through Ephesians

A Brief Overview

IN AD 62, FOUR OF THE apostle Paul's brothers in the ministry of Jesus left him in his Roman prison cell to deliver four of Paul's letters that would become significant parts of the Bible. Those letters are now known as the Prison Epistles of Paul. Tychicus took the letter to the Ephesians to Ephesus, his hometown (see Ephesians 6:21). Epaphroditus carried the letter to Philippians (see Philippians 4:18). Epaphras delivered to his hometown the epistle to the Colossians (see Colossians 4:12). And Onesimus, a fugitive slave from Colossae, returned to his hometown to deliver the epistle to Philemon, who was his owner (see Philemon 10–16).

Ephesus was second only to Rome in population and diversity. It was founded around 2000 BC by the Hittites, but the Greeks conquered it a thousand years later. Ephesus is recognized by historians as one of the wealthiest and most influential cities of the ancient world.

At the heart of the city was the Temple of Diana. For centuries it was considered one of the Seven Wonders of the Ancient World. The temple was patterned after the Parthenon in Athens but was two times larger. The art and architecture of the temple were unmatched anywhere at that time. For example, each of the 127 columns of the temple was magnificently carved. Inside the colossal edifice was a treasury of art from around the world. In the middle of the temple stood the massive statue of the goddess Diana, who had over twenty breasts, representing her role as the oriental mother goddess of fertility. Historians report that the temple was where shameful acts of immorality and abuse were displayed daily.

When Paul wrote to the Corinthians, he told them that he wanted to go to help them, then explained why he could not leave Ephesus at that time: "There is a wide-open door for a great work here" (1 Corinthians 16:9 NLT). Paul's teaching was so successful, with great numbers becoming followers of Christ and leaving idol worship, that many of the city's silversmiths, who made household idols of Diana, went out of business.

It is important to remember that in Paul's day, Christians struggled everyday against the pressures of an immoral, materialistic, and class-dominated culture. To address those issues, Paul wrote the first half of his letter about the core teachings of Jesus and the second half about how to apply Jesus's values and lifestyle to everyday living. Both are crucial for every generation.

The central message of Ephesians is clear. Those who turn from their old, self-centered way and turn to the living God through His resurrected Son Jesus will find life at its best on earth and eternal life with God. It is a picture of the other-centered life of Jesus—a life that has died to self, a life on a holy mission.

The primary Jesus-centered worldview taught and modelled by Jesus runs throughout the powerful letter. The Lord's unique way of understanding the meaning of our lives and interpreting our purpose in this life is described in phrases about denying, sacrificing, and dying to self. Such values are not popular in our self-indulgent age. But for the Lord and

Paul, this God-centered life is the driving motivation at the heart of the gospel and the soul of what it meant to be a true follower of Jesus. Jesus said, "If anyone would come after me, let him deny himself and take up his cross daily and follow me. For whoever would save his life will lose it, but whoever loses his life for my sake will save it" (Luke 9:23–24 RSV). Paul put it this way, "Submit to one another out of reverence for Christ" (Ephesians 5:21 NLT). And again, Paul explained, "Those who belong to Christ Jesus have crucified the flesh with its passions and desires" (Galatians 5:24 RSV).

For Paul, the Ephesian Christians had before them the most important choice they would ever make. They would either choose to die to their old, self-centered natures or give the Spirit of living Christ control of their lives.

An Inspirational Theme of Ephesians

Denying Self

What comes to your mind when you read in the Bible that the best way to know God and find His best is to take up your cross, give up your life, deny yourself, throw off your old self, and even die daily to self? (See similar statements in Luke 9:23–24, Ephesians 4:17–24, John 12:24, Galatians 2:20, Romans 6:11–14, 2 Corinthians 5:17, Philippians 1:21.)

I was eight when I accepted Jesus as my Savior and started reading the Bible. But every time I came across one of those verses about denying myself and dying to myself, I was confused, and it bothered me. So I went straight to my Sunday school teacher, who had led me to Jesus. As usual, he cleared up my confusion.

Since then, I've noticed not only kids but many adults get mixed up about what Jesus and others in the Bible meant about denying self and dying to self, and sometimes their confusion leads to unhealthy thinking and poor decision making. They do not have a solid understanding of these concepts. Since Adam and Eve, people have tried to make things right after doing things wrong by punishing themselves and others. World religions, political leaders, and even parents have for ages attempted to get rid of guilt by using humiliation, beating, cutting, burning, solitary confinement, and other forms of pain to make people pay for their sins.

We must not forget that in Jesus's day, crucifixions were horrible public spectacles etched on the minds of eyewitnesses. Jesus knew that His followers would face persecution. They would be abused and unfairly mistreated. Some would suffer the humiliation of being publicly stripped naked and hung on a cross. Others would feel deep sorrow from seeing the suffering of those they loved. And some would lose their lives.

So when Jesus told those who wanted to follow him they must take up their crosses and deny themselves, He was being honest and realistic, wanting them to be prepared to face abuse, humiliation, grief, and even possible loss of life. The word *deny* does not mean to hide or to pretend. Jesus was a bold realist. He never wanted anyone to live in self-denial, acting like things were okay when they were not.

Also, for Jesus, to deny the self did not mean to give up things. Jesus used phrases like *denying self* and *dying to self* to produce unforgettable pictures in the mind. He wants you to picture a guard standing at the door of your heart denying access to your old self, your old thoughts, values, and way of acting. He wants you to picture your public baptism, when you showed everyone that your old self was dead and buried in the water and your new self came alive. Paul described it this way: "Going under the water was a burial of your old life; coming up out of it was a resurrection, God raising you from the dead as he did Christ" (Colossians 2:12 MSG).

Denying self or dying to self is not a negative act. It is a positive choice of allowing the Spirit of Jesus to take control of the steering wheel of your life. Paul told the Ephesians, "Throw off your old sinful nature and your former way of life, which is corrupted by lust and deception. Instead, let the Spirit of Jesus renew your thoughts and attitudes. Put on your new nature, created to be like God" (Ephesians 4:22–24 NLT).

Will you deny others and your old self the control over your attitudes and actions today? Will you choose to give the Spirit of our living Jesus control your life? He's counting on you to make the best choice.

Related Scriptures from Ephesians

Since you have heard about Jesus and have learned the truth that comes from him, throw off your old sinful nature and your former way of life, which is corrupted by lust and deception. Instead, let the Spirit renew your thoughts and attitudes. Put on your new nature, created to be like God—truly righteous and holy.

(Ephesians 4:21–24 NLT)

Submit to one another out of reverence for Christ.

(Ephesians 5:21 NLT)

Other Related Scriptures

[Jesus] said to the crowd, "If any of you wants to be my follower, you must give up your own way, take up your cross daily, and follow me. If you try to hang on to your life, you will lose it. But if you give up your life for my sake, you will save it.

(Luke 9:23–24 NLT)

You also should consider yourselves to be dead to the power of sin and alive to God through Christ Jesus. Do not let sin control the way you live; do not give in to sinful desires. Do not let any part of your body become an instrument of evil to serve sin. Instead, give yourselves completely to God, for you were dead, but now you have new life.

(Romans 6:11–13 NLT)

What Is God Saying to You?

What does the fact that God wants His Spirit to live in you say about His heart and mind and character?

How might you explain to a child Jesus's invitation to deny self?

Paul contrasts our "old nature" (old, pre-saved self) to our "new nature" (new, saved self). What are some of the most noticeable differences in your attitude and thinking?

Dear Father, the more I get to know You, the more I see how selfless and other-centered You are. Help me to see myself as You see me and be more like You. Amen.

Get to Know God through Philippians

A Brief Overview

THE LETTER TO THE PHILIPPIANS is an emotional letter written at the end of Paul's Roman imprisonment in AD 61 or 62. It was one of his four Prison Epistles—Ephesians, Philippians, Colossians, and Philemon. But this letter was different. This letter to the Christ followers in Philippi was written out of Paul's close relationship with his friends in this first church in Europe. Paul felt closer to this small congregation than any other he had started. As you read the letter, you will notice that the Philippian believers were deeply grateful for Paul, and Paul felt the same for them.

Philippi was a Roman colony of around fifteen thousand people, most of whom were slaves and servants. The leaders took pride in the city and intended to make it a miniature version of Rome. Paul visited there on his second missionary journey, spending about three months in the city. For Paul, his visit was an especially important trip for the spread of the gospel around the world because it was the first time people in Europe heard of Jesus. From Europe, the gospel message was carried to America and then to the ends of the earth.

While Paul was in Philippi, many people became passionate Christ followers and longtime friends of the apostle. They also formed the core of a growing and vibrant congregation that would ultimately help spread the gospel around the world. The Philippian Christians were unusually close to Paul. In times when Paul felt called of God to leave them and go to help other churches, time and time again some of the Philippians followed him, taking money and supplies to help him.

Among the new believers in Philippi was Lydia, a businesswoman who sold purple dye made in that region. Paul introduced her to Jesus, and she became a follower. Shortly afterward, she was baptized publicly, and her family invited Paul and his coworkers to stay in their home while in Philippi (see Acts 16:13–15). During that same visit, many others came to Christ.

Throughout this short letter, Paul speaks of the Jesus type of joy sixteen times. He makes it clear that this special kind of joy is different from the temporary pleasures that come from acquiring things, having power, or receiving praise of people.

The inextinguishable joy and unwavering gratitude that permeate this touching letter is the same joy-out-of-gratitude attitude that Paul wished for all of those he had led to Jesus. He had taught the Philippians well by word and example. No circumstance or resistance was too hard or painful to keep him from expressing the same grateful, joyful attitude that Paul saw in his Lord Jesus.

An Inspirational Theme of Philippians

Satisfying Your Insatiable Desire for Joy

Can you say, "I'm always full of joy"? Wouldn't it be wonderful if you could? Although we all want joy, unfortunately, most people do not truly experience it.

Thomas Aquinas, one of history's most respected theologians, taught that God created humans with a built-in, insatiable desire for joy. In his *Summa Theologica* he said we "cannot live without joy." However, as much as we crave it, most of us never experience it because we accept poor substitutes that never satisfy. And over time we become addicted to those substitutes and miss out on the real thing.

Do you believe it is even possible to have the real thing—real joy—all the time? The apostle Paul claims joy is not only possible, it's what he felt all the time, and that this is the inner peace and contentment your Lord wants for you too. In Philippians, Paul's most joy-filled letter, the apostle assures his friends that they can "always be full of joy" (Philippians 4:4 NLT).

You may be thinking that this is what you desire, but it just sounds too good to be true. For years, that's what I thought. But since I learned how to have the ever-present kind of joy Paul wrote about, it has changed how I look at God and everything around me. How can you experience the kind of joy the Bible talks about? The good news is there are some things you can do to have this kind of joy.

First, *practice being humble*. When you start focusing on being humble, being joyful will start happening. Paul wanted to his Philippian friends to be joyful, so he told them to be humble and consider others more important than themselves (see Philippians 2:3). He encouraged them to take on the attitude of Jesus who, although equal with God, humbled himself and took on the role of a servant and even died for us (see Philippians 2:8).

C. S. Lewis, the brilliant Oxford professor and atheist who became an humble Christian, wrote his heart-wrenching book *Surprised by Joy*, a beautiful and touching account of his last days with his beloved wife, Joy, as she was dying died of cancer. During that time, Lewis's mind and heart were so focused on how his wife felt that he later realized he had stopped thinking about how he felt. And through that experience, he says, he was "surprised by joy." As I have noted before, Lewis wrote this truth which bears repeating: "Humility is not thinking less of yourself but thinking of yourself less."

If you want to experience joy at all times, practice being humble at all times.

Second, *practice being grateful*. It is a basic biblical truth that the more grateful you are, the more joyful you will become. Joy is the fruit of gratitude. Paul said that one of the fruits of the Spirit is joy (see Galatians 5:22).

In our house, we have a Joy Jar, just a plain, old clear jar with a flower painted on it. If you opened it and dumped it out, you would find slips of paper where we have written phrases of our thanksgivings. Maybe it was for an unexpected blessing, or perhaps for an answered prayer, but on every slip of paper is our gratitude for something God has done. We find that as our Joy Jar fills up with expressions of our gratitude, our hearts are filled with joy. Brother Steindl-Rast, a leader of the international House of Prayer movement, reminds us, "It is not joy that makes us grateful; it is gratitude that makes us joyful."

If you practice being humble and being grateful for God's presence and for His every gift, you will experience an unwavering joy regardless of your situation. Just like Jesus said, "You will be overjoyed. No one takes away your joy" (John 16:22 NLT).

Related Scriptures from Philippians

But I will rejoice even if I lose my life, pouring it out like a liquid offering to God, just like your faithful service is an offering to God. And I want all of you to share that joy.

(Philippians 2:17 NLT)

Always be full of joy in the Lord. I say it again—rejoice!

(Philippians 4:4 NLT)

Other Related Scriptures

I have told you these things so that you will be filled with my joy. Yes, your joy will overflow!

(John 15:11 NLT)

I pray that God, the source of hope, will fill you completely with joy and peace because you trust in him.

(Romans 15:13 NLT)

What Is God Saying to You?

What does the fact that God wants you to be filled with joy say about His nature?

What are some reasons you don't always have joy in your heart and mind? What are some ways you can practice being humble and grateful to the Lord?

Dear Father, the more I get to know You, the more I see that You want me to share in Your joy and that by being more humble and grateful, I can. Help me to see others as You do and be always ready to express my gratitude. Thank You. Amen.

Get to Know God through Colossians

A Brief Overview

ALTHOUGH PAUL HAD NEVER BEEN to Colossae, he was the founder of the church in that important city in the same way he was the founder of other churches across that part of the world. When Paul led people to Jesus, he stayed in their city long enough to help them get grounded in their new faith and discover whom the Lord chose to be their leaders. Before he moved on to spread the word in other cities, he tried to prepare the new Christians in the teachings of Jesus and how they could stand up to all that life and Satan would throw at them.

Many considered Colossae the doorway to the Eastern cultures of the Orient. The city was often referred to as the gateway of Phrygia, where the East and the West met. For years Colossae partnered with the other larger cities in the region such as Philadelphia, Sardis, Thyatira, and Pergamum, working together to protect themselves from militant tribes and hostile countries from the East. But by Paul's day, the entire region was more secure under the control of the Roman Empire. The once military-driven culture had become more focused on commerce, art, education, and self-serving immoral activities.

The Colossian congregation met in the home of Philemon, to whom Paul wrote his next letter. We learn from Paul's letter to Philemon that Epaphras had come to Rome to help Paul while he was in prison (see Philemon 1:23). While there,

Epaphras shared his concerns about the misleading and harmful teachings the Colossian Christians were hearing. So Paul wrote this letter to remind them their focus was to be on Jesus and who He was.

Two primary dangers caused the young Christians most of their confusion. One was the temptation to freeze and do nothing to confront the misleading teachings of the culture around them. That approach generally caused churches to become nothing more than ceremonial organizations. The other danger was to take the road of least resistance, leading the churches to become self-centered reflections of their cultures.

The main issue at the core of their confusion was the belief that Jesus was not actually God but only a holy man and a good example for people. Paul confronted the Jesus attackers, who held an elitist spirit, believing they had a corner on truth. They created their own standards of right and wrong that helped them justify their unrestrained, shameless behavior. Their faith was in their own philosophies, which taught that God was no more than an unknowable spiritual force in the universe.

For Paul, Jesus was not an unknowable force at all. He was the long-awaited Messiah, the incarnation of the Creator God, the embodiment of God born of a virgin, the visible image of the invisible God, the resurrected Redeemer, and Paul's personal indwelling Savior and Lord. These facts were nonnegotiable.

The letter to the Colossians is a summary of Jesus's authenticity and a lesson on the importance of Jesus as the most complete and clearest revelation of God possible.

An Inspirational Theme of Colossians

How Can You Be Sure of Authenticity?

Jesus claimed He was in the beginning. He was God come to earth, the Creator, the Way to heaven, the Truth, the resurrected Spirit who can live in you. Was Jesus all he said? How can you be sure?

It is important for you to be confident about Jesus, because if Jesus was not all He said, then He's just another religious teacher, and our hope for heaven is gone. C. S. Lewis summarized it in *Mere Christianity* when he said that Jesus was either a lunatic, a liar, or God. There's no middle ground.

Even with all of Jesus's amazing miracles, large followings, and scripture-backed claims, most people in His day didn't believe in Him. The same is true in our day. The number of Americans denying Jesus's claims continues to climb. Skeptical intellectuals, prejudiced religious leaders, the profit-driven media, and especially our younger generations find many reasons to reject Jesus.

When Paul learned that his Colossian children in Christ were under attack by a group of pseudo-intellectual, anti-Jesus elitists and were becoming increasingly confused about Jesus's authenticity, he quickly responded. He was determined to prepare his insecure spiritual children in how to handle such false accusations. So he wrote his now famous Colossian letter—his Declaration of Authenticity.

How did Paul know with such confidence that Jesus was absolutely authentic? He did what you and I must do. He risked reaching out to meet Jesus and then developed a close, personal relationship with him. The highly educated Paul chose to stop merely listening to opinions *about* Jesus and chose to get out of his comfort zone and get in touch *with* Jesus. If you want to be as confident *about* Jesus as Paul was, you must be as personal *with* Jesus as Paul was.

The brilliant scholar Paul stopped focusing on his own intellect to figure out *how* Jesus could possibly be the Creator and started focusing on making contact *with* his Creator. He hungered for more than an understanding *of* God. What he wanted most was a personal relationship *with* God. And he found it, just like you can.

When Paul was asked why he believed in Jesus, he surprised people by telling them how he started out believing Jesus was a fraud, how he was a Roman citizen, a highly educated teacher, and a zealous keeper of the law. Although he had never met Jesus, he would explain that he knew Jesus was a blasphemer and had done his best to hunt down and imprison every Christian he could find.

Then suddenly, no doubt with a smile on his face, Paul would tell them of his encounter with the risen Christ. His reporting went like this: "But one day, on my way to Damascus, to arrest more Christians, I met Jesus. Not in His physical body, but in His spiritual body. He had been dead for a long time. But there He was, very much alive, just like He said. Ever since that day, He's been with me and lives in me. For me to live is Christ, to die will be my gain. He's more real than anything" (see Philippians 3:7–11).

The evidence for Jesus being who He said He was is overwhelming. Thousands of prophecies were fulfilled in Him. Millions of lives through the ages have been transformed by Him, and many of those have been willing to die for Him.

Countless hospitals, orphanages, and schools have been established by these believers. And these believers have included some of the greatest minds and scientists, who had no scientific evidence but yet believed. In truth, all of these arguments for Christ can be challenged and debated, but what cannot be debated is the personal experience of one who has truly encountered the living Christ.

I once spoke in a church where no one knew me but the pastor. In my message, I told the people my wife, Phyllis, was a wonderful, gracious, unselfish, beautiful, and talented woman. Then I asked, "How can you know if I'm telling the truth? If the pastor agreed, would that make it true? Or what if my friends wrote to you and repeated what I said about Phyllis? Would that make you believe it? Or would you ask yourself if they could they be exaggerating or just be saying what I told them to say? Let's face it, you're never going to know if I'm telling the truth, and you won't know Phyllis until you actually meet her and spend time with her. Then you'll know what I know."

It is the same with Jesus. When you encounter Him, spend time with Him, get to know Him, you'll know He lives and is all He said he was. It's like my favorite hymn, "He Lives":

I serve a risen Savior, He's in the world today;
I know that He is living whatever men may say;
I see His hand of mercy, I hear His voice of cheer,
And, just the time I need Him, He's always near.
He lives, He lives, Christ Jesus lives today!
He walks with me and talks with me along life's narrow way.
He lives, He lives, Salvation to impart!

You ask me how I know He lives. He lives within my heart.

Related Scriptures from Colossians

Christ is the visible image of the invisible God. He existed before anything was created and is supreme over all creation, for through him God created everything in the heavenly realms and on earth.

(Colossians 1:15–16 NLT)

For in Christ lives all the fullness of God in a human body.

(Colossians 2:9 NLT)

Other Related Scriptures

For to me, living means living for Christ, and dying is even better.

(Philippians 1:21 NLT)

In the beginning the Word [Jesus] already existed. The Word was with God, and the Word was God.

(John 1:1 NLT)

What Is God Saying to You?

What does it say about God that He wants to reveal Himself in Jesus?

What are some things you can do to help you have confidence that Jesus is God with you at all times?

Dear Father, the more I get to know You, the more I see that Your Son, my Savior Jesus, is You, and You are with me all the time. Thank You. Amen.

Get to Know God through 1 Thessalonians

A Brief Overview

OF THE TWENTY-SEVEN NEW TESTAMENT BOOKS, Paul wrote thirteen. Nine were letters to local churches like this first missive to the Thessalonians, in which Paul focuses on his appreciation for those young Christians. The Thessalonians encouraged Paul because of their works of faith, labors of love, and their steadfastness of hope—themes that resound throughout the famous letter (see 1 Thessalonians 1:3).

Thessalonica was established in 315 BC after Alexander the Great's kingdom was split into four parts. It was an important commercial, military, and entertainment coastal city. In Paul's day, it had a population of about two hundred thousand, with a large enough Jewish community to warrant a synagogue. It was the capital of the Macedonian Province, a key region that Paul targeted for the spread of the gospel. Today, Thessalonica (also called Salonica) is Greece's second-largest city.

Thessalonica was well known for being a popular city on the Ignatian Way, a famous Roman-constructed stone road that ran from Albania to Constantinople. Paul and his fellow missionaries traveled along this road to get to Thessalonica, which was about one hundred miles from Philippi and five hundred miles from Athens. In Paul's day, the Roman Emperor Claudius I ruled the area from AD 41 to 54 and was succeeded by the crazed, youthful Nero who persecuted Jews and Christians throughout the Empire.

This first Thessalonian letter is filled with uplifting and affectionate comments like this one: "We loved you so much that we shared with you not only God's Good News but our own lives, too" (1 Thessalonians 2:8 NLT). Because of Paul's deep love and gratitude for their faithfulness, he expresses how much their work means to him and challenges them to keep up their tireless efforts for the weak and most vulnerable. He urges them to maintain their reputation of holy and sacrificial living as they wait for the coming of the Lord Jesus.

The first chapter focuses on Paul's thankfulness for their being an inspiration to him in all of his distress and pain. The second chapter is a reminder of the time Paul, Timothy, and Silas came to them and experienced their support. In chapter three, Paul refers to Timothy's previous trip to them to fortify and encourage them. He focuses on how much their steadfast love meant to him when he was so oppressed and how much he wants to see them again.

In chapter four, Paul challenges them to keep on doing what they were already doing—living holy lives, avoiding the common sexual immorality of their culture, keeping their bodies under the control of the Spirit of God, living quiet lives, working hard, and winning the respect of unbelievers.

In chapter five, Paul concludes the letter with a final word about our Lord's return and the importance of being ready. Paul cautions them to be alert and to live as if Jesus could come at any moment, like a thief in the night. He closes his letter reminding them of the importance of loving one another, living in peace, being joyful, praying always, and giving thanks in everything situation.

An Inspirational Theme of 1 Thessalonians

Keep Your Eye on the Ball

I was embarrassed when I joined our Little League baseball team at nine because I could not hit the ball. Then one day my daddy pointed out my problem. I've never forgotten when he said, "Bill, I've it figured out. You're not hitting the ball because you're not keeping your eye on the ball. You're distracted by what people may be thinking and all that's going on around you. When you step up to that plate, you've got to focus on only one thing—that ball. Focus, Bill. Focus. It's all about focus." When I learned to keep my eye on the ball, I finally knocked a homerun.

Sometimes our lives end up like that baseball game. We have so many things distracting us that we can't hit the ball—the things God has given us to do, our work and our relationships with others and Him.

Do you ever feel that way? Well, then, maybe it's time for you to stop, step back, and take a good look at what's worrying and distracting you. Maybe you need to ponder what Daddy said for a few minutes: "Focus. It's all about focus." To focus means to concentrate on that which helps you accomplish God's plan for you and to avoid those things that slow you down or prevent you from succeeding.

If you examine the lives of some of the Bible's most recognized people, like Moses, David, Esther, Mary, Paul, and Jesus, you'll notice they all continually encountered serious problems—injustice, self-serving leaders, repulsive religion, personal pain, cruel criticism, hated, jealousy, heartache, and prejudice. But if you look more closely, you'll also notice that each of them had one important spiritual discipline that helped them avoid letting their problems become distractions. Regardless of what was happening to them, they managed to accom- accomplish the task God gave them. That critical discipline was focus.

Of course, like you and me, they had their ups and downs. But their stories in God's Word tell us over and over again that through it all they kept their eyes on the ball. They kept looking to God, turning to Him, seeking Him, fixing their eyes on Him, focusing on Him. Paul said, "We [please God] by keeping our eyes on Jesus" (Hebrews 12:2 NLT.). Paul said the secret to completing God's task was staying focused on God's purposes (see Philippians 3:13).

So, when the scriptures tell us to focus on God, to look to Him, to keep your eyes on Him, to turn to Him, those verbs are picture words describing actions you can take to help you please God, get to know Him more closely, and follow His will for your life.

For example, when you are *focusing* on Him, it may mean you are taking steps to attentively read God's Word. Or it may mean you are concentrating on staying in touch with Him by briefly speaking with Him throughout your day rather than ignoring Him.

When you *look* to Him, it may mean you intentionally keep an eye out for His presence, His hand of mercy, His healing touch through one of his servants. To look to Him may mean when you look at a person, you see more than most see. You see each person as a special child of God whom He loves and cares for, as a temple where God's Spirit lives.

I vividly remember a time in the ICU when I did not know if I was going to live or die. It was dark and cold, and there were so many noisy machines. I had been in and out of consciousness for hours. But when I opened my eyes, I saw my precious wife, Phyllis. She had been patiently sitting in that same uncomfortable chair for days. When I looked into her loving face, her eyes and gentle smile said to me, "I'm right here Bill. I'm not going anywhere. I love you. God is with us, and everything will be all right." Nothing else around me mattered at that moment. I felt God's presence and was completely safe, and a quiet peace came over me. The same Spirit of our Lord who was in my Phyllis was also in that ICU room.

Helen Lemmel wrote one of my favorite hymns, "Turn Your Eyes Upon Jesus." Her text pictures that same sense of God's presence and love that will be with you no matter what you're going through when you turn to Him.

O soul, are you weary and troubled?
No light in the darkness you see?
There's light for a look at the Savior,
And life more abundant and free!

Turn your eyes upon Jesus,
Look full in His wonderful face,
And the things of earth will grow strangely dim,
In the light of His glory and grace.

Related Scriptures from 1 Thessalonians

So be on your guard, not asleep like the others. Stay alert and be clearheaded.

(I Thessalonians 5:6 NLT)

Now may the God of peace make you holy in every way, and may your whole spirit and soul and body be kept blameless until our Lord Jesus Christ comes again.

(I Thessalonians 5:23 NLT)

Other Related Scriptures

Not that I have already obtained it [this goal of being Christ-like] or have already been made perfect, but I actively press on so that I may take hold of that [perfection] for which Christ Jesus took hold of me and made me His own.

(Philippians 3:12 AMP)

So whether we are here in this body or away from this body, our goal is to please him.

(2 Corinthians 5:9 NLT)

What Is God Saying to You?

What things distract you most from keeping your eyes on Jesus?

What are some things you can do that will help you get and stay closer to Jesus on a daily basis?

Dear Father, the more I get to know You, the more I see that You are within me and want to me to give You all of my self. Help me to stay focused on You and Your purpose for my life. Thank You that You live in me. Amen.

Get to Know God through 2 Thessalonians

A Brief Overview

AS I MENTIONED IN THE INTRODUCTION to 1 Thessalonians, Paul had started the church in Thessalonica and had gotten word that they were doing well in their faith journey—except for their understanding of Jesus's second coming. The immaturity of his new converts made them perfect targets for Satan and his deceiving workers. It had only been a few months since his first letter to them, yet Paul sensed he needed to send a second one.

He wrote 2 Thessalonians from Corinth in AD 51 and repeated the same main themes his first letter had contained. No doubt he had received a second report from some of the believers there who were raising fears and questions that the brothers and sisters were having about the end times and Jesus's return.

Paul had several clear and similar purposes in writing both letters. They were the desires of his heart, not only for those in Thessalonica, but for all Christians with fears and questions, for people like those under severe persecution in countries around the world today, and people like you and me.

Paul's purposes in writing these letters came from his heart and his own personal experiences. First, Paul wanted them to know that he was grateful for their faithfulness under persecution, especially as they were young Christ followers. Second, he wanted them to return to their original authority—the words and life of Jesus—and avoid false teachers. Third, he wanted to give them some brief and simple answers about the second coming that would relieve their fears and increase their hope. And finally, Paul wanted them to refocus their attention. He wanted them to be comforted and excited about Jesus's return, but he cautioned them in the meantime not to neglect the work the Lord called them to do.

From Paul's comments, it is apparent that false teachers were confusing the young congregation by teaching lies and forging letters with Paul's name on them to make them look like they came from Paul (see 2 Thessalonians 2:2). Paul made it clear they should be cautious of evil people who would resort to any kind of deception to mislead God's children. He repeated much of what he had already written in 1 Thessalonians and emphasizes the importance of staying focused on the truth.

Second Thessalonians uses serious language to explain the seriousness of leaving the main message of the gospel and getting distracted by things of lesser importance. Paul challenges the church not to worry or be confused because the *timing* of Jesus's return is not as important as the fact *of* His return. The hope of His coming to take them home should motivate them to live responsibly and compassionately for Jesus no matter their circumstances.

Paul always provided his new converts with important lessons on the main teachings of Jesus, with practical ways they could use them in their daily lives, and with words of love and encouragement. Second Thessalonians is no exception. If you read this letter as if it were written to you personally, the Spirit of the Lord will strengthen you in your faith, give you ways to apply His truths to your life, and inspire you to be more grateful and joyful.

An Inspirational Theme of 2 Thessalonians

How to Actively Wait

If you knew Jesus was coming tomorrow, what would you do today? Would you stop doing something you're doing? Would you start doing some things you've put off for a long time? In Forrest Pollock's book *The Last Sermon I Would Preach If Jesus Were Coming Tomorrow,* he invited thirty preachers, whom he considered America's finest, to tell what they would do.

As you would expect, each of them shared something a bit different about what they would do. But all of them had these emphases in common: the fact of Jesus's return, the importance of being ready, the uncertainty of the details, the anticipation of all being made right, and most of all, the unspeakable joy of being with our Lord Jesus forever.

In Paul's absence, the Christians in Thessalonica had been falsely told that Jesus was returning within a few days. Some doubted. Some feared. Some were so excited that they sold everything, quit their jobs, and went out on the hillside to wait and watch. Paul quickly responded with a letter of correction and instructions. He said his message to them was from God and it should be shared with other Christians. That means you and me.

What did he say we should do while we wait for Jesus to return? If Jesus were coming tomorrow, what should you be doing today?

First, be *self-controlled* in your out-of-control world. Paul recognized that their lives were getting out of control because they were listening to the wrong voices. He reminded them and us to stay focused not on trying to figure out when, where, or how Jesus will come again, but on surrendering to the indwelling Spirit of Jesus who has already come into our lives.

Second, *be other centered* in your self-centered world. Paul warned them about returning to their old self-centered lifestyle. As you wait for Jesus's return, He wants you to stay focused on your new, Christ-centered, other-centered way of living.

Third, *be heaven and earth minded* in our this-is-all-there-is world. Paul reminded his Thessalonian friends that they currently lived in their physical bodies, but soon they would be given a new spiritual body. As you wait with all of life's problems—pain, tears, sorrows, injustice—remember, it won't be long before you'll enjoy the reward of your faithfulness. In the meantime, like your Lord, never neglect to fulfill God's purpose for you on earth. God wants you to stay excited about His coming and your eternal home, but He also wants you to remain His faithful, caring servants.

Ever since Jesus announced that He will come again, people have responded in different ways. Some, who don't believe the Bible is accurate, skeptically dismiss the whole idea of a second coming. Others get distracted, spending their time speculating about the details surrounding His coming. But some of us, who know we have been saved by His first coming, now anxiously anticipate his second coming. We are thrilled to know we will be reunited with those we love.

Most of all, we rejoice with the apostle Paul who said, "For now we see in a mirror dimly, but then face to face" (1 Corinthians 13:12 ESV). And "For the Lord himself will come down from heaven with a commanding shout, with the voice of the archangel, and with the trumpet call of God . . . [We] will be caught up in the clouds to meet the Lord in the air. Then we will be with the Lord forever" (1 Thessalonians 4:16–17 NLT).

Charles Hadden Spurgeon, called the prince of all preachers, often preached on the second coming. In his famous sermon, *God Our Portio*n, delivered in 1877 at the Metropolitan Tabernacle, Spurgeon explained how being with God was for him what makes heaven heaven. For him, Jesus's return was "heaven at its best. Not the harps of gold, nor the crowns unfading, nor the light unclouded is glory to me; but Jesus, Jesus Himself, and myself forever with Him." That's heaven.

When you think about Jesus coming again, what comes to your mind? And allow me to ask you what Forrest Pollock asked all those preachers: what will you do today?

Related Scriptures from 2 Thessalonians

He called you to salvation when we told you the Good News; now you can share in the glory of our Lord Jesus Christ. With all these things in mind, dear brothers and sisters, stand firm and keep a strong grip on the teaching we passed on to you.

(2 Thessalonians 2:14–15 NLT)

May the Lord lead your hearts into a full understanding and expression of the love of God and the patient endurance that comes from Christ.

(2 Thessalonians 3:5 NLT)

Other Related Scriptures

Seek the Kingdom of God above all else, and live righteously, and he will give you everything you need.

(Matthew 6:33 NLT)

We can say with confidence and a clear conscience that we have lived with a God-given holiness and sincerity in all our dealings . . . I hope someday you will fully understand us, even if you don't understand us now. Then on the day when the Lord Jesus returns, you will be proud of us in the same way we are proud of you.

(2 Corinthians 1:12, 14 NLT)

What Is God Saying to You?

What does the promise of Jesus's return to earth say about God's character?

What does the fact of Jesus's return and the end of time on earth say to you about your current priorities?

Dear Father, the more I get to know You, the more I see that Jesus's return is part of Your glorious plan for those of us who love You. Thank You. Amen.

Get to Know God through 1 Timothy

A Brief Overview

First Timothy is a personal letter written by Paul and is part of a new group of Paul's letters he wrote to Timothy and Titus. These three books are called the Pastoral Epistles. The Greek word translated *pastoral* means "shepherd"—one who takes care of the sheep. Thus, these Pastoral Epistles are personal, handwritten letters from Paul to his young converts Timothy and Titus, whom Paul trained to take care of and lead Jesus's sheep—His local congregations of believers.

The writing of the three Pastoral Epistles came after the events recorded in the Book of Acts. Paul anticipated that he would be released from his long prison term, something that probably happened around AD 62 (see Philippians 2:24). At that point he left Rome to go back to Ephesus and see to it that Timothy became the leader of that important church.

After Paul left Ephesus and preached throughout Macedonia, he heard reports of Timothy's outstanding leadership and the numerous philosophical, religious, and moral attacks against the gospel and followers of Jesus. Those reports prompted Paul to write 1 Timothy, probably in AD 63.

Timothy was Paul's spiritual child and fellow traveler in starting and training new congregations and is mentioned twenty-four times in the New Testament. In this first letter to Timothy, Paul offers him some down-to-earth, pastoral advice as Timothy begins his care for the Christians in the church at

Ephesus. The letter provides us with the most thorough and inspirational instructions for Christians who seek to be faithful to Jesus in the face of false beliefs and socially acceptable immoral behavior. It gives basic qualifications for congregational leaders and helpful insights into church discipline.

Paul's advice to Timothy emphasizes the value of purity, discipline, and Christlike behavior that should characterize all Christian caregivers.

An Inspirational Theme of 1 Timothy

Above All Else, Do What?

In 2019, the painting *Salvator Mundi* by Leonardo da Vinci was purchased for $450 million, making it the world's most expensive painting ever sold. The National Gallery of London goes to extreme measures to guard this valuable possession.

As valuable as the painting is, stop for a minute and ask yourself this question. Which is more valuable to you, the painting or knowing God in a personal way—having inner peace no matter what and experiencing His presence all the time? Paul made the comparison this way:

> I once thought these things were valuable, but now I consider them worthless because of what Christ has done. Yes, everything else is worthless when compared with the infinite value of knowing Christ Jesus my Lord. For his sake I have discarded everything else, counting it all as garbage, so that I could gain Christ and become one with him.
>
> (Philippians 3:7–9 NLT)

Knowing God in a personal way—what the Bible refers to as having Him in your heart—*is* the most valuable gift you could ever have. That's why you read repeatedly throughout the Bible that nothing should be more important to you than to carefully guard your heart. Solomon said, "Guard your heart above all else, for it determines the course of your life" (Proverbs 4:23 NLT).

It's the same thing Paul told his young friend Timothy who faced so many false teachings, personal attacks, and socially accepted but seriously corrupt and harmful beliefs hostile to Timothy's faith: "Timothy, guard what God has entrusted to you. Avoid godless, foolish discussions with those who oppose you with their so-called knowledge" (1 Timothy 6:20 NLT).

The apostle Peter also emphasized the importance of guarding your heart. He told his friends to be careful about people and things trying to confuse you, distract you, and tempt you so that you miss out on God's most valuable gift, saying, "Be on guard; then you will not be carried away by the errors of these wicked people and lose your own secure footing" (2 Peter 3:17 NLT).

What three main practical actions did Peter and Paul say you should do to help you guard your heart?

First, stand firm on God's Word. Making God's Word your final authority will help you guard your heart. The Bible says, "Your word is a lamp to guide my feet and a light for my path" (Psalm 119:105 NLT). And wise King Solomon said, "Every word of God proves true. He is a shield to all who come to him for protection" (Proverbs 30:5 NLT). Decide for yourself that God's Word is completely trustworthy, inspired by God

Himself, and is your unchanging authority in all matters of faith.

Second, choose the scars from faithfulness over the ease of cowardice. It would be easier to please the crowd and go along with popular immoral behavior than to make pleasing God and following Jesus's lifestyle your heart's desire. We should not shy away from suffering for Jesus because He suffered for us. Guard you heart by suffering for Jesus (see 1 Peter 3:17–18).

Third, simplify your inner and outer life. When Jesus was asked what is most important, He said, "Love the Lord your God with all your heart, all your soul, and all your mind" (Matthew 22:37 NLT). Simply put, Jesus says if you want to stay close to God, love Him humbly, responsibly, and as honestly as you can. Paul said when you focus on a simple inner and outer life, "You will experience God's peace, which exceeds anything we can understand. His peace will guard your hearts and minds as you live in Christ Jesus" (Philippians 4:7 NLT). Guard your heart by choosing to follow the simple example and words of Jesus.

Related Scriptures from 1 Timothy

The purpose of my instruction is that all believers would be filled with love that comes from a pure heart, a clear conscience, and genuine faith.

(1 Timothy 1:5 NLT)

They should be rich in good works and generous to those in need, always being ready to share with others. By doing this they will be storing up their treasure as a good foundation for the future so that they may experience true life.

(1 Timothy 6:18–19 NLT)

Other Related Scriptures

And you saw how the Lord your God cared for you all along the way as you traveled through the wilderness, just as a father cares for his child.

(Deuteronomy 1:31 NLT)

A good person produces good things from the treasury of a good heart, and an evil person produces evil things from the treasury of an evil heart. What you say flows from what is in your heart.

(Luke 6:45 NLT)

What Is God Saying to You?

In 1Timothy, there is an emphasis on guarding your heart, the place of all your emotions, your desires, and your will. What does this say about God's character and what He wants for you?

What kinds of things do you experience daily that make you aware that you truly do need to guard your heart?

Dear Father, the more I get to know You, the more I am aware that You give instruction so that my life will be fulfilling, peaceful, and productive for Your purposes. When I guard my heart and focus on You, I have peace and direction. Thank You. Amen.

Get to Know God through 2 Timothy

A Brief Overview

TIMOTHY HAD BEEN THE PASTOR of the Ephesian church for four years when his spiritual father, Paul, wrote him this letter. In it, Paul is more concise but full of serious advice and heartwarming concern because he is writing it from a dark Roman prison cell waiting to die. The letter indicates that Paul's death is near and he wants to share his final desires. Reports indicate that Paul was beheaded for his faith in AD 67.

No matter how challenging the task or how hateful his enemies, Paul encouraged Timothy to continue to respond to his adversaries the way Jesus did and to rest in the peace that Jesus lives in him and would take him to heaven for his reward. Even while facing impending death, Paul gave Timothy a checklist.

> Preach the word of God. Be prepared, whether the time is favorable or not. Patiently correct, rebuke, and encourage your people with good teaching. For a time is coming when people will no longer listen to sound and wholesome teaching. They will follow their own desires and will look for teachers who will tell them whatever their itching ears want to hear. They will reject the truth and chase after myths. But you should keep a clear mind in every situation. Don't be afraid of suffering for the Lord. Work at telling others the Good News, and fully

> carry out the ministry God has given you. As for me, my life has already been poured out as an offering to God. The time of my death is near. I have fought the good fight, I have finished the race, and I have remained faithful.
>
> (2 Timothy 4:2–7 NLT)

Paul gave Timothy list of attitudes as to how he should respond to his problems and enemies and carry on the work God had called him to do. Throughout this letter, he told him to:

- Be faithful in sharing the Gospel.
- Be prepared for every situation.
- Be patient with your expectations.
- Be persuasive in your sharing.
- Be firm in your convictions.
- Be encouraging in discouraging times.
- Be peaceful in chaotic situations.
- Be courageous when you're abused for Jesus.
- Be eternity-minded at all times.

An Inspirational Theme of 2 Timothy

Are You at Peace with God?

Can you imagine how you will feel when you face the end of your life here on earth and are about to enter the next? Going through the 2020 pandemic gave all of us reasons to be thinking more about such things.

In the midst of the pandemic, I had a conversation with a Christian woman I've known for many years. She believed her life here was just about over. I asked her, "How are you feeling about all that?" She calmly replied, "I feel completely at peace with God."

Don't you love it when people feel that way about such serious matters? But too frequently, that is not the way. Working as a minister for years, I often witnessed the opposite—people in their final days filled with anxiety, uncertainty, and fear.

Dr. Francis Collins, the world-renowned physician, scientist, and head of the National Institute of Health, shared his personal testimony at the BioLogos 2019 International Conference for Faith and Science. He revealed how he observed significant differences between Christians and unbelievers facing death. As a young atheist doctor on a ward of terminally ill patients, Dr. Collins noticed how peaceful his Christian patients were and wondered "If I was lying in that bed with a terminal diagnosis, how would I handle it?" He observed that the Christian patients looked forward to what would come next, and he realized he wanted what these Jesus followers had—a personal relationship with God that would bring that peace. Not long after that experience, he gave Jesus his life and found the peace he had seen in his patients.

The same thing happened to Paul. Early in his life, he was at war with God, others, and himself. He knew no peace. But when he found Jesus, he found peace. On his last days, chained to a wall in a Roman prison awaiting execution, he wrote, "My time has almost run out. Very soon now I will be on my way to heaven. I have fought long and hard for my Lord, and through it all I have kept true to him. And now the time has come for me to stop fighting and rest. In heaven a crown is waiting for me" (2 Timothy 4:6–8 TLB).

The Bible says that our heavenly Father is the God of peace. That means He is the Source of peace. There is a mistaken idea among some that peace is the absence of problems and suffering, but Jesus tell us we will always have problems on earth. But the peace He gives is His presence. With His indwelling presence, you have inner peace no matter what's happening around you.

If you know the peace of God in Jesus, pause right now and thank Him for the gift of His presence, His peace, and His promise of heaven.

If you do not yet have His peace, is there any good reason you can't pause right now and ask Him to come into your life? That's what my friend did. And that's why she had complete peace in the face of death. That's what Dr. Collins did. That's what Paul did. That's what I did and millions of others too. Make today the day you begin to be at peace with God for eternity.

Related Scriptures from 2 Timothy

The time of my death is near. I have fought the good fight, I have finished the race, and I have remained faithful. And now the prize awaits me.

(2 Timothy 4:6–8 NLT)

[Jesus] broke the power of death and illuminated the way to life and immortality through the Good News.

(2 Timothy 1:10 NLT)

Other Related Scriptures

Then you will experience God's peace, which exceeds anything we can understand. His peace will guard your hearts and minds as you live in Christ Jesus.

(Philippians 4:7 NLT)

I [Jesus] am leaving you with a gift—peace of mind and heart. And the peace I give is a gift the world cannot give. So don't be troubled or afraid.

(John 14:27 NLT)

What Is God Saying to You?

What does the fact that Paul could have peace while awaiting his execution say about the nature and character of God?

What are some things people do to try to find inner peace? Why don't they work?

Dear Father, the more I get to know You, the more I see that there is no real peace apart from Your presence. Thank You for being willing to be present in my life. Amen.

Get to Know God through Titus

A Brief Overview

TITUS WAS MENTIONED in Paul's other letters thirteen times. He was one of Paul's most trusted fellow ministers. When Paul left Antioch for the historic, doctrine-changing Jerusalem Conference, he took Titus, a Gentile, to serve as an example of one accepted by grace without circumcision (see Galatians 2:1–3). Titus worked with Paul at Ephesus and Corinth, helping the churches, and collecting money for the poor Christians in Jerusalem (see 2 Corinthians 2:12–13; 7:5–6; 8:6).

Paul then visited Crete, a mountainous and fertile island 150 miles in length and thirty-five miles in width. Paul left Titus in Crete to instruct the leaders of the several churches they had previously started.

Paul next went to Nicopolis in southern Greece (see Titus 3:12). When he learned how discouraged Titus was from his difficulties with the Cretans, Paul wrote this letter to encourage and instruct him between AD 62 and 67: "I left you on the island of Crete so you could complete our work there and appoint elders in each town as I instructed you" (Titus1:5 NLT).

Titus is valuable for us today in knowing God's principles concerning properly organizing a congregation, staying true to the teachings of Jesus, and relating to the community and world. Paul warned Titus to not be so worried with the church's structure, system, or appearance but instead to focus on its spirit, beliefs, and Christlike activities in the world.

Churches in Titus's day and ours are tempted by culture to focus more on the forms of worship—the ever-changing types of music, ceremonies, structures, and building designs—and less on the unchanging, absolute norms provided by Jesus.

As you read the letter to Titus, you begin to see the heart of God, the importance of staying true to his Word, and His way of caring for His wayward children. You'll see how Paul emphasizes the importance of balancing the right beliefs and the right spirit.

An Inspirational Theme of Titus

Can You Be Right and Wrong at the Same Time?

My southern-belle wife, Phyllis, makes the world's best pecan pie. Are you imagining it? Well then, imagine this: what if she brings the pie to me, places her right hand behind my head and smushes that fabulous pecan pie in my face. How do you suppose I would like that pie?

That's the way some Christians deliver the good food of God's truth to people with whom they disagree—family members, friends, people doing and saying bad things. No matter how good, true, or right you are, your words are no better than the way you deliver them. Even if you're trying to correct wrong, speak up against terrible teachings, or straighten out immoral behavior, how you deliver your message makes all the difference.

That's what the apostle Paul told Titus in Paul's now famous letter to the young pastor. Titus had gone to the rugged island of Crete to train the new Christian congregation in how to deal with their immoral friends and family members. Paul began his message by expressing his sympathy for Titus in dealing with rebellious, egocentric people who claimed to be Christians. Paul said, "[I know] The people of Crete are all liars, cruel animals, and lazy gluttons . . . they claim they know God, but they deny him by the way they live" (Titus 1:12,16 NLT).

But Paul gave Titus more than sympathy. He gave him some excellent advice on how to relate to such people. He said, "Remind the believers to . . . be obedient, always ready to do what is good . . . not slander anyone and . . . avoid quarreling . . . be gentle and show true humility to everyone" (Titus 3:1–3 NLT).

As in Titus's world, you and I constantly see on TV, the internet, and even in our own communities plenty of things people are doing and saying that we as Jesus followers don't just dislike but detest. If you're like me, you get emotionally upset about such wrongs. You know how shameful and harmful such things are.

But the questions you must ask yourself are this: How should I respond? How can I help make a difference and not just express my frustration? How can I disagree without being obnoxiously disagreeable?

Here are a few things Paul told Titus to do. And I believe Paul saw this same approach in the life of our Lord Jesus.

1. Show people you care. Paul said, "Be obedient" (see Titus 3:1–8). Before people will hear you or change, they most see you walk your talk. Be obedient and consistent in your Jesus-like spirit.
2. Prepare your heart. Paul said, "Be ready" (see Titus 3:1–2). You'll want to convince them they're wrong. Before

speaking, give Jesus control of your heart. Your heart must speak louder than your beliefs.

3. Look for common ground. Paul said, "Don't slander" (see Titus 3:2). Find places where you agree. Avoid shaming, putting them down, or appearing superior.
4. Appreciate their struggle. Paul said, "Avoid quarrelling" (see Titus 3:9). Arguing is of no value. Convince them you understand their position and want to be close even if you can't agree on things.
5. Ask permission to share your ideas. Paul said, "Be gentle and humble" (see Titus 3:2). Don't demand control. Be patient. Give God room to speak. Ask permission to briefly share your views and why you believe what you do. Assure them you don't expect them to agree. You just want them to better understand your ideas and heart.

The Bible says, "Each of us will give an account of ourselves to God. Therefore, let us stop passing judgment on one another" (Romans 14:12–13 NIV). If someone is saying or doing something the Bible says is wrong, you're not being judgmental in explaining to them what's right from your perspective. But you are being judgmental and wrong if your way of sharing with them makes them feel stupid, heartless, or worthless and makes you appear to be morally superior.

Charles Spurgeon said it right: "The greatest enemy to human souls is the self-righteous spirit." Decide right now to let the Spirit of Christ make you as passionate about the way you speak as you are about what you speak. And may I add, "Please, don't ever throw your good pie in anyone's face."

Related Scriptures from Titus

You must teach these things and encourage the believers to do them. You have the authority to correct them when necessary, so don't let anyone disregard what you say.

(Titus 2:15 NLT)

They must not slander anyone and must avoid quarreling. Instead, they should be gentle and show true humility to everyone.

(Titus 3:2 NLT)

Other Related Scriptures

A gentle response defuses anger, but a sharp tongue kindles a temper-fire.

(Proverbs 15:1 MSG)

You must be compassionate, just as your Father is compassionate.

(Luke 6:36 NLT)

What Is God Saying to You?

In the book of Titus, we are told how to deal with those who do not follow God's way. What do these instructions tell us about God's way of dealing with people?

Think of someone you know who has been doing something wrong for a long while. What are some things Jesus would probably say to them?

Dear Father, the more I get to know You, the more I see that it pleases You for me to act and speak with the compassion of Your Son, my Lord. Help me to allow Your spirit to work in me. Amen.

Get to Know God through Philemon

A Brief Overview

THE LETTER TO PHILEMON is Paul's shortest letter, only one chapter in our Bible. It is unique in that it was written to a new believer, a wealthy businessman who had accepted Jesus as his Savior under Paul's preaching.

The letter is a heartwarming appeal from Paul to Philemon, who, before he was saved, owned a slave named Onesimus. Slavery was a common practice in the Roman Empire at that time. In fact, there were some sixty million slaves in the Empire, which was half of the total population.

The slave owner, Philemon, lived in Colossae but had travelled on business to Ephesus, where he met Paul sharing the saving message of Jesus. When Philemon accepted Christ, he returned to his hometown and opened his house as the meeting place for the first Colossian congregation.

Prior to Philemon's conversion, one of his slaves had stolen some of his money and run away to hide in the big city of Rome. As was often the case, the slave Onesimus was caught and put in jail. Providentially, he shared the cell with Paul. As Onesimus awaited his punishment before being sent back to his owner, Paul led him to Christ.

During his time with Paul, Onesimus experienced the transformed witness of Paul, who was unlike anyone he had ever met—a man chained to a dungeon wall facing death but free in his heart and soul, and a man who spoke of real freedom and eternal life in Christ Jesus.

Eventually, Paul paid Onesimus's debt and asked him to return to his master, Philemon, and carry this letter to him. In the letter, Paul asked Philemon to forgive Onesimus and welcome him back not as a slave but as a brother in Christ. This request was Paul's way of testing the integrity of Philemon's conversion. Paul was reminding Philemon that Jesus forgave him and set him free. Now it was time for him to prove that his decision to follow Jesus was real.

The letter to Philemon is a picture of the character of God who cares more about our attitudes and actions than our appearances and words.

An Inspirational Theme of Philemon

The Proof Is in the Pudding

Have you ever chosen a dessert because it looked like it would be absolutely delicious, only to take your first bite and discover it was surprisingly tasteless? I have, and it sure is disappointing.

A lady once made a bowl of pudding, poured it into a gorgeous bowl, and served it to her guest on a beautifully decorated table. Because the dessert looked good but was simply bland, she wrote this familiar old proverb: the proof is in the pudding. Actually, I like it better the way she originally wrote it: the proof of the pudding is in the tasting.

This phrase is a way of stating a profound biblical truth that echoes throughout the scriptures—the proof that one's faith in God is genuine is in the testing. Our Lord Jesus was never impressed with appearances. Nor was He fooled by fake religion. For Him, the genuineness of one's religion, one's love, one's faith was always seen in the testing, the suffering, the cost.

Paul the apostle first learned that important lesson from understanding how much it cost our Lord to be faithful to his Father. Then Paul learned it firsthand, again and again, in the laboratory of his own faithful service.

Paul wrote this letter to test the genuineness of the wealthy businessman's faith by asking Philemon to forgive Onesimus and accept him as a free man and as a brother in Christ. Paul reminded Philemon that Jesus had forgiven him for all of his sins and set him free. So would he now do the same for Onesimus? Was his faith real or just a show? Would he reach out to his slave and treat him as an equal? It would cost him money and pride. Would his faith pass the test?

Today, the times and circumstances are different. But will your own faith pass the test? Your Lord is always gracious and faithful. You can count on Him. He doesn't just say He loves you. He is faithful to do what He says. But can He count on you?

So, the question is clear: this week, will your actions prove the genuineness of your love for God? As God's Spirit puts someone who is wounded because of life's circumstances, injustices, bad health, or bad choices near you, will you be God's Philemon by giving a helping hand, a caring voice, or a listening ear as an instrument of God?

Be sure that your faith in Jesus not only appears good but is good, too, because the proof of your faith is in the testing.

Related Scriptures from Philemon

[Philemon,] Your love has given me [Paul] much joy and comfort, my brother, for your kindness has often refreshed the hearts of God's people.

(Philemon 1:7 NLT)

If [Onesimus the slave] has wronged you in any way or owes you anything, charge it to me . . . I will repay it. And I won't mention that you owe me your very soul.

(Philemon 1:18–19 NLT)

Other Related Scriptures

These trials will show that your faith is genuine. It is being tested as fire tests and purifies gold.

(1 Peter 1:7 NLT)

[Christians] are being tested by many troubles, and they are . . . filled with abundant joy, which has overflowed in rich generosity.

(2 Corinthians 8:2 NLT)

What Is God Saying to You?

What does the story of Philemon and Onesimus tell us about God's desire regarding freedom?

What are some things that motivate you to try to help free people from the things that enslave them, restrict them, and keep them from being all God wants for them?

Dear Father, the more I get to know You, the more I see You are full of compassion and grace, freeing me to serve You and Your children. Thank You. Amen.

Get to Know God through Hebrews

A Brief Overview

ALTHOUGH THE KING JAMES VERSION of the Bible has the heading "Epistle of Paul the Apostle to the Hebrews," some question Paul's authorship. But evidence shows that most of the churches following the writing of Hebrews believed Paul wrote the book. Although the authorship is not certain, the value and inspiration of the book has always been respected as God's Word. It was written sometime between AD 64 and 70 and named Hebrews because it includes so many references to Hebrew customs and Old Testament practices.

To many, Hebrews is second in the Bible in its importance to the letter to the Romans. It clearly presents Jesus as the divine Son of God, a man who was fully human and God's High Priest to whom all people can go to discover how to have a close relationship with God (see Hebrews 4:14–16). Jesus is seen as the final and perfect High Priest offering Himself as the sinless sacrifice, taking our place and paying for our sins (Hebrews 7:24–26; 9:28).

The message of the superiority of Jesus as our High Priest was especially valued by Jewish Christians who were struggling under Nero's persecution in Rome. The book assures those believers that they do not need to return to keeping the law to be saved. They could face suffering with confidence that Jesus was with them and would reward them for their faithfulness.

An Inspirational Theme of Hebrews

First, Make That All-Important Call

My wife, Phyllis, and I like to travel to other countries and explore new places. What we don't like is getting lost, wasting time trying to figure out which way to go, or putting ourselves in unnecessary danger. So, before we take a trip, we make that all-important call to hire a guide who knows his or her way around and can keep us safe. I can assure you, there have been many times we were grateful we had a knowledgeable guide.

If you think about it, in many ways life is like a long trip. It's full of wonderful, surprising, and enjoyable experiences. But let's be honest, sometimes it also has its washed-out bridges, inconvenient roadblocks, costly accidents, and confusing and even heartbreaking situations.

In one sense, the Bible is a record of true stories about painful losses, heartbreaking conflicts, and confusing places God's children got themselves into when they chose to travel down life's rough roads without the helpful guidance God offers. But the Bible is also a record of our caring God loving us and being faithful to us even when, time and again, we've turned our backs on His leadership and foolishly struck out on our own.

If you had a serious, deadly disease, you would never consider trying to figure out what to do on your own. You wouldn't even think about taking your chances and going it alone. You would want an expert in the field, someone who had excellent knowledge, recognized skills, and had been down that road many times before. That's what the book of Hebrews is about. It's considered by some to be the most important book in the Bible in explaining how God has provided us with the perfect guide for our life journey.

In ancient times, God chose a few people to serve as priests, a word which meant people who served as navigators, mediators, or guides for people who needed direction. Priests gave up their other jobs for full-time studying of God's Word, praying, getting close to Him, learning His ways, and preparing themselves to be God's guides for His children. When the common people faced problems and didn't know which way to go, they went to their priests for guidance.

The Bible not only talks about priests but also speaks of a High Priest. The word *high* literally meant the best possible, most qualified priest, the perfect guide. That's what the Bible means when it refers to Jesus as our High Priest. In the book of Hebrews, we read:

> We have a great High Priest who has entered heaven, Jesus the Son of God, let us hold firmly to what we believe. This High Priest of ours understands our weaknesses, for he faced all of the same testings we do, yet he did not sin. So let us come boldly to the throne of our gracious God. There we will receive his mercy, and we will find grace to help us when we need it most.
>
> (Hebrews 4:14–16 NLT)

You can see why Jesus is the perfect Guide. Look at His record. He loves you no matter what you've done. He is able to do anything you need. He knows everything, including what's best for you. And He will be with you all the time and in every situation.

As you look forward to the rest of your journey, don't forget each day to make that all-important call. Ask Jesus to be your daily guide.

Related Scriptures from Hebrews

It was necessary for [Jesus] to be made in every respect like us, his brothers and sisters, so that he could be our merciful and faithful High Priest before God.

(Hebrews 2:17 NLT)

God qualified [Jesus] as a perfect High Priest, and he became the source of eternal salvation for all those who obey him.

(Hebrews 5:9 NLT)

Other Related Scriptures

I [Jesus] am the light of the world. If you follow me, you won't have to walk in darkness, because you will have the light that leads to life.

(John 8:12 NLT)

Jesus called out to them, "Come, follow me."

(Matthew 4:19 NLT)

What Is God Saying to You?

God gave us His Son as our Savior and Redeemer. What does that say about God's intention and His activity with His children?

In making everyday decisions, what are some reasons you follow your conscience rather than making sure you're following the Spirit of Jesus?

Dear Father, the more I get to know You, the more I see that You are the perfect guide for me. Help me to follow You and recognize Your voice. Thank You. Amen.

Get to Know God through James

A Brief Overview

THE EPISTLE OF JAMES is likely the first letter written that became part of our Bible's New Testament. It's part of a group called the General Epistles (which also include 1 and 2 Peter, 1, 2, and 3 John, and Jude). They are called general epistles because they are not written to any particular individual or church but to all Christians and churches for all time.

James, the brother of Jesus, was the author of this letter and a prominent leader in the mother church at Jerusalem. Members of that congregation included many of Jesus's apostles and other followers of the Lord while He was on the earth. That body of believers helped start and fund many churches in the first century.

James's recognition as a key leader among first-century Christians is especially clear because he was chosen to make a decisive speech in the famous Jerusalem Council in AD 49 where James, along with Peter and Paul, affirmed the decision to take the gospel message to Gentiles and not just to Jews. It was also at that strategic council that Peter called Paul one of the pillars of the church (see Galatians 2:9).

The book of James is written in a style much like the book of Proverbs, focusing on practical instructions and descriptions of a genuine life of faith in Christ Jesus. Like the authors of the wisdom in the Old Testament, James encourages believers to behave in a manner worthy of being called God's people. He often gives authoritative and direct commands about living holy lives. He is not apologetic about the necessity for Christians to act differently from the rest of the world. For James, if some claim to have faith in Jesus but demonstrate no evidence of a changed life, their faith is not real but is worthless and harmful to themselves and the body of the church (see James 2:17).

In his introduction, James positions himself as a bondservant, a slave of God. His self-image is unmistakably seen in the way he repeatedly recognizes the practical or servant-oriented message of the book. James hammers home his theme: authentic faith always produces authentic acts. He is committed to what he considers the central message of Jesus. In fact, at times James's message sounds similar to Jesus's Sermon on the Mount in which Jesus pointedly denounces two-faced faith—acting one way in public and the opposite in private.

Like a preacher driving home his point, James gives numerous examples to illustrate his theme: Genuine faith withstands painful trials. Authentic faith calls on God for wisdom. Real faith bridles the tongue, turns its back on evil. It visits orphans and widows. It never plays favorites. James insists that a life of true faith is comprehensive, affecting every dimension of our lives and motivating us to share the gospel message with everyone.

James is not legalistic or cold hearted. He is sympathetic with those who occasionally stumble. But he unapologetically condemns blatant hypocrisy, making it clear that people with a genuine faith in Jesus do not live duplicitous lives. They do not cohabitate with those who do not live their lives consistent with the humble, servant lifestyle of Jesus. For James, faith without Christlike behavior is deadly.

An Inspirational Theme of James

Enemy #1

What is Enemy #1 for Christianity? If you had to guess, what would you say is the number one reason unbelievers turn their backs on the church? Let me answer that question with this true story.

Mahatma Gandhi was a London-trained Indian lawyer, a dedicated Hindu, and a nonviolent resistance champion who led a successful campaign for India's independence and inspired freedom movements for people around the world. In Chuck Stanford's article in the Hawaii Tribune Herald, "Why did Gandhi say, 'If it weren't for Christians, I'd be a Christian,'" he tells about a time in Gandhi's life when he became so impressed with the teachings of Jesus that he read the Bible and decided to experience Christianity firsthand by visiting a Christian church in Calcutta. Unfortunately, when he tried to attend, he was stopped at the front door and told he could not enter because it was for whites only. From that experience, Gandhi rejected the Christian faith and later wrote those heartbreaking words: "I'd be a Christian if it were not for the Christians."

The harshest words that have ever been spoken by the Son of Man, the Lord Jesus, were about hypocrisy. In fact, the most significant words of reproof He ever uttered were toward the most religious people on the planet:

> Woe to you, teachers of the law and Pharisees, you hypocrites! You are like whitewashed tombs, which look beautiful on the outside but on the inside are full of the bones of the dead and everything unclean. In the same way, on the outside you appear to people as righteous but on the inside you are full of hypocrisy and wickedness . . . You snakes! You brood of vipers.
>
> (Matthew 23:27–28, 33 NIV)

Hypocrisy was serious business to Jesus.

James says faith is more than just intellectual knowledge. Faith is something you do. It's active, not passive. Real faith involves making a commitment to trust in Jesus. This means we cannot earn our salvation. The Bible says, "For it is by grace you have been saved, through faith—and this is not from yourselves, it is the gift of God—not by works, so that no one can boast." (Ephesians 2:8–9 NIV). What James is saying is that our belief and commitment to Jesus are reflected in the things we do. Our good deeds are evidence of our real and trusting faith.

Maybe you're struggling to make sense of why your relationship with Jesus doesn't seem to be working. Could it be you're not putting your faith into practice? Consider James's explanation: "Just as the body is dead when there is no spirit in it, so faith is dead if it is not the kind that results in good deeds" (James 2:26 TLB).

The word you see James use over and over is *do*. His message is clear: real faith shows up in your lifestyle. Your faith should change you and the things you do. On this earth, even with God's grace and instruction, no one will ever be perfect, but we must strive to make our walk and talk be the same and pleasing to our God.

Hypocrisy causes some people to turn their backs on the church and on Jesus. No one wants to be the reason another refuses Jesus. The secret to avoiding being a hypocrite is to practice humility and do your best to please God. As you begin each day, confess your faults, weaknesses, and sins to God. Throughout the day practice comparing yourself only to Jesus. Find a way to do some small act of kindness for someone without expecting anything in return. Each day, promise your Savior, Jesus, "I will not be a stumbling block to anyone."

Related Scriptures from James

Faith by itself isn't enough. Unless it produces good deeds, it is dead and useless.

(James 2:17 NLT)

So you see, we are shown to be right with God by what we do, not by faith alone.

(James 2:24 NLT)

Other Related Scriptures

If you love me, obey my commandments.

(John 14:15 NLT)

Loving God means keeping his commandments, and his commandments are not burdensome.

(1 John 5:3 NLT)

What Is God Saying to You?

What does God's view of hypocrisy in the book of James say about His character?

What are you doing to make sure that your faith is alive and vibrant and healthy?

Dear Father, the more I get to know You, the more I see that You always do more than just speak to me. You show me Your love in acts of love. Help me to do the same. Thank You. Amen.

Get to Know God through 1 Peter

A Brief Overview

UNLIKE THE LETTERS BY PAUL that were written primarily to individuals or churches, the book of 1 Peter was written to all believers in general. It was written around AD 60, making it one of the earlier letters in the New Testament. Peter's three main purposes in writing this letter were to encourage suffering Christians by providing them with hope, to call them to personal holy lives in the face of their immoral cultures, and to assure them that each person is a chosen child of God.

In chapters 1 and 2, Peter reminds us that as God's chosen, all Christians should expect suffering. We ought to consider suffering and persecution a normal part of living, as it was for Jesus. Peter explains that we are completely secure in Christ as we go through all forms of suffering because "[Jesus] personally carried our sins in his body on the cross so that we can be dead to sin and live for what is right. By his wounds you are healed" (1 Peter 2:24 NLT).

In chapters 3 to 5, Peter encourages those going through difficult times to focus on living holy lives. God had chosen Israel as the nation through which He would bring His Son to earth. He chose them to be a light to the world. But being chosen came with requirements just as it did with the Christ followers in Peter's day. They were to be holy. By *holy*, Peter means to live lives that are separate, noticeably different from one's culture. He says, "In your hearts revere Christ as Lord.

Always be prepared to give an answer to everyone who asks you to give the reason for the hope that you have. But do this with gentleness and respect" (1 Peter 3:15 NIV).

He also warns Christians dealing with suffering and personal attacks to "Stay alert! Watch out for your great enemy, the devil. He prowls around like a roaring lion, looking for someone to devour" (1 Peter 5:8 NLT). Peter also offers encouragement and hope to those who are suffering with seemingly no way out. He tells them to remain faithful as witnesses for God and to trust Him with their souls because they have a sure home with Jesus in heaven.

Peter wrote his letter shortly after the bloodthirsty Emperor Nero came to the throne and began the most brutal and widespread persecution Christians had ever known. While reading 1 Peter, it is important to remember that his words were not theory. They were written for people facing possible death by a man who soon faced death as a martyr.

An Inspirational Theme of 1 Peter

No One Ever Chose Me

Most children can hardly wait for recess and game time during the school day. I was different. I hated first grade because of recess and game time. I was shy, skinny, unathletic, and nonaggressive—not the kind of guy to be first choice for the team. Or any choice. So game time meant that I would be sidelined, left to stand alone while the others had a fun time and even jeered at me. Not being chosen leaves you feeling sad and worthless.

Peter knew about being chosen. Here he was, an uneducated, ordinary fisherman going about his daily work and trying to provide for his family. He probably studied the weather and learned the best places to cast his net. Dealing with smelly fish, often pulling in empty nets, and repairing them was not exciting work, but Peter trudged on day after day—that is until the day he met Jesus on the shores of the Sea of Galilee.

Something drew him to Jesus, and when Jesus invited Peter to join him to be a fisher of men, Peter left his nets and followed. He did not know then all that it would mean to have Jesus choose him, but he followed anyway (see Matthew 4:18–20).

Perhaps Jesus looked at Peter and thought about what it took to be a fisherman—patience, endurance, willingness to do the dirty work, discernment, and determination. He knew that every day fishermen risked their lives to do their jobs. Those were the kind of followers Jesus chose. And later in Jesus's ministry, He told Peter, whose name meant "rock," that it was Peter's rock-solid kind of faith that He would use to build His church, so that it could never be destroyed. We can imagine that Peter had a new sense about being chosen.

Possibly today, you're feeling bored or desolate with your life and relationships. Maybe you do not have the good feelings that come with being special or chosen, and you do not sense that you have much worth. You may be feeling that life is not fair. Those are feelings. The truth is no one else may choose to give you an award or put you on the team, but God has chosen you. He made you different from anyone else who has ever walked on this planet—a different personal history, personality, life experiences, abilities, and characteristics. And the one thing you are better at than anyone else is being you—the you God designed you to be. No one else on earth can do that and fulfill His purpose for your life.

Just remember, before you even considered choosing God, He had already chosen you: "God the Father knew you and chose you long ago, and his Spirit has made you holy" (1 Peter 1:2 NLT). He loves you, has great expectations of you, wants to live in you and take you to heaven to be with Him for eternity. So if you're standing on the sidelines today feeling like you're not special or worthy, spend some time reading what God's Word has to say about that and talk to Him about your feelings. After all, you've already been chosen by the God of the universe.

Related Scriptures from 1 Peter

You are a chosen people. You are royal priests, a holy nation, God's very own possession.

(1 Peter 2:9 NLT)

But now you must be holy in everything you do, just as God who chose you is holy.

(1 Peter 1:15 NLT)

Other Related Scriptures

Even before he made the world, God loved us and chose us in Christ to be holy and without fault in his eyes.

(Ephesians 1:4 NLT)

Since God chose you to be the holy people he loves, you must clothe yourselves with tenderhearted mercy, kindness, humility, gentleness, and patience.

(Colossians 3:12 NLT)

What Is God Saying to You?

When Jesus chooses an ordinary fisherman like Peter to be His disciple, what does that say about God's character and His plan?

No matter how poorly you may be treated on this earth, what are some reasons you can be confident that God has chosen you and considers you special to Him?

Dear Father, the better I get to know You, the more I see that You have chosen me even when I do not feel special at all. Thank You. Amen.

Get to Know God through 2 Peter

A Brief Overview

THERE ARE MANY SIMILARITIES in 1 and 2 Peter. But the primary difference in Peter's second letter is his emphasis on eternity, that precious gift of eternal security through our Lord Jesus even when we face suffering. Peter uses the Greek word we translate *precious* only twice in 1 Peter but sixteen times in his second letter. Peter was known for being a big, rough fisherman. So when he continually talks about what is precious to him, it is worth taking note.

As the severity of the Christian persecution in the final years of the tyrant Nero's reign increased, Peter decided to write his second letter. In it, he sought to share God's compassionate support and instruction to the first-century Christians. He encouraged believers not to passively endure suffering but to be assertive in their faith by living holy lives of service and witness in the middle of their suffering. While many saw only gloom, Peter saw reasons for Christians to look beyond their suffering to eternity.

Not long before this persecution, Peter had been by Jesus's side every step of Jesus's journey to the cross. By observing Jesus's every act and attitude, Peter knew firsthand what it meant to live a holy life amid a hate-filled and hurtful culture. Jesus set the example for all of us, and Peter used Jesus as our example. He reminds us that Jesus always has an eternal perspective. While helping people and staying true to His God-give mission, Jesus kept His eye on this destination—heaven.

Second Peter was written for all Christians in all times, not just a local group in the first century. When he wrote this letter, Peter had not yet been arrested. But shortly afterward, Peter was martyred around AD 66 to 68. Yet his letter remains with its powerful yet simple message that gives us hope no matter what happens: be faithful to your Lord, always keeping your heart on your eternal home.

An Inspirational Theme in 2 Peter

Everything You Need

I had a close friend in the ministry whom many would consider a modern-day Job, his family's story making headlines during the AIDS crisis. The suffering, the sickness, and loss he experienced over a few years were unfathomable, yet I observed that his faith and purpose remained strong as he continued to live out his calling from God. He walked in grief and sadness, but he also walked in peace and with grace. His life taught many of us a valuable lesson in dealing with adversity.

The truth is there is no human who has not experienced difficult circumstances, fears, and loss. Jesus forewarned us that it would be that way in this world. So if you cannot avoid the pain and suffering, what is it that you need most when you're staring them in the face? Relief? Hope? A shoulder to cry on? Someone to listen to you? Someone to deliver you from the mess you're in? Something in the future to look forward to?

In his second letter, Peter was writing to people who were suffering and being persecuted by a deranged and hate-filled

Roman emperor. They were looking for relief and a hope to hold on to. Peter was no stranger to perilous times. He had walked with Jesus and had seen how humans treated the Son of God. He had followed Jesus up the hill of Golgotha to witness the unimaginable humiliation and pain inflicted upon Him. Peter lived in the shadow of knowing that he might follow the same route of persecution His Lord had endured. Be assured the words he wrote in this letter were not theoretical, theological, scholarly phrases using well-chosen and lovely words. They were the rough-hewn thoughts of a man who was living it. He knew what worked and what would see these people through their hard times.

Peter was a rugged man, big and strong, an outspoken fisherman, but it was not his strength that motivated Jesus to change his name from Simon to Peter. It was Peter's faith, his commitment, his deep and personal relationship with Jesus. It was that relationship and the promise of an eternity in heaven with Jesus that kept Peter forging ahead. And that is what Peter wrote to these early Christians and to us, always reminding us to keep our focus on Jesus and our eternity. Peter knew that focusing on Jesus and heaven enables us to look through and beyond our present circumstances, as horrible as they may be. We can look forward in hope with gratitude, generosity, and graciousness instead of fear, anger, and cynicism. We have a choice as to how we live with and through our situations.

Do you believe Jesus can provide what you need? Peter did. He banked his life on it. He said, "For as you know [Jesus] better, he will give you, through his great power, *everything you need* for living a truly good life: he even shares his own glory and his own goodness with us!" (2 Peter 1:3 TLB, emphasis mine). He also said, "We are looking forward to the new heavens and new earth he has promised, a world filled with God's righteousness" (2 Peter 3:13 NLT).

You can have peace no matter your circumstances, and you can have the assurance of your eternity in heaven. The choice is yours.

Related Scriptures from 2 Peter

So don't lose a minute in building on what you've been given, complementing your basic faith with good character, spiritual understanding, alert discipline, passionate patience, reverent wonder, warm friendliness, and generous love, each dimension fitting into and developing the others.

(2 Peter 1:5–7 MSG)

We are looking forward to the new heavens and new earth he has promised, a world filled with God's righteousness.

(2 Peter 3:13 NLT)

Other Related Scriptures

For we know that when this earthly tent we live in is taken down (that is, when we die and leave this earthly body), we will have a house in heaven, an eternal body made for us by God himself and not by human hands.

(2 Corinthians 5:1 NLT)

Be happy! Yes, leap for joy! For a great reward awaits you in heaven.

(Luke 6:23 NLT)

What Is God Saying to You?

What do the promise of His presence and the assurance of heaven that Jesus gives us say about our God?

When you are suffering, what are some things you can do to help you stay close to Jesus and keep your focus on heaven?

Dear Father, the better I get to know You, the more I see that You want to be close to me and want me to keep my heart set on my eternal home with You. Thank You. Amen.

Get to Know God through 1 John

A Brief Overview

THE AUTHOR OF THIS LETTER WAS JOHN, the beloved apostle who was considered the disciple closest to our Lord. Because of John's unique relationship with Jesus, his letter had significant authority in the early church. Also, John spoke with unusual personal passion and influence as seen in his book now known as the Gospel of John. John's focus in writing was always as a reporter. He saw himself as a blessed eyewitness to the life, ministry, miracles, and words of Jesus, stating, "We proclaim to you what we ourselves have actually seen and heard" (1 John 1:3 NLT).

First John was written around AD 90 while John was exiled to the island of Patmos. It was also from there that the elderly John wrote the Revelation. In his lifetime, he had witnessed the remarkable growth of the church and the body of believers throughout that part of the world, but he had also seen the hardships Christians faced in those early years of development.

In this first letter, John expressed some of these struggles through parallelisms that describe the challenges we all face: Christ versus antichrists, light versus darkness, truth versus falsehood, righteousness versus sin, love of the Father versus love of the world, and the new birth in Christ versus the old way of works. His list of contrasts was not meant to be comprehensive, but it did reveal the complicated and counterculture world Christ followers faced.

Although John was realistic about the problems of his day, he was also realistic about the certain knowledge we have in God's love. John made it clear by his deliberate repetition that true love and true knowing can only come from having a personal relationship with God. John used the translated word *know* thirty-one times in this short letter. He encouraged all Christ followers to demonstrate their loving knowledge of God by loving one another: "Dear friends, let us continue to love one another, for love comes from God. Anyone who loves is a child of God and knows God" (1 John 4:7 NLT).

John was consistent and persistent. He wanted his fellow believers to experience true fellowship with God and one another and to have a solid foundation upon with they could handle their sufferings. But he knew all that was possible only if Christians removed their own selfishness in favor of knowing God intimately and putting Him first. To enable the struggling young Christians to reach that goal, John focused on three main issues: demonstrating true, Christlike love toward one another, standing firm in the teachings of Jesus in the face of false teachers, and reaffirming to weak believers that they can know they have eternal life.

First John has some of the most quotable verses in the New Testament. For centuries it has been a favorite of Christians the world over because it is succinct, powerful, heartfelt, and contains possibly the most concise presentation of the gospel message found anywhere in the New Testament.

An Inspirational Theme of 1 John

How Can You Be Sure?

My doctor insists on an annual checkup. That means a personal visit, an interrogation, an examination, and the all-important bloodwork. I can try to convince the doctor that I am doing well and that I am following my diet and doing my exercises, but the bloodwork will tell the absolute story. Those labs will reveal many things about my health: nutritional deficiencies, the presence of inflammation in my system, the amount of cholesterol in my blood stream, kidney function, liver function, and the presence of chemicals and enzymes in my body. The results of those labs will let my doctor know if what I am saying about my health is accurate.

Sometimes, I wish there was a test to evaluate my relationship with Jesus, to see how truly close I am to Him, and to see if I am doing the right things to foster that relationship. Well, John says there is such a test:

> Dear friends, let us practice loving each other, for love comes from God and those who are loving and kind show that they are the children of God, and that they are getting to know him better. But if a person isn't loving and kind, it shows that he doesn't know God—for God is love.
>
> (1 John 4:7–8 TLB)

John says to truly know God, who is Love, means we will love each other.

If there was such a thing as a Know-and-Love Meter that tested the way we know and love, I am certain the world's meter would register differently than God's. Pop culture would have you think that love and intimacy are just feelings—emotional, transitory highs having more to do with a physical connection with someone. But God's ideas of intimacy and love are so much deeper and more satisfying. Knowing God and loving Him have a direct correlation to our relationships with others.

Do you want to be sure that you have a knowing, loving, intimate relationship with God that will carry over in your relationships with those He puts in your life? John gives us some guidelines. Ask yourself these questions.

- Am I keeping God's commandments?
- Do I confess that Jesus is God's Son and unashamedly talk about this with others?
- Do I desire God's will above what the world tells me to think?
- The Bible says perfect love casts fear away. Do I have fears?
- Do I have hatred in my heart for anyone?
- Do I see people in need and pass them by?
- Do I pray for others?
- Am I willing to invest myself in others as God invests Himself in me?

God desires a close, loving, intimate relationship with you: "What marvelous love the Father has extended to us! Just look at it—we're called the children of God! That's who we really are!" (1 John 3:1 MSG). That is almost beyond our comprehension—that we truly are the children of our most loving God.

John says, "No one has ever seen God; but if we love one another, God lives in us and his love is made complete in us" (1 John 4:12 NIV). God wants your life to reflect Him. He wants others to see the difference in your life through the way you live and love. So check your Know-and-Love meter, and then go. Live. Love. And rejoice that you are His child.

Related Scriptures from 1 John

So now we can tell who are children of God and who are children of the devil. Anyone who does not live righteously and does not love other believers does not belong to God.

(1 John 3:10 NLT)

If someone claims, "I know him well!" but doesn't keep his commandments, he's obviously a liar. His life doesn't match his words. But the one who keeps God's Word is the person in whom we see God's mature love. This is the only way to be sure we're in God. Anyone who claims to be intimate with God ought to live the same kind of life Jesus lived.

(1 John 2:4–6 MSG)

Other Related Scriptures

Learn to know the God of your ancestors intimately. Worship and serve him with your whole heart and a willing mind.

(1 Chronicles 28:9 NLT)

I am the Vine, you are the branches. When you're joined with me and I with you, the relation intimate and organic, the harvest is sure to be abundant.

(John 15:5 MSG)

What Is God Saying to You?

What does that fact that you can be a child of God say about His character?

When you are under pressure, what are some things you can do to help you stay close to Jesus in an intimate, loving way?

Dear Father, the better I get to know You, the more I see that You want to be close to me and You want my life to reflect my loving relationship with You so that others may see who You are. Help me to show Your love to the people You put in my life. Amen.

Get to Know God through 2 John

A Brief Overview

THE APOSTLE JOHN CLEARLY IDENTIFIED the primary recipients of his second letter: "I am writing to the chosen lady and to her children, whom I love in the truth—as does everyone else who knows the truth" (2 John 1 NLT). For many since the first century, that was a mysterious phrase. Was the chosen lady an actual woman, or did it serve as a metaphor for a church? No one can be sure, but regardless, the purpose and significance of God's Word through this letter is the same.

John wrote the letter from the island of Patmos in AD 90 shortly after his first letter. Focusing on the same themes, he strongly encourages believers throughout the region to maintain the same position he taught them in the first letter regarding the enemies of the truth. The main difference in the two letters and the motivation for the second letter is this: 1 John focuses on the importance of us having a close, loving relationship with God and one another, whereas 2 John focuses on guarding the truth of the gospel and helping to keep fellow Christians safe from false and misleading teachings. John even warns believers to protect their brothers and sisters in the faith and not to allow false teachers to teach in their gatherings: "If anyone comes to your meeting and does not teach the truth about Christ, don't invite that person into your home or give any kind of encouragement" (2 John 10 NLT). Because there were so many deceiving teachers, many of whom had penetrated the church, the apostle warns those who believe in Jesus and the gospel John has taught them to stay away from such frauds. He also encourages them to lovingly accept one another, but within the limits of truth.

The tiny letter reveals John's big heart. He had a sincere, pastoral concern to protect God's children from the harmful influence of Satan and his workers. As he did in his gospel and 1 John, the elder apostle continues to resound his main desire for them: "I am writing to remind you, dear friends, that we should love one another. This is not a new commandment, but one we have had from the beginning" (2 John 5 NLT). This clear reminder echoes the Lord Jesus's two greatest commandments—to love God and love one another (see Mark 12:30–31).

An Inspirational Theme of 2 John

How Can You Spot a Fake?

My first job was working in a Ben Franklin five-and-dime store, and one of the first things the manager taught me was how to spot counterfeit money. He taught me that most people who make counterfeit bills are good at it, and the only way to really spot a counterfeit bill is to know what a real one looks and feels like. Had I not received the training, I would have never noticed the difference between a fake and a genuine US treasury bill.

Do you know the name Glafira Rosales? In 2016 Maria Konnikova, author of *The Confidence Game*, told the story of how Rosales fooled the world's most sophisticated art collectors with her eighty-million-dollar art scam—the biggest fake-art con job in modern US history. Konnikova wrote of how

Rosales peddled the counterfeit artwork of Chinese immigrant Pei-Shen Qian, who imitated the styles of art masters, then aged the paintings using substances like tea or dirt from a vacuum cleaner. Imagine an imitator using dirt to fool even seasoned art dealers. Finally, the scam was revealed by those who knew the difference—the art experts who knew what the original true art pieces were.

Unfortunately, the same is true when it comes to spotting counterfeit beliefs—beliefs that are close to the truth but are not the truth, beliefs that look and sound good at first glance and first hearing but are harmful and deceptive. The only way to spot the counterfeit is to know what's really real. If experts can be fooled, how are the rest of us supposed to know the difference?

That was one of the main reasons the elder John wrote his second letter to the Christians—to instruct them how to know what was real. These early Christians had become confused as they were tempted to accept life-principles and beliefs that were not consistent with the words and life of Jesus. John warned them about such people: "If anyone comes to your meeting and does not teach the truth about Christ, don't invite that person into your home or give any kind of encouragement" (2 John 10 NLT).

But the question is this: how will you spot a fake if you are not certain of the truth? The answer to that is you won't. Not knowing the truth leaves you vulnerable to falling for foolish, dangerous ideas. Mark it down! If you don't nail down the truth, you will never be able to spot the fake stuff. Then the question becomes how do you nail down the truth?

The Bible says that the clearest way of nailing down the truth is to look to Jesus, who is the Truth. He claimed, "I am the truth" (John 14:6 NLT). Any teaching, beliefs, ideas, or practices that do not look and sound like Jesus are not the truth. They are fakes.

Knowing the truth is simple. It's simple because it does not require you to memorize doctrine or learn a thousand rules or study one hundred volumes on theology. It's simple because what is required is knowing Jesus intimately. But that's not so easy because knowing Jesus requires something of you. There's no way around it. You cannot know the truth accidentally or automatically. You must spend time immersing yourself, studying, listening, and meditating on Jesus's words, His life, and His stories. You must spend time with Him, talking and listening to Him. Read the writings of respected Bible teachers who encourage you to apply Jesus's teachings to your life. Knowing God's truth and applying it to our lives are not casual things.

Just remember, in our culture, counterfeiters, false teachers, and charlatans may come knocking on your door, but you don't have to invite them in and ask them to stay.

Related Scriptures from 2 John

Grace, mercy, and peace, which come from God the Father and from Jesus Christ—the Son of the Father—will continue to be with us who live in truth and love.

(2 John 3 NLT)

Anyone who wanders away from this teaching has no relationship with God. But anyone who remains in the teaching of Christ has a relationship with both the Father and the Son.

(2 John 9 NLT)

Other Related Scriptures

We are made right with God by placing our faith in Jesus Christ. And this is true for everyone who believes, no matter who we are.

(Romans 3:22 NLT)

It is this Good News that saves you if you continue to believe the message I told you—unless, of course, you believed something that was never true in the first place.

(1 Corinthians 15:2 NLT)

What Is God Saying to You?

What does John's message on the importance of truth say about God's character?

When you hear someone tell about their belief and you know it is not true, how do you come to that conclusion?

Dear Father, the better I get to know You, the more I see that You are my source for Truth and I can always count on You. Thank You. Amen.

Get to Know God through 3 John

A Brief Overview

THE APOSTLE JOHN WROTE this final of his three letters as he neared the end of his life. He had come a long way in his service of his Lord Jesus since the day Jesus called him and his brother James to leave their occupations as fishermen and become fulltime workers in his ministry. Records indicate that James was the first of the twelve apostles to die for his commitment to Jesus, but John lived longer than any other apostle and was looked up to with great respect and admiration. Peter said that John was "the one Jesus loved" (John 21:20 NLT). Clearly, the disciples felt that Jesus was closer to John than all the other eleven.

John wrote this challenging letter in AD 90 from his prison quarters on the island of Patmos, from which he also wrote his other letters and the Revelation. He addressed this letter to Gaius, a leader of one or more of the churches on the mainland. He commended Gaius for the hospitality and support he was giving to traveling Christian teachers.

In all of John's three letters, he focuses on the importance of the church leaders and families maintaining a loving and faithful fellowship patterned after the life and teachings of Jesus. Especially in his third letter, John asked the congregations to provide support and encouragement to those who were going out across the mainland spreading the message of Jesus.

John had also received a report about problems the pastors and followers were having because of a man named Diotrephes, who was misusing his leadership position. This kind of dissension among church leaders and brothers and sisters in Christ prompted John to write to Gaius, earnestly asking him to encourage all Christ followers to be true to the teachings and spirit of Jesus. He wrote, "Please continue providing for such teachers in a manner that pleases God" (3 John 6 NLT).

An Inspirational Theme of 3 John

Is Your Faith Inspiring or Infecting Others?

Not all bullies give black eyes. Some of them wound hearts and damage fellowship. It seems there was such a person in a church in Asia Minor. The apostle John had heard of the trouble this man named Diotrephes was causing and used him as an example of how misguided, prideful leadership can destroy the fellowship and witness of a church.

It appears that Diotrephes had qualities that led the Christians in his area to put him in a place of leadership. But as his authority grew, he began to misuse it, letting his power go to his head. He had become arrogant, dictatorial, and even refused to listen to the elder John's advice: "Diotrephes, who loves being in charge, denigrates my counsel" (3 John 9 MSG).

It was a common practice in that day for the local church to provide hospitality and support for fellow Christians who were what we would call missionaries. The local believers would invite the travelers into their homes and offer them hospitality and support for their work and travels. But Diotrephes refused to support these fellow believers. John wrote, "As if that weren't bad enough, he not only refuses hospitality to traveling Christians but tries to stop others from welcoming them. Worse yet, instead of inviting them in he throws them out" (3 John 10 MSG). In essence, Diotrephes had used his faith and his position to become a self-serving bully.

John wrote this letter to Gaius, the leader of a group of churches in this area, to remind him of a crucial truth: "Anyone who does what is good is from God. Anyone who does what is evil has not seen God" (3 John 11 NIV). The kind of good John spoke of was not just an occasional good deed, it was a life practice of doing good the way Jesus did. Diotrephes was not out and about doing good. His faith had become self-serving.

When Mother Teresa gave her life in sacrificial work helping impoverished people in India, people said it was a result of her faith. We are not all called to do what she did, but we are called to do good wherever we are. What about your faith? Is it healthy? Is it self-serving or other-serving? Are you motivated to do good so that others will see how good you are, or are you motivated to do good because you are grateful for God's goodness to you?

The best way to tell if we need to make changes to how we express our faith is not to compare it to some definition or to someone like Diotrephes but to compare it to the faith life of the One who is worthy of our faith—Jesus, the Son of God. When people witnessed the kind of faith He had in His Father, they were inspired to put their faith in Him. His faith was healthy and health producing. Jesus was welcoming, encouraging, truthful, humble, and inspiring. He was never discouraging, deceptive, or degrading.

Be careful of the dangers of spiritual pride. Don't allow it to make you self-serving. Instead, let your faith motivate you to be other-centered, always about doing good out of your gratitude for God's goodness to you. May your faith walk be one that would make John say, "Nothing could make me happier than getting good reports that my children continue diligently in the way of Truth!" (3 John 4 MSG).

Related Scriptures from 3 John

Friend, don't go along with evil. Model the good. The person who does good does God's work. The person who does evil falsifies God, doesn't know the first thing about God.

(3 John 11 MSG)

I have no greater joy than to hear that my children are walking in the truth.

(3 John 4 NIV)

Other Related Scriptures

Finally, all of you should be of one mind. Sympathize with each other. Love each other as brothers and sisters. Be tender-hearted, and keep a humble attitude.

(1 Peter 3:8 NLT)

You must have the same attitude that Christ Jesus had.

(Philippians 2:5 NLT)

What Is God Saying to You?

What does this book and the story of Diotrephes tell us about God's character and His expectation of His children?

As you think about the way Jesus expressed and lived His faith, what were some ways He demonstrated a humble attitude and a firm belief at the same time?

Dear Father, the better I get to know You, the more I see that You walked this earth in humility and You were always about doing good. Help me to be faithful as You were faithful. Help me to be about doing good, encouraging other believers, and engaging those who do not know You. Please let my faith and my practices reflect Your goodness. Thank You. Amen.

Get to Know God through Jude

A Brief Overview

THIS LETTER IS MOST LIKELY the last letter that became part of our Bible. The author was Jude, who like James, was the half brother of Jesus. Both James and Jude waited until after Jesus's crucifixion and resurrection to make their public commitment to Him as their Savior and Lord. It is believed by many Bible scholars that Jude became a missionary of the gospel and a powerful leader in the early church.

The book of Jude is similar in content and style to 2 Peter and was probably written around the same time between AD 67 and 80. Like Peter, Jude was serious about the dangers of false teachers who were confusing young Christians and weakening the witness of the gospel throughout the region. Jude instructed God's people to be diligent about denouncing what these teachers were saying, correcting them, and removing them from the church if they would not repent.

Jude was noticeably a man of few words. He had little patience towards those who were misleading God's children and living lives unbecoming of a follower of Jesus. He especially despised the fact that the liars rejected the authority of the apostles and sought to please themselves. In response to their apostasy, Jude marshaled various forms of biblical imagery to make clear what he thought of it all—anything from Cain killing his brother Abel to the punishment of the sinful people who populated Sodom and Gomorrah (see Jude 7, 11).

Jude had two main reasons for writing his letter: to uncover false teachers who were infiltrating the meetings of the believers, and to encourage Christ's true followers to stand firm in the faith given them from the words and life of Jesus.

As a foundation, supporting his two main reasons for writing his letter, Jude reminded the believers and leaders of how important it was to build each other up through the teaching of Jesus's words and activities as presented by those believers and eye witnesses who had been with Jesus.

An Inspirational Theme of Jude

What Fires You Up?

I was in the first grade when the teacher caught me drawing a picture on my paper while I was supposed to be practicing writing the alphabet. He took a wooden ruler with a metal edge and punished me in front of the class by striking my hands with the ruler until the skin was broken and they bled. Later that afternoon when I got home and asked my mama to put some medicine on my hands, I got the interrogation only a mother can perform. After my report, I saw a side of my sweet mama I had never seen before. She was fired up—so fired up that she put me in the car and went to the schoolhouse. Somehow, I think that teacher got rid of that ruler after Mama finished with him. Nothing fired her up as much as someone harming her children. I knew without even a vapor of a doubt that she was my defender and protector.

Jude saw himself as defender of the reputation of Jesus and the gospel message. And when he learned that there were people teaching things that were self-serving and contradictory to the words, the stories, and the life of Jesus, Jude got passionately fired up. He knew these false teachings would spread like a harmful virus, sickening the faith of God's children, and weakening the church. His passion fueling him, he could not sit idly by, so he wrote this letter. He reminded the believers of God's activity in their history, warned them about the false teachers, and admonished them to defend the gift of their faith.

> Dear friends, I've dropped everything to write you about this life of salvation that we have in common. I have to write insisting—begging!—that you fight with everything you have in you for this faith entrusted to us as a gift to guard and cherish. What has happened is that some people have infiltrated our ranks (our Scriptures warned us this would happen), who beneath their pious skin are shameless scoundrels. Their design is to replace the sheer grace of our God with sheer license—which means doing away with Jesus Christ, our one and only Master.
>
> (Jude 3–4 MSG).

Jude was a fired-up defender of Jesus.

What fires you up? Is it politics, sports, your health, your work, or something else? Whatever gets you going reveals your passions, your desires, and your heart. I knew I was in my mama's heart. The recipients of Jude's letter knew what was in his heart.

So the question really is: what is in your heart? In the Bible, the heart represents the core of who you are—your emotions, values, desires, passions, and your greatest love. All through the Bible we read the words of Jeremiah, John, Paul, Peter, and even Jesus telling us our hearts are where the things we treasure most are. So I ask you again, what fires you up? And like Paul, "I pray that from his glorious, unlimited resources he will empower you with inner strength through his Spirit. Then Christ will make his home in your hearts as you trust in him. Your roots will grow down into God's love and keep you strong" (Ephesians 3:16–17 NLT).

Related Scriptures from Jude

But you, dear friends, carefully build yourselves up in this most holy faith by praying in the Holy Spirit, staying right at the center of God's love, keeping your arms open and outstretched, ready for the mercy of our Master, Jesus Christ. This is the unending life, the *real* life!

(Jude 20–21 MSG)

Now all glory to God, who is able to keep you from falling away and will bring you with great joy into his glorious presence without a single fault.

(Jude 24 NLT)

Other Related Scriptures

With all these things in mind, dear brothers and sisters, stand firm and keep a strong grip on the teaching we passed on to you both in person and by letter.

(2 Thessalonians 2:15 NLT)

As slaves of Christ, do the will of God with all your heart.

(Ephesians 6:6 NLT)

What Is God Saying to You?

What are some things that fire you up most? What does your list tell you about your love, your priorities?

What are some areas of your life where you struggle to stand up for what you believe? Why do you think your feel the way you do?

Dear Father, the better I get to know You, the more I see that Your love for me is without reservation. Help my love for You be that way too. Amen.

Get to Know God through Revelation

A Brief Overview

THE APOSTLE JOHN WROTE THE REVELATION around AD 96 from a prison. In the evening, as he looked through the bars in the window of his cell on the island of Patmos, he could see the lights of Ephesus in the distance. For thirty years he had been the church's pastor. He had a heavy heart for his persecuted spiritual family as he wrote to them and to the other six churches in that region—Smyrna, Pergamum, Thyatira, Sardis, Philadelphia, and Laodicea.

The title *Revelation* comes from the Greek word that means to uncover, unveil, or bring to full light that which is hidden or not clear. It is most fitting since God uses the Revelation to make clearer than ever before the importance of choosing Jesus and the significant difference between the eternal rewards for people of faith and the eternal separation for those who are not.

As I have studied, thought, and prayed about how to best give an overview of this last and grand book in the Bible, I have mixed feelings. My concern is primarily because over many centuries, so many people have had so many different interpretations of the book that it would be easy to focus on all the controversies and miss the main point. I do not want any to miss God's main message by focusing on details in the book rather than its message and purpose.

Too, if we read Revelation with little knowledge of the historical context of the sixty-five books that precede it, the heavy symbolism and many biblical references may be seem confusing. But remember, this writing was not confusing to its recipients.

With all that in mind, I believe you should focus on the basic truths that are consistent with the other sixty-five books and be aware of the few things that are unique to Revelation. What are some of the consistent truths found between Genesis to Revelation?

- The central place of Jesus, the Word who was from the beginning, the Creator Savior
- The character of God as all-loving, all-knowing, all-powerful, and always present
- The desire of God that we choose to have a loving relationship and eternal life with Him

What are some ways the Revelation is different from the other books of the Bible?

- It focuses more on the end time and eternity
- It is more symbolic in style for people in that time and for people of all times
- It predicts a more severe persecution of Christians before the end of time
- It contains the most beautiful depictions of heaven with God for His children

John reminded his readers that Jesus was God in flesh. God created everything, had a good plan for His children, and gave us a free will to choose to follow His plan. He also reminded them that God is going to complete His plan in what John calls the end of time. God *is* the Alpha and Omega—the Beginning and the End.

John used many symbols and metaphors in the Revelation that are not clear in our day, but what is clear is that Jesus is the ultimate solution to all of our needs, desires, and eternity. And, as the Creator of everything, He will end what He began.

An Inspirational Theme of Revelation

All Good Things Must Come to an End. Really?

"All good things must come to an end" is an old adage or proverb that had its beginnings with Chaucer in the 1300s, and we still hear it today. As Christ followers, we can be grateful good things for us never come to an end.

You have made it to the sixty-sixth book, and I am praying that every book of the Bible has revealed something of God's character, His nature, and His desires for you. So now we come to the final book. God must have had His good reasons for assigning the book of Revelation this last position in His Word—a *The End* of sorts.

We began in Genesis where Moses wrote, "In the beginning God . . ." (Genesis 1:1 NLT). And when we reached John's gospel, we read, "In the beginning was the Word, and the Word was with God, and the Word was God" (John 1:1 NIV). And now in Revelation, John wrote about the ending. John had been with Jesus, learned His ways, ministered with Him, watched Him die, and greeted Jesus after the Resurrection. John took his assignment from Jesus seriously and stayed the course for decades. He knew about beginnings and endings and recognized that he was nearing his own end on this earth.

And now he wrote the Revelation about the end of time, trying to describe something indescribable, something too grand and glorious for the limitation of language. It is most difficult to describe supernatural, spiritual things in concrete terms, but let us not miss John's message.

I remember walking on the beach early one morning, observing a father with his young son. The child had become quite captivated by the small shells that had washed up on the beach, and he planted himself in the sand. Meanwhile, his dad tried to get the child to look at the sunrise and the glorious clouds and the gilded skies of morning and the sea gulls soaring around them. Nothing doing. The boy was so focused on the tiny shells that he missed the magnificence of the morning his dad wanted him to see.

Let us not miss the indescribable magnificence here. In Revelation, John talks about heaven and tells us about another book, maybe the most important book ever—the Lamb's Book of Life: "Nothing evil will be allowed to enter, nor anyone who practices shameful idolatry and dishonesty—but only those whose names are written in the Lamb's Book of Life" (Revelation 21:27 NLT).

All through the Bible, we read of God's plan and His invitation to you. He longs for you to accept His invitation so that He can write your name in His book. And when the end of your life comes, whether it is through the return of our Lord Jesus or when He reaches down and takes your hand to bring you home, you can be assured that you will spend eternity in heaven, the home you were made for. John describes it as the place where "God shall wipe away all tears from their eyes; and there shall be no more death, neither sorrow, nor crying, neither shall there be any more pain: for the former things are passed away" (Revelation 21:4 KJV). Oh, that wonderful place!

It seems to me that many of the stories and fairytales we read as children even speak to this God-given longing we have for that perfect place where all is well. Many of the fairytales ended with these words: "And they lived happily ever after. *The End.*" We Christ followers know that perfect place as heaven, and we can be grateful that God's Word is no fairytale. God is real. His plan is real. His heaven is real. And His love for you caused Him to step down out of His heaven and walk this earth, giving Himself for you.

At home in Heaven, all good things do not come to an end, for we truly will live happily ever after with our Lord.

Related Scriptures from Revelation

Mighty your acts and marvelous, / O God, the Sovereign-Strong! / Righteous your ways and true, / King of the nations! / Who can fail to fear you, God, / give glory to your Name? / Because you and you only are holy, / all nations will come and worship you, / because they see your judgments are right.

(Revelation 15:3–4 MSG)

The main street of the City was pure gold, translucent as glass. But there was no sign of a Temple, for the Lord God—the Sovereign-Strong—and the Lamb are the Temple. The City doesn't need sun or moon for light. God's Glory is its light, the Lamb its lamp!

(Revelation 21:23 MSG)

Other Related Scriptures

Don't let your hearts be troubled. Trust in God, and trust also in me. There is more than enough room in my Father's home. If this were not so, would I have told you that I am going to prepare a place for you? When everything is ready, I will come and get you, so that you will always be with me where I am. And you know the way to where I am going.

(John 14:1–4 NLT)

For the wages of sin is death, but the free gift of God is eternal life through Christ Jesus our Lord.

(Romans 6:23 NLT)

What Is God Saying to You?

When you think of heaven, what are some things that you look forward to most?

The Revelation says we will not need a moon or sun for light in heaven because Jesus will be our light. What are some things that means to you?

Dear Father, the better I get to know You, the more see that heaven is being with You in an unhindered way forever. How grateful I am that You, the great I AM, want me to be with You for eternity, and that You sacrificially made a way for me to belong to You always. Thank You. Amen and amen.

CONCLUSION

IF YOU'RE READING THIS CONCLUSION, you have made it through God's sixty-six books, and you have spent hours with Him, allowing His Spirit to speak to you through His Word. I hope you've enjoyed this journey through the books of the Bible with me, meeting the men and women who, like us, daily sought out God and found the difference He makes. Perhaps in some way your story has resonated with the stories I shared of real people in my life, both family and friends.

I hope in your study that you have seen the patterns of God's grace, His unfathomable love, and His desires that His children live in harmony with Him as they serve and love one another.

In the Bible and in the life of Jesus, God tells us and shows us that He has been active in human history since creation, and He is still active today as His Spirit lives and works through His children. I pray for readers like you to come to know God in a deeply personal and intimate way so that you will recognize Him more often as He moves in your life. He is real. His love for you is real. The peace He offers you is real. Take a step of faith and take His hand. He will be with you every moment, leading, encouraging, comforting, and the best news ever is that He will lead you Home.

ABOUT THE AUTHOR

BILL ADOPTED HIS PERSONAL MISSION STATEMENT decades ago: Helping people to reach their full potential in Christ. He lives that as a pastor, seminary professor, television executive, and author.

Dr. Nichols holds a MDiv and Ph.D. from Southwestern Baptist Theological Seminary, the nation's largest protestant seminary, where he taught Christian Philosophy, Apologetics, Evangelism, and World Religions. He began his pastoral ministry in 1965 and continued as senior pastor of three churches until 1982, when he was called to help found ACTS (American Christian Television System), the first faith and family television network representing the nation's mainline denominations. He went on to be a founder of Kaleidoscope Television Network, the country's first cable television channel featuring health and disability programming.

Bill has received numerous television, communications, and faith-related recognitions and awards: the Barbara Jordan Award, James Brady Award, Juvenile Diabetes International Special Service Award, The Religion in American Life RIAL Board Award, and the The Inter-Faith Network Council Award.

He is the author of four made-for-television movies, numerous Bible and discipleship booklets, and his book, *Healthy Faith: A Strategic Lifestyle Plan to Transform Your Head, Heart and Hands*. He also enjoys painting portraits and landscapes. He and his wife Phyllis live in the Texas Hill Country where they enjoy spending time with their two married daughters and three grandchildren, writing, painting, traveling, and continuing to do Kingdom work.

Website: HealthyFaith.net
Facebook: facebook.com/Bill Nichols
Twitter: twitter.com/cslchsnmore

Made in the USA
Middletown, DE
07 December 2020